Canadian Writers and Their Works

CANADIAN WRITERS AND THEIR WORKS

FICTION SERIES • VOLUME SEVEN

 EDITED BY

ROBERT LECKER, JACK DAVID, ELLEN QUIGLEY

INTRODUCED BY GEORGE WOODCOCK

ECW PRESS, 1985

CANADIAN CATALOGUING IN PUBLICATION DATA

Main entry under title:

Canadian writers and their works : essays on form,
context, and development : fiction

Includes bibliographies and indexes.
ISBN 0-920802-43-5 (set). – ISBN 0-920802-86-9 (v.7).

1. Canadian fiction (English) – History and criticism –
Addresses, essays, lectures. * 2. Authors, Canadian
(English) – Biography. * I. Lecker, Robert, 1951–
II. David, Jack, 1946– III. Quigley, Ellen, 1955–

PS8187.C36 1982   C813'.009   C82-094801-2
PR9192.2.C36 1982

V. 7

49, 464

Copyright © ECW PRESS, 1985

The publication of this series has been assisted by grants from the
Ontario Arts Council and The Canada Council.

This volume was typeset in Sabon by Compeer Typographic
Services Limited, designed by the Porcupine's Quill, and printed
and bound by Hignell.

Published by ECW PRESS, 307 Coxwell Avenue,
Toronto, Ontario M4L 3B5.

The illustrations are by Isaac Bickerstaff.

CONTENTS

PREFACE

Canadian Writers and Their Works (CWTW) is a unique, twenty-volume collection of critical essays covering the development of Canadian fiction and poetry over the last two centuries. Ten volumes are devoted to fiction, and ten to poetry. Each volume contains a unifying Introduction by George Woodcock and five discrete critical essays on specific writers. Moreover, each critical essay includes a brief biography of the author, a discussion of the tradition and milieu influencing his/her work, a critical overview section which reviews published criticism on the author, a long section analysing the author's works, and a selected bibliography listing primary and secondary material. The essays in each volume are arranged alphabetically according to the last names of the writers under study.

This is Volume Seven in the Fiction Series of *Canadian Writers and Their Works*. Other volumes in the series will be published as research is completed. The projected completion date for the entire series is 1987.

The editors wish to acknowledge the contributions of many people who have played an important part in creating this series. First, we wish to thank the critics who prepared the essays for this volume: Barry Cameron, Hallvard Dahlie, Keith Garebian, Douglas Rollins, Stephen Scobie, and George Woodcock. Our sincere thanks also go to Ken Lewis, and his assistant Scott Mitchell, for their excellent technical editing.

RL/JD/EQ

Introduction

GEORGE WOODCOCK

IN THE ESSAY on Alice Munro which he has contributed to this volume, Hallvard Dahlie seems to set the keynote for one's reading of the whole cluster of writers here represented when he remarks,

> Alice Munro occupies a solid position in that group of writers whose careers coincided with the artistic, cultural, and political coming-of-age of Canada after World War II, a period during which the intrinsic value of Canadian experience came to be taken for granted. Unlike those writers who attained their maturity between the two world wars, or who were conditioned by Old World attitudes, sentiments, and values, this younger group felt no obligation or compulsion to see their world in any other terms than those defined by their own vision and experience.

If there is a sense in which these writers do move beyond "their own vision and experience," it is to be found in the fact that they represent the coming into Canadian fiction, during the 1950s and subsequent decades, of the tradition of modernism, a tradition that had already begun to influence Canadian poetry at least two decades earlier, in the 1930s. And here there is another appropriate quotation, from Stephen Scobie writing on Sheila Watson:

> To speak of Watson's "tradition and milieu" is, in effect, to speak of the whole culture of modernism, which was obsessed equally by the impulse to order and by the desire, in Ezra Pound's phrase, to "make it new." It was in some ways a very conservative culture, looking back to all-encompassing world views, steeped in the literature and mythology of previous ages; yet, for its contemporaries, it was also revolutionary, an avant-garde, the latest thing.

What most strikingly characterized modernism was the fact that, though its practitioners were not without strong views on politics, religion, and morality, they were concerned, first of all, and in an especially austere way, with aesthetic values and their renewal. In so far as they were writers, Saint John the Evangelist could be taken as their patron saint: "In the beginning was the Word..." and through the word the thought was made manifest, so that the writer should be concerned with his prose and allow his lessons to emerge from the rightness of his words and the vision they projected.

There are many ways in which the writers here discussed — Clark Blaise, Hugh Hood, John Metcalf, Alice Munro, and Sheila Watson — show the characteristic signs of modernist influence: in their close concern for the texture of prose; in their quasi-Imagist awareness of the revealing detail; in their interest — a varying one indeed — in verbal experimentation and their desire to "make it new" in the sense of presenting fresh and individual visions; and perhaps, most of all, in what André Gide would have called their *disponibilité*, their freedom of commitment to extraliterary bonds and preconceptions, their clear-eyed openness to experience. Political insights may *emerge* from their works, as they do, for example, from Hood's *You Cant Get There From Here* and from Metcalf's *General Ludd*, with all the Stendhalian emphasis of "a pistol-shot in the middle of a concert, something loud and vulgar, and yet a thing to which it is not possible to refuse one's attention."[1] But one does not consider Hood or Metcalf as primarily political novelists since they have not started off with the intent of teaching political lessons. The lessons have emerged after the event, as it were: from the novelists' observation of the effect of politics on human behaviour and human destiny.

In the same way, it is impossible to associate any of these writers with nationalist intentions, as one can associate an earlier novelist like Hugh MacLennan, who deliberately set out to exemplify in books like *Two Solitudes* and *Return of the Sphinx* the problems of Canadian identity and unity; nor can one view any of them from a regionalist standpoint, as one can so many other Canadian writers of their generation. Sheila Watson made a point I think could be made for all when she said that writing *The Double Hook* began "in answer to a challenge that you could not write about particular places in Canada: that what you'd end up with was a regional novel of some kind."[2] It was a very modernist viewpoint: that by faithfully rendering the particular, one touches the universal without the need for any mediating factor like the region or the nation. That is, of course, a debatable attitude, based on a highly personal and almost solipsist attitude towards vision, and I do not share it unreserv edly, but I think it more or less works for the five writers we are considering.

Some of them, indeed, are very localized in the places they write about: Sheila Watson rendering in *The Double Hook* her long-ago experience of Dog Creek, British Columbia; Alice Munro writing all her best work about the seedy town edges of southern Ontario, where she grew up; and Hugh Hood concentrating much of his fiction in his longtime home of Montreal. Others are broader in their choice of terrain, Clark Blaise usually alternating between Florida and Canada but sometimes venturing as far as India, and John Metcalf continually reverting to his English past while also writing in the Canadian present. What unites them is the sharp and concrete particularity with which experience is rendered wherever it takes place, and the particularity of experience is one of the essential assumptions of modernism.

Equally essential to modernism, whether in literature or in the visual arts, is an assumption of the universal validity, and therefore the universal availability, of form. This made the masters of the movement choose their own masters with the splendid eclecticism that so enriches *The Waste Land* and the *Four Quartets*, and the *Cantos*, *Ulysses*, and *The Apes of God*.

The same might be said of the five writers represented in this volume. To begin, one of their most striking common characteristics is their apparent lack of models among Canadian writers. Undoubtedly they have been stimulated by the energies that since the 1950s have created in Canada an ambiance favourable to literature of a kind unknown before. Relatively easy publication in books and periodicals, an emergent body of intelligent critics, and a growing audience provide the kind of setting in which writers can operate with increasing confidence. But such confidence also leads writers away from the special preoccupations and problems of a nascent literature.

Nobody is concerned any longer, like poets earlier in the century, with expressing Canadian experience in its own authentic language or, as Grove was in the Prairies or Buckler in the Maritimes, with bringing an undescribed landscape, an uncelebrated pioneer way of living, into literature. These basic functional problems and the worst economic problems of publishing having been solved to the satisfaction of everyone except Robin Mathews, Canadian writing has become increasingly free to variegate, to find its own ways in content and style, and now the kind of writers who were once seen as models, like Hugh MacLennan and Morley Callaghan and W. O. Mitchell, have in fact turned into hindering and increasingly ignored stereotypes.

Keith Garebian, for example, remarks that Hugh Hood

> does not invite comparison with Canadian literary predecessors or contemporaries, but this is not because of any colonial romanticism or vain self-aggrandizement. It is simply because he does not believe that there has been any Canadian writer good enough to have served as an influence.

And, disproportionate though Hugh Hood's opinion of himself may often seem to be, the fact is that, with the possible exception of a slight touch of Callaghan, one can detect no identifiable influence of any other Canadian writer in his work. There are times when he and Mordecai Richler may seem to echo each other, but that is almost certainly because of the experience of Montreal which these two nearly exact contemporaries, born in 1928 and 1931 respectively, have shared from different viewpoints, one Anglo-French Catholic and the other half-assimilated Jewish.

In fact, in the case of every writer discussed in this volume, the important formative influences and the important role models have been those of foreign writers. The study of Wyndham Lewis, that accidental Canadian and great international modernist, has been Sheila Watson's most enduring preoccupation. Hugh Hood looks to Marcel Proust as the greatest novelist of modern times and describes *A la recherche du temps perdu* as "the modern epic of the individual consciousness which aims at the discovery of the fundamental laws governing the human mind."[3] Alice Munro, though her characters speak in the vernacular of southern Ontario, has found her strongest affinities in American writers like James Agee and particularly Eudora Welty. Barry Cameron remarks of Clark Blaise that

> ...the literary and philosophical tradition to which Blaise feels the greatest affinity is neither Canadian nor American but what he has called "the discursive tradition," "literature compounded of cold observation *and* subjective passion," in sensibility if not completely in fact a French tradition: Pascal, Flaubert, Proust, Céline, Mann, and Kerouac, among others.

John Metcalf, like most of the other four writers, has always been annoyed at attempts to find Canadian models for his work, and, as Douglas Rollins points out, he has declared in an interview with Barry Cameron that

> writing is an international business. There is no such thing as a national literature.... The influences are from whoever is good and whoever is being innovative anywhere.[4]

Elsewhere Metcalf has argued that "we need foreign models..,"[5] and one of the most interesting and important passages in Rollins' essay is that in which he takes the argument back to the matter of modernist affinities with which I began this Introduction and suggests how "Metcalf's early admiration of the Imagist poets and their principles established the base from which all his work has developed." What he goes on to say about the manner in which Metcalf shows the influence of the Imagists applies also in broad terms to the other writers discussed in this volume:

> Metcalf's rejection of abstraction (in an interview he echoed the cry "No ideas but in things"), the precision and economy of his prose, and his sensitivity to the sound and rhythmic flow as well as the meaning of words illustrate the degree to which his practice squares with Imagist theory.

Clear and particular vision, precise and economic prose, and a care for its sound and texture, plus a sharp individuality of vision, are the characteristics which all our five writers share. Reading them one has a sense that they are constantly exploring not only the human mind and the universal order it reflects, but also the language itself, and this generates a kind of participatory excitement which perhaps explains the unusual degree of empathetic understanding that all the present critics have shown in their essays.

Modernism, of course, is no longer the sharp spearhead of the literary avant-garde; that role has been taken over in notably various ways by the post-modernists, who have been emerging — and often vanishing — with considerable rapidity over recent years, and who often seem devoted to experiment as an activity so autonomous that its results often pass far beyond the ever-refined precision demanded by modernism into realms of esoteric obscurity the modernists would have found repellent. In such experiment for experiment's sake, none of the present writers has indulged. Even John Metcalf does not carry the principle of "No ideas but in things" to the extent of French *choseistes* like Alain Robbe-Grillet, for whom the things became so important that persons were reduced to their reflections. And the kind of inventive mingling of genres and even arts practised by Canadian writers like Michael Ondaatje, bpNichol, and bill bissett, who experiment in the areas between prose and verse and between the visual and the verbal, has not attracted any of the writers now being discussed. They are fiction writers, and if they derive techniques from other genres, as Metcalf, and I suspect also Watson, did from Imagist poetry, then these are turned to fictional ends. They experiment with a purpose, which is to make their prose more precise and revelatory, not for the sake of experiment itself, and this often means that their structures, as distinct from their textures, tend to be traditional where, as in the case of Alice Munro, for example, the traditional framework continues to be serviceable. Classic modernism, as T. S. Eliot and its other exponents made clear, never involved a mindlessly complete rejection of tradition.

Modernism, of course, was never a closely linked school of writers dominated by a clearly defined theoretical approach like Surrealism or Black Mountain poetry-writing, even though it did include in its broad scope short-lived groups with special aims like the Imagists and the Vorticists. The movement was a matter of shared attitudes rather than shared techniques, which was why it embraced figures so various as T. S. Eliot and James Joyce, as Herbert Read and Wyndham Lewis, as H. D. and Richard Aldington and Ezra Pound. These writers certainly knew each other, and each in his or her own way sought to "make it new," but they worked in increasing isolation. And the late modernist approach, shared in Canada by writers as various as Louis Dudek, the McGill poets, and the prose writers in this book, is manifest in links between writers which are those of affinity rather than of any kind of formal alliance.

It is true that for a while John Metcalf, Clark Blaise, and Hugh Hood, with other writers, were associated in The Montreal Storytellers Fiction Performance Group, but this was less a literary coterie in the classic sense than a kind of missionary effort aimed at organizing prose readings to spread awareness of Canadian writings and writers through the educational system. It is perhaps equally significant that *White Pelican*, the Edmonton literary magazine, whose most active editor was Sheila Watson, appears to have included no contributions from Hugh Hood, John Metcalf, Alice Munro, or Clark Blaise. These writers in no way put themselves together; yet juxtaposed, as they are here, by editorial fiat, they fit in with each other amazingly well.

If they are not a school, they do not form a generation either in the temporal sense, for Sheila Watson, born in 1909, is thirty-one years older than Clark Blaise (born in 1940) and twenty-nine years older than John Metcalf (born in 1938). But affinities, in Canadian writing at least, do not always go by age groups. It is too new a tradition for seniority patterns to have imposed themselves. Thus poets like Earle Birney, Dorothy Livesay, and P. K. Page, returning with a second wind at what to ordinary people would be retirement age, have astonished us by writing verse so new and contemporary that it stands admirably beside the poetry much younger people were writing at the same time. In a similar way, Sheila Watson's austerely scanty production of one small novel and five short stories, most of them written almost a quarter of a century ago, still appear with extraordinary freshness and individuality among later works by much younger writers.

Sheila Watson is the writer in this group who has the most direct links with the classic modernist movement because of her long and sustained interest in Wyndham Lewis and the fact that she first began to study him under his student and associate, Marshall McLuhan. Expressed in this way, it sounds as if one were claiming an apostolic succession, but Watson's own works are the evidence of the permeative influence of the earliest modernists, and of the Imagist poets — H. D. perhaps even more than Pound — as well as of Lewis.

Stephen Scobie says in his essay that "the major fact about Sheila Watson's biography is that she does not have one; or, rather, that she would regard it as irrelevant." Doubtless, indeed, biography is irrevelant to the extent that Watson is in no sense an autobiographical writer, and therefore there is no point in seeking in her life the parallels to what her imagination has produced in the way of fiction. Yet two biographical facts do remain of crucial importance. One is that almost obsessive interest in Lewis, the author-artist whose writings were always permeated with the visuality and the imagery that came from his other life as a painter. The other is the vital two years she spent teaching during the 1930s in the little lost village of Dog Creek in the Cariboo ranching country.

At Dog Creek she was among people who lived a stark and deprived life in close contact with often violent natural forces; it was a setting of sharp, hard visual images as well as of powerful and often negative human emotions, and it stayed in her mind until it finally emerged as the subject for an only novel that was also a masterpiece and virtually — in Canadian terms — an immediate classic. In recollection, as Scobie quotes, she said of the Dog Creek experience and its relation to *The Double Hook*,

> I'd been away for a long time before I realised that if I had something to say, it was going to be said in these images. And there was something I wanted to say: about how people are driven, how if they have no art, how if they have no tradition, how if they have no ritual, they are driven in one of two ways, either towards violence or towards insensibility — if they have no mediating rituals which manifest themselves in what I suppose we call art forms.[6]

Explanations of any work of art in terms of a theoretical approach tend to take one away from a real sense of the work itself, its atmosphere and its vision, from the archetypal figures like Mrs. Potter, the old fisherwoman, and James, her son and murderer, and Greta, her daughter, who burns the house and herself rather than letting either be possessed by strangers, and holy Felix, and blinded voyeur Kip, whose inner selves stumble in ignorance, shadowed by the evil will of Coyote. They move in and out of a bright mythological light and yet, at the same time, in outward appearance, are the kind of cattle-raising people one might encounter any day riding on the back roads of the Cariboo country. The clue that unites the theory and the achievement lies in the phrase "these images."

For though there have inevitably been eager scholars seeking the symbolic patterns in *The Double Hook*, Sheila Watson was not really one of those who walked through Baudelaire's *forêt de symboles*. The symbolic pattern in the novel is simple: the fish of Christian, and Coyote of Indian, mythology. The double hook itself, I would say, is emblematic rather than symbolic, a sharply visual presentation of the rival forces in the hook and their interdependence: "That when you fish for the glory you catch the darkness too. That if you hook twice the glory you hook twice the fear."[7] But, for the most part, the book is carried in the dense pattern of its images, which allow an extreme minimalization of the discursive element in the prose, for they cohere as naturally as images in a haiku:

James turned on his heel. But when he turned, he saw nothing but the water-hole and the creek and the tangle of branches which grew along it.

Ara went down the path, stepping over the dried hoof-marks down to the creek's edge. She, too, saw nothing now except a dark ripple and the padded imprint of a coyote's foot at the far edge of the moving water.

She looked up the creek. She saw the twisted feet of the cottonwoods shoved naked into the stone bottom where the water moved, and the matted branches of the stunted willow. She saw the shallow water plocking over the roots of the cottonwood, transfiguring bark and stone.

She bent towards the water. Her fingers divided it. A stone breathed in her hand. Then life drained to its centre.[8]

The cumulation of images, and the very clarity with which they are seen, builds up to a climactic part of the novel. They are used not merely for descriptive effect; each has its correlation to the emotions that are moving between people and leading to fatal action. Here and there Watson breaks with strict Imagist theory by introducing a simile: *like* is a word used quite often. But even then, the simile is so sharply visualized that it reinforces the pattern of images.

Nothing like *The Double Hook* had been written in Canada before. Its effect on younger writers has been permeative and persistent, though critics were first reluctant to recognize it. In 1977, when I said that *The Double Hook* was "one of the most important books for itself and in terms of influence" published in the 1950s,[9] I was reproved by no less a figure than Sheila Watson's fellow neo-modernist, Louis Dudek. But many of the younger critics clearly agree with me. Frank Davey recently described *The Double Hook* as "the first truly modern Canadian novel,"[10] and Stephen Scobie, in this volume, puts the point in an equally impressive way when he says, "Speaking for myself, both as a writer and as a critic, it is the Sheila Watson generation that I belong to."

Sheila Watson's own claims for the work, in keeping with her austere view of selfhood, have been much more modest. As we have seen, she says she wrote *The Double Hook* "in answer to a challenge that you could not write about particular places in Canada: that what you'd end up with was a regional novel of some kind."[11] That, of course, is another way of stating the important truth modernism gave to literature: that in close attention to the particular you arrive at the universal, with no need for mediation — the "World in a grain of sand" of that great pre-modernist William Blake.

It would be hard to find a greater contrast than that which one perceives between Sheila Watson and Hugh Hood: she modest in claims and works, he voluminous and somewhat vain. Except for one story that got left out, Watson's life's work — apart from *The Double Hook* — fits into a single 190-page special issue of *Open Letter*. At the last count I made, Hood had published six volumes of short stories, two volumes of essays, a book on ice hockey, and one on Seymour Segal's painting, four individual novels, and the first five volumes of his "prose epic," The New Age / Le nouveau siècle, whose various parts, he has promised us, will keep on appearing until the twelfth volume in the millennial year 2000. I am the last man to throw stones through the walls of the glass house where I live by objecting to a writer being prolific, yet I know from experience the perils that gift may involve; one of them is a diffusion of intent.

Such a diffusion emerges in Hood's various attempts, as quoted in Keith Garebian's essay, to define his roles as a writer. He sees himself as "an epic novelist, a maker of catalogues and encyclopedias and compendia of syntax-forms, and vocabularies of names and a story teller and etc.,"[12] and again as "*both* a realist and a transcendentalist allegorist,"[13] and again as "a moral realist, not a naturalist nor a surrealist...or *avant-garde* writer."[14] The most obviously appropriate of these copious self-descriptions is that of the "maker of catalogues and encyclopedias" for the immediately striking feature of Hood's stories and novels — and even of the putative prose epic, The New Age — is the remarkable sense of the detail of everyday life presented with what Frank Davey once called "invisible craftsmanship." Davey went on to say that Hood's work "gives the illusion of being journalistic reportage — chatty, matter of fact, and unplanned; the casual voice of a somewhat unsophisticated but sensible narrator can be heard throughout.... the reader is led to trust every detail that Hood offers."[15]

And the detail comes in abundance, for Hood, even if he makes no claims to being an "*avant-garde* writer," is a modernist at least in his devotion to the particular as a means of approaching the universal. Garebian takes Robert Fulford to task for his definition of Hood as "a superior journalist" being "slowly strangled by an inferior novelist."[16] Yet part of Fulford's statement is obviously true. Hood does excel in those very activities he shares with journalists and social historians: the precise detailing of the actual process of living. No novelist — Canadian or other — whom I know of enters so subtly into the occupational lives of his characters and describes them with such precise and convincing detail; but Hood is by no means so convincing when he enters the emotional lives of the same people, which he tends to see *sub specie aeternitatis* rather than in diurnal terms, and therefore not quite humanly. Garebian is quite right to say that "as a didactic writer, Hood has few equals anywhere," but didacticism is no unequivocal virtue for a writer, and in Hood's work it introduces a discursive Victorian element that clashes with the modernist urge to deal with people and their relationships, which are the stuff of novels, in terms of the concrete and particular imagery he applies to the material framework of their lives.

Looking through the volumes of his dodecalogy, The New Age, that have so far appeared, it seems as though Hood's problems are partly those of the culture to which he belongs. For this "prose epic," which we were led to believe might be the North American equivalent of Proust's masterpiece, in fact resembles it in only two ways: it is long; and its narrator and protagonist is obviously one of the author's personae, so that it is virtually, if not literally, autobiographical. But the texture of The New Age, its cultural substantiality, its explorations into the rhythms of human minds and feelings, and even the quality of its presentation of a living society, fall so far short of the great European fictional epics, like *Ulysses* and *A la recherche du temps perdu*, that one is led to assume such works can only successfully be written in the context of ancient and elaborate cultural traditions, traditions moreover at the point of decay.

It is significant in this connection that the first and still the best work of modernist fiction written in Canada — *The Double Hook* — should have been short and concise (a poetic novella rather than a novel in the true sense), that Hood's own best works so far should be the stories, where his talent for precise, quasi-reportorial detail can best be deployed, and that the three remaining writers discussed in this volume should all be primarily short-story writers whose novels show in their episodic structures a continuing adherence to the shorter form.

Alice Munro is one of those writers who at first sight appear to be working in a style of clear and lucid realism — the style that critics find it hardest to deal with since everything seems so precisely and naturally there. But very soon one becomes aware of the forms moving beneath that translucent surface, so that, as Hallvard Dahlie says of the stories in *Dance of the Happy Shades*, one finds oneself facing "a recognizably realistic world whose components never leave one entirely comfortable, a situation rendered both ambivalent and complex by Munro's sensitive use of irony, paradox, and understatement." And as one goes further on into Munro's writing career, one finds that, as with some abstract painters, what is absent becomes as important as what is there. What Dahlie terms "the inability to communicate, the reduction to silences, [and] the futility of words" become unavoidable elements in the process of actual communication between writer and reader as well as factors of noncommunication between characters: so much in these splendid stories goes by implication.

This is why Alice Munro, since she became established as a writer, has always made a dual appeal. On the one hand, she is in Canadian terms a best-seller, even achieving publication by large paperback houses in the United States, and that is because of the immediate, on-the-surface appeal of her books, in which readers — and women especially — find that she is presenting what in realistic terms seem to be situations with which they can identify, and is reflecting their own perplexities when they come to realize, as Dahlie puts it, "that morality itself is an elusive aspect of reality, and that human relationships create by their very interaction a perpetually shifting dimension of this morality." On the other hand, Munro has always been admired by her fellow writers for the extraordinary lucidity of her prose, for her precise handling of sensual data, and for her skilful use of the short-story form in its most effective way — again in Dahlie's words — "to attach added intensity to the dilemmas her protagonists face, or, perhaps more accurately, to leave them with those tensions suspended that a novel more typically would resolve."

If Alice Munro combines rather enviably the two roles of a moderately popular story writer and a writer's writer, both Clark Blaise and John Metcalf, with their deliberate and at times rather vocal preoccupation with the problems of the literary artist, are still very much writers' writers, as the great modernists of course also were until history lifted them on its tide by turning them into classics and therefore indispensable reading.

Clark Blaise's work largely derives its interest from the fact that it belongs in a middle land of fiction between the short story and the novel. Even in what look like collections of short stories, such as A North American Education and Tribal Justice, there will be groups of items with a common central character, and this character will provide the continuity in what would otherwise be a discontinuous world, a "culturally disparate" world as Barry Cameron describes it, whose divisions are symbolized by the divided origins and loyalties of the central figure, and by the geographical dispersion of the action; there are always journeys to be made, roads to be followed to indefinite destinations.

The sense of alienation, of being a stranger in a strange world, that has been so strong in the French writers Blaise admires — from Pascal (another Blaise!) down to Alain-Fournier and Camus — is carried in his writing perhaps farther than in the work of any other Canadian writer. Everywhere he is dealing with outsiders — Floridans in Montreal, Montrealers in the South, North Americans in India — but the outsider status is as much spiritual as geographical. And, through the compelling confidentiality with which Blaise writes, that status is made universal as well. Blaise is virtually telling the reader, as Barry Cameron remarks, "...you too are a voyeur; you too are forever an alien." Yet there is more to these strange books than mere alienation, for one of the essential characteristics of the voyeur, after all, is that he *sees*. And if Blaise writes largely, as he has said, of a world in which so much is a matter "of the sinister and of duplicities and dualities,"[17] he is still a revealer of mysteries; and, as Dennis Duffy has said, "...the essential theme of exploration and delicate adjustment, concluded often with a vision of loneliness, abides throughout his work."[18]

John Metcalf is an interesting mixture of the high artist and the satirist, which means that he combines a strong element of the didactic with his formal preoccupations. We have already seen how resistant he is to any nationalist approach to literature, how he sees writing as international and his own roots going down wherever good writing is being done. He has also declared, in refreshing exception to the pseudopopulist trends of the time, "I want to write elitist art. It's the austere that appeals to me more than anything else in art" (Cameron, p. 411).

Metcalf's derivations from Imagism, already noted, have led him into a sharp prose in which particulars are carefully recorded and almost mosaically constructed into the frameworks of episodes whose placing together becomes an important structural element in his work. The short story, a clear and quickly apprehensible frame of incident, is both the form he likes most and the one in which his particular gifts as an artificer of fiction are perhaps best used.

He has always resented the conventions of the ordinary traditional novel. Douglas Rollins appositely quotes Barry Cameron's interview with Metcalf, in which he intimated that the episodic structure of his first novel, *Going Down Slow*, resulted from his impatience at "having to put connecting bits in and continuing the story. It was the set pieces of the book...that [he] really enjoyed because they were the closest to the short story form" (Cameron, p. 403). Metcalf has made no bones about the deliberate character of his writing, no pretence of writing "naturally." It is all avowedly artifice and manipulation, both of the prose and of the reader's reactions. And so he could admit frankly to Cameron that he started on *Going Down Slow* largely because he had been told that writing a novel would further his career.

But, despite the episodic character of *Going Down Slow*, this novel and its successor, *General Ludd*, do add up to a great deal more than episodic sequences, since it is in these books that Metcalf's comic and satiric gifts have emerged. He has said — like Orwell — that "...all writing is political, all great writing subversive,"[19] which means that, despite his concern for the artifice of writing, he adopts no narrowly aestheticist stand. His books are intended, if not to teach, certainly at times to preach, and he is quite ready to use his sharp-edged prose to expose the flaws of a society he largely despises. *Going Down Slow*, essentially a fictional attack on the Canadian educational system, reminds one in more than its title of the "angry young men" who were prominent in England during Metcalf's boyhood there, but it is in *General Ludd* that he really comes into his own, using his talent for creating convincing episodes to construct a true picaresque, the ideal form for a comic fiction. *General Ludd* is a book of outlandish imagery and scornful prose, in many ways reminiscent of Céline's masterpieces, *Voyage au bout de la nuit* and *Mort à crédit*, and like those books it offers, as John Moss has said, "a vision that is at once hilarious and chilling" in its exposure of a society dying for the lack of art. Moss considers it "probably the finest comic novel ever published in Canada,"[20] and such perhaps it is, if one excepts Wyndham Lewis' *Self Condemned*, which, though about Canada, was first published elsewhere.

I have no reason for suggesting that *General Ludd* may have been influenced by *Self Condemned*, but there are strong parallels between the views the two novels present of the philistine ugliness of Canadian urban existence and the hollow pretentiousness of its academic life. And it seems appropriate to end by pointing out the affinities of a contemporary Canadian novelist with the classic modernist who indirectly, through Sheila Watson, contributed to the modern trend in Canadian fiction.

NOTES

[1] This description by Stendhal of "politics in a work of literature" is quoted in Irving Howe, *Politics and the Novel* (New York: Meridian, 1957), p. 15.

[2] Sheila Watson, "What I'm Going to Do," *Open Letter*, 3rd ser., No. 1 (Winter 1974–75) [*Sheila Watson: A Collection*], p. 182.

[3] Pierre Cloutier, "An Interview with Hugh Hood," *Journal of Canadian Fiction*, 2, No. 1 (Winter 1973), 52.

[4] Barry Cameron, "The Practice of the Craft: A Conversation with John Metcalf," *Queen's Quarterly*, 82 (Autumn 1975), 412–13. All further references to this work (Cameron) appear in the text.

[5] John Metcalf and Clark Blaise, Introd., *Here and Now*, ed. John Metcalf and Clark Blaise (Ottawa: Oberon, 1977), p. 6.

[6] Watson, "What I'm Going to Do," p. 183.

[7] Sheila Watson, *The Double Hook* (Toronto: McClelland and Stewart, 1959), pp. 4–6.

[8] Watson, *The Double Hook*, p. 29.

[9] George Woodcock, "Possessing the Land: Notes on Canadian Fiction," in *The Canadian Imagination: Dimensions of a Literary Culture*, ed. David Staines (Cambridge: Harvard Univ. Press, 1977), pp. 93–94.

[10] Frank Davey, "Watson, Sheila," *The Oxford Companion to Canadian Literature*, ed. William Toye (Toronto: Oxford Univ. Press, 1983), p. 822.

[11] See above, note 2.

[12] "Hugh Hood and John Mills in Epistolary Conversation," *The Fiddlehead*, No. 116 (Winter 1978), p. 136.

[13] "Hugh Hood and John Mills in Epistolary Conversation," p. 145

[14] Hugh Hood, "The Ontology of Super-Realism," in *The Governor's Bridge Is Closed* (Ottawa: Oberon, 1973), p. 127.

[15] Frank Davey, "Hugh Hood," in *From There to Here: A Guide to English-Canadian Literature since 1960* (Erin, Ont.: Porcépic, 1974), p. 138.

[16] Robert Fulford, "Hugh Hood's Misused Talent," rev. of *The*

Camera Always Lies and *Around the Mountain*, by Hugh Hood, *Toronto Daily Star*, 11 Oct. 1967, p. 43.

[17] Geoff Hancock, "An Interview with Clark Blaise," *Canadian Fiction Magazine*, Nos. 34–35 (1980), p. 54.

[18] Dennis Duffy, "Blaise, Clark," *The Oxford Companion to Canadian Literature*, ed. William Toye (Toronto: Oxford Univ. Press, 1983), p. 74.

[19] John Metcalf, "Soaping a Meditative Foot (Notes for a Young Writer)," in *The Narrative Voice: Short Stories and Reflections by Canadian Authors*, ed. John Metcalf (Toronto: McGraw-Hill Ryerson, 1972), p. 154.

[20] John Moss, *A Reader's Guide to the Canadian Novel* (Toronto: McClelland and Stewart, 1981), pp. 200, 197.

Clark Blaise (1940–)

BARRY CAMERON

Clark Blaise (1940–)

BARRY CAMERON

Biography

"I'M A KIND OF TROPICAL TREE with an awful lot of shallow roots and I can easily be blown over. On the other hand, I can survive a lot of changes. I adapt very easily to just about anything around me"[1] — Clark Blaise speaking of the double-edged legacy bequeathed to him by his wandering parents: a sense of ultimate rootlessness coupled with a positive ability to adapt, a sense of vulnerability coupled with an instinct to survive. Blaise was born on 10 April 1940, in Fargo, North Dakota (from where he moved six months after birth), to Canadian parents — his mother, English-Canadian from Manitoba, and his father, French-Canadian from Quebec — who had come to the United States in search of the American ideal of success.[2] Because his father's career as an itinerant furniture salesman took him there, Blaise spent a part of his childhood in the Deep South of Alabama and Georgia, but most of it in central Florida.[3] According to the dust jacket of *A North American Education: A Book of Short Fiction* (1973), Blaise's first book, he "attended twenty-five schools" during this period of time. That fact alone, if one were seeking direct autobiographical influences on Blaise's work, might account for the predominance of alienation and dislocation as psychological and metaphoric motifs in his fiction.

Blaise's childhood, particularly in Florida, gave him his first apprehension of "a continuity between the moral and the physical,"[4] a perception that would be reexperienced and deepened when he moved to Montreal. Landscape and cityscape are, as John Metcalf has said (Metcalf, p. 77), moral landscapes in Blaise's fiction. Setting in a Blaise story, down to the minutest detail, is consistently metaphoric, often synecdochic, correlative in a variety of ways to the human "action" of the story. For Blaise, as for many other writers, the South as a region and

Montreal as a city "are places where setting is not merely an excuse, but where setting is in fact the mystery and the manner" (Metcalf, p. 78). In an interview with Geoff Hancock, Blaise speaks revealingly of the formative quality of his Florida experience:

> . . . Florida was physically, morally and historically an apt place for me: I exploited it ruthlessly and it exploited me in turn. It was a location (thinking back now to the still-rural, Deep South Florida of the mid- and late-40's) that was made for the hounding out of some central worm-like creature in myself.
>
> Florida was foreign to everything in my nature. It was a brutal confrontation, but it was physically so interesting and physically so unforgettable that it linked up forever a notion of nature, of water, of solitariness, and a kind of harshness that I lost myself in for hours every day. . . . in Florida . . . you literally passed through a wall at seven in the morning and came back at dusk and were out in it all day walking through jungle and water and you never felt as though you were in particular danger. Yet you were always seeing things that were dead or dying, or crawling up from the mud or down from the trees. You saw putrefaction, you saw the tropical world in which all the processes are speeded up and [in] which the chain of exploitation is just so much more vivid than it is up here.
>
> So I was the beneficiary of that and later on . . . I came to see the social and historical and economic analogues to that kind of nature. The myth was laid down for me pretty early, and it was a matter of feeding into the myth with plots and psychologies and characters.[5] (Hancock, p. 48)

After spending 1950 and 1951 in Winnipeg, to where he had moved from Florida, Blaise moved to the American Midwest, living for some time in Springfield, Missouri, and Cincinnati, Ohio, and then in 1953 settling in Pittsburgh, Pennsylvannia, where he attended high school.[6] In 1957 he went to Denison University in Granville, Ohio, where he first majored in geology and then, after eight months out of university, switched his major to English. It was during this period that Blaise first began to write intensely and to read "serious" fiction:

In the eight months I was out of school I read never less than a book a day, and often two or three. Nothing heavy; I was still courting facts, and the only writers I really valued were those who described experiences, appearances, or states of mind that I knew to be true. Theodore Dreiser, Sinclair Lewis, and Thomas Wolfe were obvious early favourites; they reaffirmed the helplessness I felt; the venality of my petty-bourgeois surroundings, and the noble calling of "writer." At the close of that period I discovered the French: Flaubert (not of *Madame Bovary*, but of *The Sentimental Education*), Alain-Fournier's *Le Grand Meaulnes*, Zola, Céline and Stendhal. I even liked Camus, something I would now avoid. . . . Lawrence and especially Faulkner became even more important . . . "influential" . . . since I had begun to write by then, out of the same desire to capture moments of myth acting through nature, as Lawrence had, and to capture as intensely as Faulkner did the palpability of time-passing in a geographical and historical milieu that I too knew very well. Thomas Mann had been with me from the beginning.[7]

After graduation from Denison with a B.A. in 1961, Blaise went to Harvard, where he attended Bernard Malamud's class in creative writing.[8] In February 1962 he moved to the University of Iowa Writers' Workshop. At Iowa, he met in 1962 and married in 1963 (during their lunch hour on the first day of the academic year) Bharati Mukherjee, the talented Bengali-Canadian novelist of *The Tiger's Daughter* (1972) and *Wife* (1975). The Iowa experience was important for Blaise, for, like others who attended the Workshop in the 1960s,[9] Blaise learned "a sense of obligation to craft and community and standards and articulateness about aims" (Metcalf, p. 77).

After graduation from Iowa in 1964 with an M.F.A. — his thesis was a story collection entitled "Thibidault et fils" — Blaise taught at the University of Wisconsin in Milwaukee; but because he had "dreamed restless dreams of Canada, especially of Montreal," and because "he felt it was the place that would let him be himself,"[10] he emigrated to Montreal in 1966 and became a Canadian citizen in 1973. Except for sabbaticals in India during 1973–74 and 1976–77, Blaise remained in Montreal for twelve years, teaching modern fiction and creative writing at Sir George

Williams University (subsequently Concordia University). In 1978 he moved to York University to become a Professor of Humanities; in 1980 he left Toronto to share a teaching position with his wife at Skidmore College in Saratoga Springs, New York;[11] and in 1983 he moved on again to join his wife and two sons — with interruptions for short stints of teaching, and reading tours — in Iowa City.

Tradition and Milieu

In Montreal, Blaise became part of "The Montreal Storytellers Fiction Performance Group" — to use its official name — which also included John Metcalf, Hugh Hood, Ray Smith, and Ray Fraser. Metcalf and Hood formed the group during the winter of 1970–71 "to promote Canadian prose to as large an audience as possible by bringing the writers into direct contact with students in high schools, colleges and universities."[12] Because neither the media nor the publishing industry itself seemed to be promoting Canadian literature and because of the "paucity of Canadian literature in high schools and university English courses," Metcalf believed that writers themselves would have "to create and educate an audience for Canadian fiction."[13] The group was forced to disband after a few years[14] but not before it had implicitly proven to the Canada Council, through highly entertaining and instructive performances, that prose readings as well as poetry readings should receive financial support. The struggle to create and educate an audience for Canadian fiction, alas, continues.

The continental range of Blaise's personal history, its culturally disparate quality, is the framework or "shell" — at least until very recently[15] — of his fiction. "Canada, America, French, English, north, south, and a kind of reflective, observant, fat and phlegmatic child" (Hancock, p. 58) — into these "frames," Blaise places his "totally invented" plots:

> If you have a basically passive and observant, fearful child, then you can create vivid, lurid nightmares for him to fall into. If you create the tension of a responsible and respectable mother and irresponsible, unrespectful father,

you can create confrontations between them. . . . If you're talking about such vast geographical compass points as Manitoba, Quebec and Florida, you can talk quite legitimately about North America. So I've been quite happy accepting the givens of my life autobiographically but I have not been dependent upon the contents of my own life. . . . if all the things that I've written about had actually happened to me, then I would obviously be a very different person than I am. They are merely all within me.

. . . .

I've only written of three characters really and that's my mother, my father and myself. I am utterly dependent upon the family situation and the family conflicts as the source of my fiction. Now the "myself" character is sometimes female, sometimes male and the myself character is sometimes acutely analytical and cynically intelligent, and sometimes it's reflectively and passively intelligent, sometimes it's only cynical and worldly and abusive, but all those are within myself and I can as easily be one of them as another. The father character stands as all males, older, with authority, with physical power, with experience, with sexual charm, with confidence, with a fearlessness before the law, with a kind of lawlessness, people who *define*, or, who are continually pushing out against definitions. And my mother-figures are always the ones who are pulling in within definitions, anticipating, so acutely aware of restrictions and anticipating rebuffs, anticipating them so sensitively that you internalize them before you ever do anything. So that is my landscape, my moral landscape. . . . (Hancock, pp. 58–60)

Blaise began publishing stories in the early 1960s in various academic and literary quarterlies, but his most important short fiction (some of it previously published in literary journals) appears in two deliberately constructed "books of short fiction": *A North American Education* (1973), which won the Great Lakes College New Writers' Award, and *Tribal Justice* (1974), which won the Saint Lawrence Award for Fiction.[16] *Days and Nights in Calcutta*, a journal based on the experiences of a sabbatical year in India, the first part written by Blaise and the second part by

Bharati Mukherjee, with an epilogue by each author, appeared in
1977 and won the "Asia Week" Award. Blaise's fourth book, a
novel entitled *Lunar Attractions*, was published in 1979 and won
the *Books in Canada* First Novel Award.[17] A second novel, *Lusts*,
appeared in 1983. All these books were published simultaneously
in Canada and the United States, and *Lunar Attractions* was also
published in England.

In a remark quoted earlier, Blaise speaks of the early influence
Lawrence and Faulkner exerted on his writing. Like Lawrence,
Blaise often attempts "to capture moments of myth acting
through nature," or — to expand this notion — as the epigraph
from Sartre for "The Thibidault Stories" in *A North American
Education* has it, "to condense into a single mythic moment
the contingencies and perpetual rebeginnings of an individual
human history."[18] Like Faulkner, Blaise — especially in his fiction
set in Florida of the mid- and late 1940s — tries to capture "the
palpability of time-passing in a geographical and historical
milieu."

Several other literary, philosophical, and aesthetic points of
reference suggest the directions from which Blaise's fiction is
moving. Early in his life, for example, Blaise was affected by the
twelve-volume *Collier's Encyclopedia*, especially the biogra-
phies, which he read through perhaps twice a year: ". . . even at
nine or ten I could not imagine living a life that would not
someday be glorified in the encyclopaedia" (Martin, p. 34). Even
more significant as a biographical context for such works as
Lunar Attractions, "The Thibidault Stories," and the story
"Grids and Doglegs" in *Tribal Justice* is the atlas:

There was only one book in my life, at least up to the age of
twelve, and that was the Atlas. From it I typed out, at the
age of eight and nine, a 120-page compilation of all the
salient descriptive facts about the surface of the earth. By
six I had known all the state and provincial capitals (thanks
to maps my mother had always hung in the kitchens of our
Florida apartments); by seven I'd added the world capitals;
by eight all cities in the world (1930 census, alas) with over
fifty thousand, with their exact population; by nine I knew
all the U.S. counties in every state and their county seats,
and by ten I had abandoned the known world for world

maps and country maps of my own invention, hand-painted with invented mountain ranges, cities, and rivers, all very precisely named in languages of my own invention, with appropriate altitudes and populations. Of course I think of it now as a writer's natural evolution, from passionate but passive observation and unconscious mimicry, through to the creation of a personal mythology. (Martin, p.34)

Yet the literary and philosophical tradition to which Blaise feels the greatest affinity is neither Canadian nor American but what he has called "the discursive tradition," "literature compounded of cold observation *and* subjective passion,"[19] in sensibility if not completely in fact a French tradition: Pascal, Flaubert, Proust, Céline, Mann, and Kerouac, among others.

Blaise feels a strong philosophical-religious kinship with Pascal: Pascal's existentialist tendencies and Jansenist sympathies; his emphasis on the wretchedness and anguish of man without grace, without God; his awareness of the random, accidental quality of life and his sense of the inevitable; and his belief that the ambiguously irrational in man is in fact his "essence" and that reason can only end in doubt and leave unsatisfied our deepest concerns:

Pascal, that old *Québecois*, would insist that infinity suspends reason and that to cope with the "infinity of things" lying beyond reason requires grace. And if faith or grace is not forthcoming, silence and fear alone are possible. No one raised in the shadows of French Canada is immune to Pascal, no matter in what form or language he might have absorbed him. . . . It is the hint of unfathomable complexity, the insolent infinity that defeats our humanity, that interests me. . . .[20]

Flaubert and Proust appeal to Blaise first of all, I think, because they are romantic paradigms of the dedicated writer: men to whom art seems more valuable than life itself or to whom life is incapable of meaning unless it be in some way transformed or shaped by art. But Blaise also shares much with Flaubert emotionally, and his sensibility is essentially Proustian, albeit in a minor key. In many ways, too, Blaise is just as thematically preoccupied as Proust with the ways in which the past permeates the present and with the implication in Proust's distinction between "voluntary" and "involuntary" memory that we live mechanically in the present, tragically unaware of the essence of our lives. Consider, for example, Blaise's choice of epigraphs from Pascal for "The Montreal Stories" and "The Keeler Stories" in *A North American Education*, which function as thematic directives for reading each group of stories, though their application need not be restricted to those groups:

So we never live, but we hope to live; and, as we are always preparing to be happy, it is inevitable we should never be so. (p. 1)

We do not rest satisfied with the present. We anticipate the future as too slow in coming, as if in order to hasten its course; or we recall the past, to stop its too rapid flight. So imprudent are we that we wander in the times which are not ours, and do not think of the only one which belongs to us; and so idle are we that we dream of those times which are no more, and thoughtlessly overlook that which alone exists. (p. 39)

Blaise has said he would like to be "a dirty saint" like Céline, to smudge his minor Proustian sensibility in a Célinesque way, perhaps to portray, as Céline, the vileness of humanity.[21] Mann is attractive to Blaise for several reasons: Mann's preoccupation with "the other side," with dualities, with antitheses — discipline and passion, spirit and matter, civilization and the primitive, art and life — and with convergences. In addition, like Flaubert and Proust, Mann represents for Blaise a type of the dedicated artist.

Jack Kerouac is in many ways, I think, both Blaise's alter image and his ironic *Doppelgänger*: Jean-Louis Lebris de Kérouac, born an American of French-Canadian parents; Kerouac, perversely precocious as a child; Kerouac, sports fan, athlete, and inventor of sports games; Kerouac, that "strange solitary crazy Catholic mystic"; Kerouac, that "madman bum and angel,"[22] another dirty saint of sorts. Kerouac's innovative use of a personalized narrator in *On the Road*, in which he presents himself unequivocally as the one who observed it and wrote it all down, is also a technical tradition out of which Blaise writes. Kerouac's subject matter in such books as *The Town and the City, Dr. Sax*, and *Satori in Paris* reflects some of Blaise's concerns too — Kerouac's search for his roots in Brittany in the last, for example.

Because they are "texture-workers" like himself, Blaise is attracted to the fiction of John Hawkes, Richard Yates, Tillie Olson, Cynthia Ozick, and Bernard Malamud.[23] Implying "both vitality and unevenness," texture is, for Blaise, "detail arranged and selected and enhanced. It is the inclusion of detail from several planes of reference: dialogue, fantasy, direct passive observation ('I am a camera'), allusion, psychic wound, symbol, straight fact, etc. etc. — the sum of all that is *voice*" (Metcalf, p. 78). For Blaise, "to present texture and design without distortion" is "the job of fiction";[24] he wants "to view life through a microscope so that every grain gets its due and no one can confuse salt with sugar" (Metcalf, p. 78). Voice, for Blaise, refers to "the control, what is commonly referred to when we mention the 'world' of a certain author; the limits of probability and chance in his construction, the sanctions he leaves us for our own variations, what we sense of his own final concerns and bafflements" (Metcalf, p. 78). A concept not unlike Wayne Booth's notion of "the implied author,"[25] voice "allows the reader a confidence that he is in a shaping vision with a tone coloration that is different from the actual 'character's'" (Metcalf, p. 78). This distinction is particularly important in Blaise's fiction because so much of it is first-person narration, autobiographical in mode and framework if not, as Blaise has said, in fact. Indeed, voice allows for "the *suggestive* space between quite ordinary facts" (Hancock, p. 52) that distinguishes fiction from other sorts of writing.

Blaise's concern with voice, however, does not imply an interest in "character." The "construction of 'character'" is "an honourable but not necessarily compelling occupation" (Metcalf, p. 78). For Blaise, character is really nothing more than "that force which tries to maintain balance" between the "delicate interplays of action and description"[26] that constitute the essence of story: "The centre of my stories is not in my characters. The centre is elsewhere and so I do not set out to create character. I do not set out to write a psychological case study. I am really trying to talk about . . . the world, the nature of event, happenstance, accident, beauty, permanence, change, violence . . ." (Hancock, p.59).

It is a matter of texture to select details, then, and a matter of voice to allow for a wider interpretation. To render the texture of a situation, to make the reader experience details in all their particularity and cumulativeness so that a larger and deeper life may be revealed, Blaise must himself experience the depth of that situation, must see, in fact, "the other side of it":

> Unless I feel that I have seen behind the stage (so to speak) or grasped the texture of a given situation, I won't be content simply to say, here's a street, a house, a car, an attractive young couple. . . . I have to have some *other* sense about that street: what is the last thing I can say about this place? Until I've come to that point I'm not interested in rendering any of it. But once I have come into that awareness, then I can't stop from writing it. It simply grips me and that's it, I'm in its full power.
>
> The first-person narrator is a way of controlling its power by limiting the world outside the self. (Hancock, p.51)

It is this power and Blaise's unwillingness to let anything intrude on voice that account for the sparseness of dialogue in his stories: "Dialogue is a terribly inefficient way to set up anything or to impart information. It only works for me as an instance of inadvertence, or pressure released" (Metcalf, p.79). He is, however, moving more and more away from first-person; in recent stories, Blaise uses third-person: "Third-person opens up many, many aspects because the tone of voice can be varied" (Hancock, p.51). In these new stories, Blaise wants "to link up an individual life with many things outside that life" (Hancock, p.51). The most appropriate point of view for this task is third-person because it represents "a mode of community" — unlike first-person, which is "the voice of isolation" (Hancock, p.51). Yet language is essentially visual for Blaise: "Only the word . . . is truly visual"; and consequently when he writes a story, in either first-person or third-person, he *sees* the story "in terms of its images and situations, the tone and texture and discovery that seems immanent in that situation" (Metcalf, p. 78).

Given Blaise's aesthetic of texture, the most appropriate way to read any of his stories is according to what he calls "the slow approach": through "its associations, its 'world' and its minute details" (Metcalf, p. 77). A Blaise story should be viewed essentially as "a single metaphor and the exfoliation of a single metaphor through dense layers of submetaphors" (Hancock, p. 56), and in this respect Blaise's stories show their kinship to poetry. As John Metcalf has observed, "The 'plots' of [Blaise's] stories are carried [along] by an unobtrusive chain of images much in the manner of poems" (Metcalf, p. 79), and for Blaise "plot is the revelation of inevitability, the slow disclosure of something beautifully obvious, though hidden" (Hancock, p. 61).

The sense of a Blaise story as poem is reinforced by his theory of the function of first paragraphs and first sentences in fiction. No matter how skilful or elegant the other features of a story may be, the first paragraph should give the reader "confidence in the power and vision of the author" ("To Begin, to Begin," p. 24). Genesis is more important to Blaise than apocalypse, for a Blaise story is often, if not always, its beginning amplified or expanded:

> The first sentence of a story is an act of faith — or astonishing bravado. A story screams for attention, as it must, for it breaks a silence. It removes the reader from the everyday. . . . It is an act of perfect rhythmic balance, the single crisp gesture, the drop of the baton that gathers a hundred disparate forces into a single note. The first paragraph is a microcosm of the whole, but in a way that only the whole can reveal. . . . It is in the first line that the story reveals its kinship to poetry. Not that the line is necessarily "beautiful," merely that it can exist utterly alone, and that its force draws a series of sentences behind it. The line doesn't have to "grab" or "hook" but it should be striking. ("To Begin, to Begin," p. 22)

Premature first sentences begin where they should end, and casual and *in medias res* openings are just as damaging. An effective first sentence in a story should, as in poetry, imply its opposite:

If I describe a sunny morning in May . . . I am also implying
the perishing quality of a morning in May, and a good
sensuous description of May sets up the possibility of a May
disaster. It is the singular quality of that experience that
counts. May follows from the sludge of April and leads
to the drone of summer, and in a careful story the action
will be mindful of May; it must be. May is unstable,
treacherous, beguiling, seductive, and whatever experience
follows from a first sentence will be, in essence, a story
about the May-ness of human affairs. ("To Begin, to
Begin," p. 23)

A writer is always trying to suggest the *other* side of things.
He's trying to create a subject and an object, not only the
centerpiece but the frame, and sometimes he feeds the
frame first and withholds the picture. Other times he gives
the picture and withholds the fact that he's going to hang it
in the garage next to an old nudie calendar. Sometimes it
may be a very beautiful thing to be deliberately destroyed.
. . . It's always a matter of working by indirection and by
surprise and by suggestion, which means that everything
you state directly has a shadow meaning, implied. (Hancock, p. 54)

Finally, a good first paragraph should tell us, "in effect, that 'this
is how things have always been,' or at least, how they have been
until the arrival of the story," until the point when "plot intrudes
on poetry" ("To Begin, to Begin," pp. 24–25).

Critical Overview and Context

Although the reviews of Blaise's books in both Canada and the
United States have been generally favourable — for the most part
only appreciative, however, not balanced by genuine critical
analysis[27] — there is no substantial criticism of any of Blaise's
work in print.[28] W. H. New's comments on Blaise in the *Literary
History of Canada: Canadian Literature in English* cover only
A North American Education in his chapter on prose fiction and
are of necessity limited.[29] John Moss devotes a few, at times

confusing, pages to Blaise in *Sex and Violence in the Canadian Novel*.[30] Like Russell M. Brown in his review of *A North American Education*,[31] Moss sees rhetorical problems where there are none in the relationship between the narrator and reader in Blaise's fiction. Moss wants us to enter certain of Blaise's stories through a sympathy and identification with the narrator that Blaise actually invites in only a qualified way. For instance, the story "Grids and Doglegs" in *Tribal Justice*, which Moss uses as an example of the reader's being excluded, is intended for a specific fictional audience — "Are there others, still, like me, in Pittsburgh? This story is for them"[32] — a situation, however, which does not necessarily preclude universal responses. Blaise is, in fact, as I shall show, quite often at pains to suggest the paradigmatic nature of his stories.

Contrary to Moss's feeling of being excluded and made a mere watcher, Brown feels he is being forced into an author-reader intimacy "with an author who does not like himself very much" (p. 115), and he doesn't like it. That is really a moral judgement about a rhetorical situation disguised as a critical assessment; he also complains of a pseudoproblem of unity in *A North American Education*. Brown does make, nevertheless, some important observations about Blaise's fiction: that what might be called the "pseudoepiphanies" of Blaise's stories often "serve not to reveal something, but to lead the reader back into the depths of the story, leaving him to reflect on the experience more than to understand it"; that Blaise's endings are not really resolutions but emblems, often "encapsulating the emotional mood of the story"; and, finally, that Blaise works more often by "juxtaposition" than "straight-forward narrative" (p. 114).

Frank Davey's comments on Blaise in both *From There to Here* and in his essay "Impressionable Realism: The Stories of Clark Blaise"[33] are, it seems to me, very misleading — an unusual circumstance since Davey is frequently an astute critic. He is, for example, as I have already suggested and shall amply demonstrate, erroneous in such remarks as the following: "The form of most of Blaise's stories is casual, straightforward, factual narrative. There is very little reliance on symbolism or imagery; the only 'images' in the stories are the very ordinary physical objects encountered by the characters";[34] Blaise avoids "metaphor, simile, and romantic imagery," although, "curiously, stories which are notable for their lack of metaphor become as units metaphors for continental issues";[35] and, last, speaking of the "masses of detail" in Blaise's stories, Davey says, ". . . they are contaminated by little connotative attribution or by any hint of pathetic fallacy. The narrator projects none of himself into them; he yields to them, allows them to pass through him."[36] Davey's comments about the beginning of Blaise's stories and his argument that Blaise's tone is analogous to that of anecdotal journalism or the reflective essay are also, as we shall see, off the mark. Davey had, it seems, somehow failed completely to respond to Blaise's voice.

Blaise's Works

> If I have any kind of "vision" it's a naturalistic vision. Everything shall be worn down; every life will be worn down . . . the way continents are reduced to bedrock. Everything that's been suppressed will eventually be exposed. Every doubt will be tested. Every weakness will eventually be exploited. (Hancock, pp. 56–57)

The sense of inevitability permeates Blaise's fiction and nowhere more so than in his first book, *A North American Education: A Book of Short Fiction*, which presents us with a vision of loss and defeat resulting from a sudden but inevitable contact with the "insolent infinity" beyond man's control. With a three-part structure — "The Montreal Stories," "The Keeler Stories," and "The Thibidault Stories" — the book is in effect a collage of various mythic moments in the life of North American man held together by theme, tone, and style, but especially by voice as a unifying and controlling instrument.

The protagonist in the three Montreal stories is called Norman Dyer, though the narrators in the second and third stories of the group, "Eyes" and "Words for the Winter," are unnamed, an absence suggesting a loss of identity. Something has happened, we infer, in the white space between the first story, "A Class of New Canadians," and "Eyes," the second story — some movement down, some humiliation, some form of disintegration or loss. The protagonist in the three Keeler stories is Paul Keeler, though, again, two of the stories, the first two, "Extractions and Contractions" and "Going to India," have unnamed narrators. Once more some loss of identity is suggested, for these two stories are "the present" of Keeler's life, while "Continent of Strangers," in which he is named, is his "past." It is significant that the two stories in which the central character is named are, in contrast to the others in their respective groups, in the third person: the sense of identity in these stories does not emanate from an "I," a self. The central character of the four Thibidault stories is Frankie Thibidault, who is named in every story. In terms of the reverse chronology of the three groups of stories taken together, beginning with adult experience and moving back through adolescence or young manhood to childhood, Blaise is suggesting a progressive disintegration of self. The older we get, the more our sense of identity is eroded, yet that sense of identity, of self, is, as the Thibidault stories make clear, a fragile illusion in the first place.

The pattern of the stories, then, may be seen as a retreat into the past only to reveal the same tragic condition of alienation. The name, age, geographical environment, and circumstances of the central character may change in *A North American Education*[37] — and only because of the particular phase of the tragic pattern Blaise happens to be exploring — but he remains an isolated, alienated, culturally and psychologically displaced, rootless individual, a dreamer unable to come to terms with reality. Each story is a metaphor of man's alienated condition, and each story functions as a thematic and structural analogue to each of the other stories in the book. *A North American Education* thus maps out "a man's life" from the present (Dyer has no past) backwards into the past (Thibidault is all past), and the title refers to education into North America in the broadest sense: its surface and its other side.

"A Class of New Canadians" is to the other stories in the book somewhat as the poetic moment is to plot in Blaise's theory about the beginning of stories: it is "the drop of the baton that gathers a hundred disparate forces into a single note" ("To Begin, to Begin," p. 22). The themes, images, and major metaphors that run throughout the book are all basically deployed here as we watch Norman Dyer, significantly through a controlled third-person point of view. (A voyeur motif is subtly announced and

then picked up more loudly later in this story and especially in
"Eyes.") Dyer, whose name suggests one who dyes, one who
appropriates disguises, one who changes colours, is an English
instructor in Montreal, and we see him during one evening in his
life that is a mythic moment revealing all. He is a man trying hard
to maintain an illusion, to sustain a dream of identity, of home,
of place; "a semi-permanent, semi-political exile" from the
United States; a white, middle-class liberal who is "proud of
himself for having steered his life north, even," he thinks,
unaware of his patronizing attitude, "for jobs that were menial
by standards he could have demanded" (p. 3):

> Besides the money, he had kept this second job because
> it flattered him. There was to Dyer something fiercely
> elemental, almost existential, about teaching both his
> language and his literature in a foreign country—like Joyce
> in Trieste, Isherwood and Nabokov in Berlin, Beckett in
> Paris. Also it was necessary for his students. It was the first
> time in his life that he had done something socially useful.
> What difference did it make that the job was beneath him, a
> recent Ph.D., while most of his colleagues in the evening
> school at McGill were idle housewives and bachelor civil
> servants? It didn't matter, even, that this job was a perver-
> sion of all the sentiments he held as a progressive young
> teacher. He was a god two evenings a week, sometimes
> suffering and fatigued, but nevertheless an omniscient,
> benevolent god. His students were silent, ignorant, and
> dedicated to learning English. No discussions, no demon-
> strations, no dialogue. (p. 5)

The ironic deflation in the final two sentences here anticipates
the more intense deflation that Dyer will experience later in the
evening.
    There are several related metaphoric patterns in the story,
which in their effect are functionally poetic: the notion of good
and bad taste as a way to see, evaluate, and transform the world;
a sense of taste as it applies to food, clothing (camouflage and
illusory protection), social position, and linguistic and rhetorical decorum; language as an epistemological, cultural, and
elemental existential force; and surfaces or appearances. All

these motifs appear in the first paragraph of the story. As we do
on two subsequent occasions, once in the middle of the story,
strategically, and once at the end — "He hurried ahead to the
room, feeling that he had let Montreal down"; "He hurried now,
back down Sherbrooke Street to his daytime office . . ." (pp. 10,
14) — we see Norman Dyer at the very beginning of the story as a
man in a hurry ("He had no time for dinner tonight . . ." [p. 5]),
trying as he moves "down" to protect himself from elemental
forces; "this is how things have always been" ("To Begin, to
Begin," p. 24):

> Norman Dyer hurried down Sherbrooke Street, collar
> turned against the snow. "Superb!" he muttered, passing a
> basement gallery next to a French bookstore. Bleached and
> tanned women in furs dashed from hotel lobbies into
> waiting cabs. Even the neon clutter of the side streets and
> the honks of slithering taxis seemed remote tonight through
> the peaceful snow. *Superb*, he thought again, waiting for a
> light and backing from a slushy curb: a word reserved for
> wines, cigars, and delicate sauces; he was feeling superb
> this evening. After eighteen months in Montreal, he still
> found himself freshly impressed by everything he saw. He
> was proud of himself for having steered his life north, even
> for jobs that were menial by standards he could have
> demanded. Great just being here no matter what they paid,
> looking at these buildings, these faces, and hearing all the
> languages. He was learning to be insulted by simple bad
> taste, wherever he encountered it. (p. 3)

Not really a full participant in the city but forever a voyeur, an
outsider, Dyer is impressionably responding only to the surfaces
of Montreal — "looking" at the "buildings" and "faces" and
only "hearing" the "languages" — only to the superficial, metaphorically implied in the adjectives "bleached" and "tanned"
and suggested in the social pretentiousness and mock romantic
glamour of the entire sentence "Bleached and tanned women in
furs dashed from hotel lobbies into waiting cabs." But the
chaotic and the sinister lie beneath this illusory image — "Even
the neon *clutter* on the side streets and the honks of *slithering* taxis *seemed* remote tonight through the peaceful snow"

(emphasis mine)—and Dyer must back away from the reality of a "slushy curb." Then we have the use of the word "superb" three times — a deflating pattern being suggested as we move from the muttered *superb* through the thought *superb* to the felt *superb*—and Dyer's definition of its rhetorical decorum in terms of social pretentiousness: "a word reserved for wines, cigars, and delicate sauces." Finally, for the third time, the notion of social pretension is sounded in the irony of Dyer's arrogant stance of superiority in the final sentence of the paragraph: "He was learning to be insulted by simple bad taste, wherever he encountered it."

Dyer's implicit search for "the authority of simple good taste" (p. 4) in food, drink, films, literature, and someday, he believes, clothing becomes the ironic vehicle of his search for identity, ironic because a mere sophisticated veneer, an illusion of identity. We learn early in the story, too, through such details as his cultivation of ethnic restaurants, that Dyer is trying hard to suppress his past, to suppress what he was and thus what he is. However, as he immerses himself in the cosmopolitan surface of Montreal, there is a strong suggestion that he has never known who he is:[38]

> Since leaving graduate school and coming to Montreal, he had sampled every ethnic restaurant downtown and in the old city, plus a few Levantine places out in Outremont. He had worked on conversational French and mastered much of the local dialect, done reviews for local papers, translated French-Canadian poets for Toronto quarterlies, and tweaked his colleagues for not sympathizing enough with Quebec separatism. He attended French performances of plays he had ignored in English, and kept a small but elegant apartment near a colony of *émigré* Russians just off Park Avenue. Since coming to Montreal he'd witnessed a hold-up, watched a murder, and seen several riots. When stopped on the street for directions, he would answer in French or accented English. . . . He had no intention of returning to the States. (pp. 3–4)

Although Dyer is in a hurry, he must stop at "the window of Holt-Renfrew's exclusive men's shop" because the clothes on the "tanned mannequin" in the window epitomize the false identity, the unwitting disguise, that Dyer is in a hurry to achieve. The mannequin, a mere dumb imitation of a human being, is Dyer's alter ego and is identified later in the story with one of Dyer's students, "the vain and impeccable Spaniard," Miguel Mayor, who is in several ways Dyer's ironic *Doppelgänger* in the flesh. When Dyer arrives at class, he begins, as suggested in an earlier quotation, to romanticize his position and function as a teacher, because he has an identity problem:

> *I love them*, he thought. They need me.
> . . . .
> *They love me*, he thought, taking off his boots and hanging up his coat; I'm not like their English-speaking bosses.
> *I love myself*, he thought with amazement even while conducting a drill on word order. I love myself for tramping down Sherbrooke Street in zero weather just to help them with noun clauses. I love myself standing behind this podium and showing Gilles Carrier and Claude Veilleux the difference between the past continuous and the simple past; or the sultry Armenian girl with the bewitching half-glasses that "put on" is not the same as "take on"; or telling the dashing Mr. Miguel Mayor, late of Madrid, that simple futurity can be expressed in four different ways, at least.
> This is what mastery is like, he thought. Being superb in one's chosen field, not merely in one's mother tongue. A respected performer in the lecture halls of the major universities, equipped by twenty years' research in the remotest libraries, and slowly giving it back to those who must have it. Dishing it out suavely, even wittily. Being a legend. Being loved and a little feared. (pp.5–6)

Despite all this love, Dyer immediately proceeds to patronize[39] his students mockingly by intimidating them with ambiguous or ambivalent sentences from Faulkner's *Absalom Absalom!*, although on the surface his action is meant as a joke:

> "Can anyone here tell me what the *impregnable citadel of his passive rectitude* means?"

"What, sir?" asked Mr. Vassilopoulos, ready to copy.
"What about *the presbyterian and lugubrious effluvium
of his passive vindictiveness?*" A few girls giggled. "O.K.,"
said Dyer, "take your break." (pp. 6–7)

The discussion of language here and in the previous passage
metaphorically suggests, as the rest of the story makes clear, the
cultural and existential conditions of man's alienated life. The
reference to "put on," which is discussed again later in the story
(p. 10) — both "to get dressed" and "to fool someone," maybe
even oneself — is significant because it identifies clothes, foolishness, and false identity or appearances. And, of course,
"superb" is sounded again in the process of Dyer's transforming
experience once more into arrogance, superiority, and pretentiousness: "Dishing it out suavely, even wittily." The notion of
suave is also associated with Miguel Mayor, for whom, as Dyer
ought to realize for his own future, "simple futurity can be
expressed in four different ways, at least."

Dyer tries hard during the evening to maintain his illusion of
Montreal because it is an illusion of identity, of self, but that
sense of self is continually being undermined. Dyer, defensive,
begins metaphorically to get a "sour taste" in his mouth: "He
began the second hour with a smile which slowly soured as
he thought of the Israelis" (p. 10). From Mr. Weinrot, who
has, significantly, emigrated from Israel (a country presumably
founded by the dispossessed of the world) and who, on the ironic
basis of his social appearances ("Something about him suggested
truck-driving, perhaps of beer . . ." [p. 7]), Dyer decides, cannot
"supply the name of a good Israeli restaurant" (p. 7), he hears,
among other disconcerting revelations, this: "Two years in a
country I don't learn the language means it isn't a country," and
"What I was wondering, then . . . was if my English is good
enough to be working in the United States. You're American,
aren't you?" (pp. 8, 9). Weinrot and, as we shall see in a moment,
Mayor are of course moving in the very direction from which
Dyer has fled and from the place he wishes to embrace:

He hurried ahead to the room, feeling that he had let
Montreal down. He wanted to turn and shout to Weinrot
and to all the others that Montreal was the greatest city on

the continent, if only they knew it as well as he did. If they'd just break out of their little ghettos. (p. 10)

Finally, Dyer faces the intimidating, "the dashing Mr. Miguel Mayor, late of Madrid" (p. 6), the details of whose appearance immediately echo the details of dress on the mannequin we have seen earlier in Holt-Renfrew's window ("a brash checkered sportscoat with a burgundy vest and dashing ascot" [p. 4]):

> "Sir," he began, walking stiffly, ready to bow or salute. He wore a loud gray checkered sportscoat this evening, blue shirt, and matching ascot-handkerchief, slightly mauve. He must have shaved just before class, Dyer noticed, for two fresh daubs of antiseptic cream stood out on his jaw, just under his earlobe.
> "I have been wanting to ask *you* something, as a matter of fact," said Dyer. "Do you know of any good Spanish restaurants I might try tonight?"
> "There are not any good Spanish restaurants in Montreal," he said. (p. 11)

Despite Mayor's "prosperous" and "confident" appearance, the "two fresh daubs of antiseptic cream" undermine his image, suggesting that he is vulnerable, that he can be wounded, that he is imperfect; and he immediately and directly assaults Dyer's image of himself by his blunt answer to Dyer's question about Spanish restaurants. As I have suggested, he is Dyer's ironic *Doppelgänger*, an image of what Dyer would like to be: "For an instant Dyer felt that his student was mocking him, somehow pitting his astounding confidence and wardrobe, sharp chin and matador's bearing against Dyer's command of English and mastery of the side streets, bistros, and ethnic restaurants" (p. 13).

Because Dyer feels that he is being "abused by the very people he wanted so much to help" (p. 14) and because the American "superstructure of exploitation," he rationalizes, has "to end someplace" (p. 14), he corrects Mayor's letter of application for a job in the United States only to the extent of scratching out "the second 'humbly' " (p. 14) — a word that reminds us of the whole false pride motif that runs throughout the story — in effect fore-

stalling if not preventing Mayor's opportunity for a job interview. Dyer resents Mayor's wearing of such clothes because he
feels that he himself has not worked hard enough to deserve
them and that Mayor has worked even less hard and is thus even
less deserving: "Dyer realized now that it was comic, even
touching. Miguel Mayor had simply tried too hard, too fast, and
it would be good for him to stay in Montreal until he deserved
those clothes, that touching vanity and confidence" (p. 15).

Dyer, of course, is no less pretentious than Mayor. But what
the clothes represent is an illusion, a veneer, a false identity,
another embracing of surfaces. The story ends with Dyer
hurrying again "back down Sherbrooke," with his illusions
reestablished, and, voyeur that he is, he pauses to look in the
window of Holt-Renfrew's once again, where, however, he now
sees the tanned mannequins as "legless dummies" — some
deflation, some movement in perception towards reality has
taken place[40] — and overtly identifies Mayor with one of them:

> Montreal on a winter night was still mysterious, still
> magical. Snow blurred the arc lights. The wind was dying.
> Every second car was now a taxi, crowned with an orange
> crescent. *Slushy curbs had hardened* [emphasis mine]. The
> window of Holt-Renfrew's was still attractive. The legless
> dummies invited a final stare. He stood longer than he had
> earlier, in front of the sporty mannequin with a burgundy
> waistcoat, the mauve and blue ensemble, the jade cufflinks.
>
> *Good evening, sir*, he could almost hear. The ascot, the
> shirt, the complete outfit, had leaped off the back of Miguel
> Mayor. He pictured how he must have entered the store
> with three hundred dollars and a prepared speech, and
> walked out again with everything off the torso's back.
> I want that.
> What, sir?
> *That.*
> The coat, sir?
> Yes.
> Very well, sir.
> And *that.*
> Which, sir?
> All that.

"Absurd man!" Dyer whispered. There had been a moment of fear, as though the naked body would leap from the window, and legless, chase him down Sherbrooke Street. But the moment was passing. . . . With one last look at the window, he turned sharply, before the clothes could speak again. (pp. 14–15)

The moment of fear speaks of Dyer's real condition of alienation, and perhaps, if the clothes could speak again, that is what they too would say. Montreal is both a metaphor for North American society and the human condition. Dyer is really "out of place," as we all are.

I have spent a considerable amount of space on "A Class of New Canadians" not only because it is the first story in A North American Education, establishing the basic metaphoric and thematic motifs in the book, but also because it is a story that serves well to illustrate Blaise's aesthetic of texture, beginnings, and voice and the way in which a Blaise story should be read as a poem, that is, in terms of "its associations, its 'world' and its minute details" (Metcalf, p. 77). I do not have the space here to treat Blaise's other stories in such detail, but I do want to point out the major metaphoric patterns shaping them and to suggest the ways in which they work.

The title of the second of the Montreal stories, "Eyes," establishes its central metaphoric pattern, and the voyeuristic motif initiated in "A Class of New Canadians" is particularly prominent. The story is in the present tense, and the point of view is second-person: somewhere between "he" and "I," somewhere between "A Class of New Canadians" in the third person and "Words for the Winter" in the first person. The effect of the present tense is a sense of immediacy, and the second person, which is here implicitly a direct address to the reader, not only involves the reader directly but thereby makes the central character's experience universal or exemplary: you too are a voyeur; you too are forever an alien. Paradoxically, the reader ceases to be a detached observer (his position in "A Class of New Canadians"), a voyeur, of the narrative action to become a participant in it — perhaps even to a greater extent than a first-person point of view might invite.

The first paragraph of the story makes emphatic the unnamed

central character's condition of alienation. He is unnamed because he lacks a sense of identity, and there is the suggestion that, in the context of a descent image, he is a foreign body in the bloodstream of Montreal. The first sentence dramatizes the paradox of his dilemma:

> You *jump* into this business of a new country *cautiously* [emphasis mine]. First you choose a place where English is spoken, with doctors and bus lines at hand, and a super-market in a *centre d'achats* not too far away. You ease your-self into the city, approaching by car or bus down a single artery, aiming yourself along the boulevard that begins small and tree-lined in your suburb but broadens into the canyoned aorta of the city five miles beyond. And by that first winter when you know the routes and bridges, the standard congestions reported from the helicopter on your favorite radio station, you start to think of moving. What's the good of a place like this when two of your neighbors have come from Texas and the French paper you've duti-fully subscribed to arrives by mail two days late? These French are all around you, behind the counters at the shop-ping center, in a house or two on your block; why isn't your little boy learning French at least? Where's the nearest *maternelle*? Four miles away. (p. 16)

And so he moves to "a small side street where dogs outnumber children and the row houses resemble London's, divided equally between the rundown and remodeled" (pp. 16–17). A "street where dogs outnumber children" is one of those Blaisian details of texture that reveals so much, and because cityscape in this story, as in the other Montreal-set stories, is correlative to the moral and psychological condition of the protagonist, "the rundown and remodeled" houses are metaphors of the central character's sense of being.

Plot intrudes on poetry in the next paragraph with Blaise's use of that "simple terrifying adverb: *Then*" ("To Begin, to Begin," p. 25), as we watch with the protagonist a voyeur who is watching his wife:

> Then comes the night in early October when your child is coughing badly, and you sit with him in the darkened

nursery, calm in the bubbling of a cold-steam vaporizer while your wife mends a dress in the room next door. And from the dark, silently, as you peer into the ill-lit fire alley, he comes. You cannot believe it at first, that a rheumy, pasty-faced Irishman in slate-gray jacket and rubber-soled shoes has come purposely to *your* small parking space, that he has been here before and he is not drunk (not now, at least, but you know him as a panhandler on the main boulevard a block away), that he brings with him a crate that he sets on end under your bedroom window and raises himself to your window ledge and hangs there nose-high at a pencil of light from the ill-fitting blinds. And there you are, straining with him from the uncurtained nursery, watching the man watching your wife, praying silently that she is sleeping under the blanket. (p. 17)

But because you are an alien in this world of terror and fear,

. . . what can you do? You know, somehow, he'll escape. If you hurt him, he can hurt you worse, later, viciously. He's been a regular at your window, he's watched the two of you when you prided yourself on being young and alone and masters of the city. He knows your child and the park he plays in, your wife and where she shops. He's a native of the place, a man who knows the city and maybe a dozen such windows, who knows the fire escapes and alleys and roofs, knows the habits of the city's heedless young. (p. 18)

Then, repressing the knowledge that we are all voyeurs, all tourists, you move again, ironically thinking that you can escape the voyeurs — in effect, escape yourself:

It's health you've been seeking, not just beauty; a tough urban health that will save you money in the bargain, and when you hear of a place twice as large at half the rent, in a part of town free of Texans, English, and French, free of young actors and stewardesses who deposit their garbage in pizza boxes, you move again. (p. 19)

But in this new "city of Greeks" you are even more estranged, even more a nonparticipant. At the movies, an incident which reiterates the voyeuristic motif:

> You understand nothing, you resent their laughter and you even resent the picture they're running. . . . After an hour the movie flatters you. No one knows you're not a Greek, that you don't belong in this theater, or even this city. That, like the Greeks, you're hanging on. (p. 20)

Outside the theatre, the voyeuristic motif sounding again:

> . . . you come upon a scene directly from Spain. A slim blond girl in a floral top and white pleated skirt, tinted glasses, smoking, with bad skin, ignores a persistent young Greek in a shiny Salonika suit. "Whatsamatta?" he demands, slapping a ten-dollar bill on his open palm. And without looking back at him she drifts closer to the curb and a car makes a sudden squealing turn and lurches to a stop on the cross street. Three men are inside, the back door opens and not a word is exchanged as she steps inside. How? What refinement of gesture did we immigrants miss? You turn to the Greek boy in sympathy, you know just how he feels, but he's already heading across the street, shouting something to his friends outside a barbecue stand. You have a pocketful of bills and a Mediterranean soul, and money this evening means a woman, and blond means whore and you would spend it all on another blond with open pores; all this a block from your wife and tenement. (p. 21)

You continue to watch life during the next few months — for example, your child who "is becoming Greek, becoming Jamaican, becoming a part of this strange new land" (p. 22), as you never will.

Finally comes the day of the "Byzantine moment" at the butcher's when you find yourself attracted to the boxes outside the store:

> Staring out are the heads of pigs and lambs, some with the eyes lifted out and a red socket exposed. A few are loose and the box is slowly dissolving from the blood, and the ice beneath.

The women have gathered around the body; little pieces are offered to them from the head and entrails. The pigs' heads are pink, perhaps they've been boiled, and hairless. The eyes are strangely blue. You remove your gloves and touch the skin, you brush against the grainy ear. How the eye attracts you! How you would like to lift one out, press its smoothness against your tongue, then crush it in your mouth. And you cannot. Already your finger is numb and the head, it seems, has shifted under you. And the eye, in panic, grows white as your finger approaches. You would take that last half inch but for the certainty, in this world you have made for yourself, that the eye would blink and your neighbors would turn upon you. (pp. 23–24)

Removing your gloves is to remove a barrier but also to be unprotected, and to crush the eye would be to cease to be a voyeur, would be to act, to participate, even as the Greek women do. But you cannot: a final image of fear and alienation "in this world you have made for yourself."

The point of view in "Words for the Winter," the last of the Montreal stories, is basically first-person (sometimes plural), modulating occasionally into second-person where the effect is similar to that in "Eyes." The reader is invited to be involved, and the unnamed narrator's experiences, it is suggested, are typological or paradigmatic. The major metaphoric pattern shaping the story involves various images of descent, which also occur in the first two stories but are intensely articulated here. They are complemented by images of disintegration, destruction, and death — ultimately, of the self. The slow descent from the mountains in the north to the city in the south is metaphorically a descent from dreams, from "charade," to reality, from the illusion of security and a sense of identity (represented in the story by keys and objects for those keys — a car, a flat, an office, a cabin — as well as by mail) to, by the end of the story, the almost complete disintegration of self.

The story begins with an image of descent, September, the autumn of life, implying winter, death:

September, month of the winding down. For a month we've lived the charade of ruddy good health up in the mountains north of Montreal. Swimming, rowing, tramping up the mountain just behind our cabin, baking trout over the coals at night. Drinking from the last pure-water lake in the Laurentians, reading by sunlight on the dock, sleeping in the cool mountain air from dark till the sunrise at 5 A.M. This is how I dreamed it would be: water, trout, and mountains. And in this small way, I have succeeded. (p. 25)

But that small success is immediately undermined by the narrator's sense of inferiority (". . . I'm only a teacher too young to have suffered and deserved the lake, but too old to ever learn the proper physical skills" [p. 26]) and subsequently turned to complete defeat by the end of the story. As we move through the story, we experience a densely textured number of details about the neighbourhood and building in which the central character (who wishes "to sink into the city" [p. 30]) and his family live—a building of "sub-divided" flats, in winter the street a "one-lane rut." All of them are metaphorically related to the narrator's psychological and cultural condition, and we learn of the mice slowly, symbolically, eating away their lives, destroying their past and the meaning of their lives, and of how the flat, except for the illusion of beauty in the front room, has "defeated" them.

Then, towards the end of the story, we are presented with the death of Nikos, a boy of six who "falls" to his death from a second-story balcony next door, the narrator the only witness. In his attempt to help, he is physically and psychologically assaulted, an image of horrible alienation:

But they were like the insane, their faces twisted around their open mouths and accusing eyes. *Oh, God, I had dreamed of loving the Greeks*, and now I wished to annihilate them. One of theirs lay injured and I stood accused—a man, a foreigner, tall and blond—and they attacked. From below my shoulders they leaped to hurl their spittle, to scratch my face, to rip my shirt and trenchcoat. I was consumed with hatred for them all, a desire to use my size and innocence, my strength and good intentions, to trample them, to will them back to Greece and their piggish lives in the dark. They pecked like a flock of avenging sparrows, and one finally broke through to throw herself on the child and roll his body over. (p. 33)

We also see Irene — "Her voice was a woman's; her face, Anne Frank's" (p. 35) — whom the narrator suspects of shredding his and his family's mail (their personal lives) and who in the final scene of the story becomes the instrument of the narrator's resentment and alienation because he believes she has stolen his keys, an image of the almost complete destruction of his identity. Significantly, he descends "downstairs" in this final scene to the basement apartment to inquire whether he may leave his son while he goes in search of his wife and a key to the flat. The apartment is an epitomizing image of disintegration, of chaos, and, in his frustration, his pain, he turns self-destructively inward by lashing out in his attitude and behaviour towards his son. The final scene is both grotesque and pathetic:

> I run from the basement, from Kit's screaming, the twin halves of my trenchcoat flapping on my back like the pattern for an immensely fat man's pair of pants. *My keys, my keys*. Car, house, office and cabin. The locker in the basement, the trunks in the locker. The cabin is elaborately locked; I will have to smash a window. The car is locked, rolled up tight. Again a window. The front of my shirt is stained, the Greeks at the bus stop are staring at me.
>
> At this moment, Irene must be in the flat. There is much to steal that we will never miss. Something infinitely small but infinitely complicated has happened to our lives, and I don't know how to present it — in its smallness, in its complication — without breaking down. I who live in dreams have suffered something real, and reality hurts like nothing in this world. (p. 37)

The second group of stories in *A North American Education*, "The Keeler Stories," are overtly arranged in reverse chronological order. We move from Keeler's present in the first two stories, "Extractions and Contractions" and "Going to India" — and we sense that further disintegration has taken place in the white space between these stories — in which, lacking a sense of who he is, he is appropriately unnamed, to his "recent past" in "Continent of Strangers" only to discover the same condition of insecurity, sense of inadequacy and inferiority, isolation, and dislocation. The epigraph from Pascal, which I quoted earlier, provides a thematic focus for the group, though its application need not be restricted to only this middle group of stories in the book. We are forever living in dreams of the past and the future, not in the reality of the present.

In the first story, "Extractions and Contractions," a mythic concentration of a man's lifetime into one day, Blaise is openly insisting on "the disruptive non-sequential nature of teasingly similar events" (Metcalf, p. 78) by his use of collage. While we may live one detail of our lives at a time, we are forever repeating ourselves. Life is not one big dramatic event, but a series of many different events linked together, and "every second in a life relates to the beginning and to the end of that life" (Hancock, p. 57).

The title of the story mocks our expectations in that the narrator's tooth is not extracted and his wife's contractions do not lead to a birth. There is thus a sense of nonaccomplishment, of failure, suggested, reinforced by our sense that in each of the twelve titled sections the narrator lacks control of his situation. The title also points to other thematic and metaphoric motifs and to Blaise's method in the story: *extraction* — to pull out with effort, to obtain from a substance by some process such as distillation, (ethnic) origin, or descent; *contraction* — to draw closer together, to make smaller in length or width or volume, a legal agreement. All these ideas run throughout the story, a contracted narrative of a life distilled. Keeler himself is contracted in more than one sense and desperately trying to extract meaning from his fragmented, disintegrating, decaying life — the collage form itself suggests fragmentation.

The first scene, "Student Power" — the titles are emblematic in their effect — sets the tone for the whole piece. It presents an image of descent, decline, fear, paranoia, helplessness, guilt, humiliation, dislocation, claustrophobia, and contraction; a metaphor of the narrator's condition in Montreal and man in the modern world:

Leaving my office on the twelfth floor and boarding the elevator with ten students, I have this winter's first seizure of claustrophobia. Eleven of us in heavy overcoats, crammed shoulder-to-shoulder in an overlit stainless steel box, burning up. The elevator opens on 11 and two students turn away, seeing that it's full. We stop on 10 but no one is waiting. We are trapped by the buttons other people press before they take the stairs. We will stop on every floor, it is one of those days, though we can take no one in and all of us, obviously, are dressed for the street. On 8 as the doors open and no one presses "C" to close them quickly, I have a sense of how we must appear to any onlooker — like a squad of Gothic statuary, eyes averted upward, silent, prayerful. On 7 I sense there will be a student waiting as the door opens. He looks in, smiles, and we smile back. The doors do not close and we wait. He opens his briefcase and assembles a machine gun. We cannot move; we are somehow humiliated by over-crowding. No one presses "C." A burst of fire catches us all, economically gunned down by a grinning student. The doors close and do not open again until we tumble out in the main lobby. (pp. 41–42)

Winter is a bleak psychological landscape in the story even as dentistry is a metaphor for psychological torture and pain, the narrator's tooth a symbol of the disintegration of self: "The cold wind on a bad tooth anticipates so much" (p. 42). At the end of the section "The Dentist" is one of the major images of decline and decay in the story:

"Success," he pronounces. He is happy, the tooth will drain, in a week he'll pack it. Leaving, I have my doubts. No John Wayne, certainly, I'm beginning to feel like Norman Mailer. A nerve ripped from my body at thirty. I am a young man, haven't deteriorated much since twenty-one, expect to remain the same at least till thirty-five. But somehow, some day, some *minute*, the next long decline begins to set in. At forty I will be middle-aged. At forty-five, twenty-five years from my grave. When does it start — with a chipped tooth? A broken nose? A broken leg even? Oh, no. It begins in choices. The road downhill is slick with fat and fallen hair and little pills. Bad styles and bad convictions. Pain killers, contraceptives, tranquilizers, and weak erections. Pulled nerves. (p. 45)

Forever an immigrant, he will never be at home in the world, in Montreal where life is at best "a low-grade art experience" (p. 52).

Then, after his confrontation outside the university with an Indian, "A brown angel, not of death but perhaps of impairment?" (p.54), in which his guilt ("I could die tonight of a dozen things, all deserved" [p.53]) and paranoia ("Why seize me, I want to cry . . .?" [p.53]) are dramatized, we are presented with an epitomizing image of assault, disintegration, degradation, humiliation. The narrator begins at three in the morning ("The time of the crack-up" [p.55]) to clean up his young child's unintentionally dropped excrement on the rug:

> For a minute or two it goes well, then I notice glistening shapes staggering from the milky foam; the harder I press, the more appear. *My child has roaches*, his belly is teeming, full of bugs, a plague of long brown roaches is living inside him, thriving on our neglect. The roaches creep and dart in every direction, I whack them with the wooden brush but more are boiling from the foam and now they appear on my hand and arm. I see two on the shoulder of my white shirt. I shout but my throat is closed after an evening lecture — I sputter phlegm. These are not my son's; they are the rug's. The other side of this fine Irish rug that we bought for a house in the suburbs that we later decided against, this rug that we haven't turned in months and haven't sent out to be cleaned, is a sea of roaches. I drop the brush and look underneath. Hairpins and tufts of tissue: an angry wave of roaches walking the top of the brush and glistening in the fibers like wet leaves beginning to stir. *My brush*, I want to cry: the brush was my friend. I pick it up and run with it down the hall, the filthiest thing I've ever held. I hear the roaches dropping to safety on the floor. It occurs to me as I open the apartment door and then the double doors of the foyer, and as I fling the brush over one curb of parked cars, that a drop of soapy water anywhere in this apartment would anger the roaches: the drawers, the mattresses, the good china, the silverware at night. First brushes, then rugs, and anything fine we might possibly buy or try to preserve; everything will yield to roaches. All those golden children of our joint income, infested. (pp.56–57)

The story closes with a final, emblematic image of pain, frustration, and pathos:

After such roaches, what improvements? A loft, a farmhouse, a duplex five miles out? Five years in this very place
living for the city, the city our prize. For what we've caught,
stopped, saved, we could have camped along St. Catherine
Street. Holding onto nothing, because we were young and
didn't need it. Always thinking: no compromise. Always
thinking: there is nowhere else we'd rather be. Nowhere
else we can be, now. Old passports, pulled nerves, resting in
offices. I think of my friends, the records they cry over, silly
poems set to music, and I could cry as well. For them, for
us. (pp. 57–58)

"Going to India" consists of thirteen numbered sections
(Blaise, in fact, first entitled the story "Thirteen Ways of Going to
India"). The effect is somewhat like a collage, but the story is
really more a series of inexorable, fearful steps towards the inevitable — towards, the narrator senses, psychological, if not
physical, death. The story begins with an image of horror, a
journey towards death, of man helpless:

A month before we left I read a horror story in the
papers. A boy had stepped on a raft, the raft had drifted
into the river. The river was the Niagara. Screaming, with
rescuers not daring to follow, pursued only by an amateur
photographer on shore, he was carried over the Falls.

It isn't death, I thought, it's watching it arrive, this
terrible omniscience that makes it not just death, but an
execution. The next day, as they must, they carried the
photos. Six panels of a boy waving ashore, the waters
eddying, then boiling, around his raft. The boy wore a
T-shirt and cut-off khakis. He fell off several feet before the
Falls. Who would leave a raft, what kind of madman builds
a raft in Niagara country? Children in Niagara country
must have nightmares of the Falls, must feel the earth
rumbling beneath them, their pillows turning to water.

I was raised in Florida. Tidal waves frightened me as a
child. So did "Silver Springs," those underground rivers
that converge to feed it. Blind white catfish. I could hear
them as a child, giant turtles snorting and grinding under
my pillow. . . . I am death-driven. I feel compassion, grief,
regret, only in the face of death. (pp. 59–60)

Man's fearful, vulnerable condition is the same no matter what the physical or cultural environment, which functions merely as the source of his symbols of fear. The entire image is both an expression of the narrator's present fear and an anticipation of the fearful events to come: "A month from now we'll be in India. I've begun to feel it, I've been *floating* for a week now, *afraid to start anything new*" ([emphasis mine], p. 60).

Throughout the story, we see the narrator in various conditions and degrees of imbalance, fear, and alienation, concerned with time, with his past, trying to hold on to that which is identifiable as he inexorably moves towards the mysterious East and down into the unknown. (Significantly, he is unnamed, in stark contrast to his Indian wife, Anjali Chatterjee, who is.) It is a psychological journey, as well as both a spatial and temporal one. At one point in this descent into darkness, as the world of his past begins to intersect with his future, as his orbit begins to conflict with his Indian wife's, he realizes that even imagination, which before had provided some kind of defence, some kind of order, against the chaos of personal experience, is now inadequate (p. 73). The story ends with an ultimate image of fear and alienation, a paralyzing inability to act, to face reality, the present, the future, the self:

> Other thoughts are coming to me now: not the howling sand of Kuwait—*mud*. Not the empty desert—*people*. Not the wind—*rain*. I want to scream: "*It's four in the bloody morning and I'm soaking with sweat. Somebody do something!*" Even in the open bus as we zip down the runway there's no breeze, no relief. Anjali's hair, cut and set just before we left has turned dead and stringy, her sari is crushed in a thousand folds. This is how the world will end.
>
> ·
>
> We have come inside. Harsh lights, overhead fans. Rows of barriers, men in khaki uniforms behind each desk, desks laden with forms and rubber stamps. The bureaucracy. Behind them the baggage, the porters squatting, the Customs, more men, more forms. Then the glass, the waiting crowd, the parents, the embraces, the right words, the corridors. *I'm not ready*, I want to scream, *turn this plane around*. I've stopped walking, the passports are heavy in my hand. I've never been so lost.

"Darling, what's the matter?" she asks, but she has already taken my hand, taken the passports, the declarations, and given me the flight bag in their place. Ananda stands before me, the beautiful child in his yellow slicker, black hair plastered to his forehead. I take his hand, he takes Anjali's, and I think again: *I'm not prepared*, not even for the answer which comes immediately: and if you're not, it says, who is? (pp. 82–83)

Written from a controlled third-person point of view — the effect is a distancing one — "Continent of Strangers: A Love Story of the Recent Past" is the most conventional and, I think, the least subtly textured story in *A North American Education*. As the title blatantly suggests, it is a story about alienation and problems of communication. On his journey towards his baptism into experience, Paul Keeler, a self-deprecating dreamer, "a stumbler at the dance" of life and love (p. 105), finds himself confronting a series of barriers along the way: language, culture, knowledge, humiliation, age, time, vision (artistic and fantastic), and his own body. Until now a voyeur of life, as his innocent romantic illusions about Europe, love, and the self are one by one shattered, he slowly descends into reality, taking the final plunge, becoming a participant, in the last scene of the story. But, of course, Keeler has paid a price. He is, as we know from the first two stories in the group, taking his first big step towards a Pascalian abyss of wretchedness.

Like "Continent of Strangers," the third group of stories in *A North American Education*, "The Thibidault Stories," are less densely textured than any of the Montreal-set stories in the book, perhaps because they were reworked from a failed novel: "The parts of the novel that I worked into the stories . . . were the 'remembered' parts of the novel; the 'present action' of the book never really built on its 'textured' foundation . . ." (Metcalf, p. 77) — a fact all too evident in the story "Thibidault et fils,"[41] the material Blaise managed to salvage from the "present action" of the novel. "In rewriting the fragments of the novel into stories," Blaise "concentrated on the handling of *time*, trying to make for each of them a self-contained temporality that was lacking in the larger context of the novel. That accounts for the playing with time in three of those stories — the historical / episodic in the little [sic] story ['A North American Education'],

the woven back-to-front quality in 'The Salesman's Son Grows
Older,' and the rather more elliptical nature of 'Snow People' "
(Metcalf, p. 77). Time is a major component of Blaise's natural-
istic vision, which, with a sense of the inevitable, permeates all
four of these stories, in which we see Frankie Thibidault at
different stages in his childhood and in varying degrees and situations of alienation and anguish.

"The Bridge" is a first-person collage of three mythic moments
in which "the contingencies and perpetual rebeginnings" of
Frankie's "individual human history" have been condensed
(Sartre, from the epigraph to "The Thibidault Stories," p. 131).
We witness the precariousness and wretchedness of the terms
(both psychological and cultural) of Frankie's existence. His
dilemma is epitomized in the central image of the incident on the
bridge.[42] Helpless, tempted by the illusory peace and security
implied in nonexistence, death by drowning, he is trapped, in
the metaphors of extremity the story uses, between the icy,
"numbing cold" of the water and the burning, "scalding sun,"
between Canada and Florida (p. 136). By sheer but inevitable
happenstance, he is rescued, ironically, in the final scene of the
story by his father and his father's mistress. That, as we learn in
subsequent stories, is no real redemption whatsoever.

Three related motifs in "The Bridge" are carried forward
prominently in the following Thibidault stories: the various roles
Frankie must play as the salesman's son; Frankie's real and ironic
relationships with his father, especially through Frankie's sexual
awakening; and the notion of the "illicit."

In "The Salesman's Son Grows Older," the privileges of a
salesman's son are ironically a metaphor for the son's lonely,
isolated, displaced condition. Forever seeking deference, if not
sympathy, he feels every bit as foreign, as alienated, in the "cool,
confident, and British" world of Saskatchewan (p. 150), to where
he has involuntarily withdrawn with his mother, as he was in
Florida: "So many new things to be ashamed of—my accent, my
tan, my chubbiness" (p. 153). These feelings are dramatized,
respectively, in the incident of the leaking pen and the kick-
the-can episode. While we may discover that Frankie's father is
not dead, we see Frankie, only age eight, dying psychologically.
The story ends with the adult Frankie — having stumbled "back
to Montreal a middle-class American from a broken home, after
years of pointless suffering had promised so much" (p. 155) —

asking questions, trying to make sense of his apparent meaning-
less movements across North America, trying to come to terms
with his sense of loss, his only answer the accidental, nonrational
quality of life. Like his mother, in whose face he long ago saw
that ". . . *life is long and many things happen that we can't
control and can't change and can't bring back*" (p. 145), Frankie
now knows too that ". . . many things have gone for good"
(p. 161).

Another collage of various but connected moments in Frankie's
life of alienation, "A North American Education," as Blaise
points out, is structured in a "historical / episodic" pattern, and
it explores the real and ironic affinities between "Thibidault et
fils." A dreamer, Frankie is interested in history and his roots. He
reflects on his tenuous sense of identity, most obviously in his
wish to believe his grandfather "extraordinary" — "the face that
seems lifted from the crowd, from history, the face that could be
dynastic" (p. 164). Fishing, an activity ironically binding father
(who is no fisherman) and son, is a recurring metaphor for a
pattern of hope followed by failure that permeates their lives. It is
a structure also identified with Frankie's voyeurism as he finally
does glimpse the naked Annette, his next-door neighbour (who
is, significantly, like Joan in "The Bridge," French-Canadian
from New England), but in his own bathroom, not hers, and
illicitly with his father.

The pivotal event of the story is Frankie's sordid, painful, and
humiliating "North American Education" into sex when his
father takes him to see Princess Hi-Yalla, a lewd, debasing
experience during which he involuntarily ejaculates. Repudi-
ating him, his father banishes Frankie to the realm of the
abnormal, and the ultimate effect is that "sex, despite my dreams
of something better, something nobler, still smells of the circus
tent, of something raw and murderous. Other kinds of sex, the
adjusted, contented, fulfilling sex of school and manual, seems
insubstantial, willfully ignorant of the depths" (p. 173). The story
closes with an emblematic image, both ironic and pathetic—"the
best day of fishing we'd ever had" — of father and son walking
"hand in hand for the last time, talking excitedly, dodging
coconuts, power lines, and shattered glass, feeling brave and
united in the face of the storm. My father and me. What a day it
was, what a once-in-a-lifetime day it was" (p. 184).

"Snow People," the final story in the Thibidault group and in the book and one of the only three stories in *A North American Education* in the third person, does not differ substantially in length or format from the other stories, but Blaise has nevertheless subtitled it "A Novella." Apparently the story had been cut by twenty pages, but for Blaise ". . . the notion of 'Snow People' as a denser and longer piece stuck in my mind, the thing that must be read in the book if you're to get as many of the tones of 'North America' and 'Education' as I could put in" (Metcalf, p. 77).

   "Snow People" points back to the Montreal stories. For this is a story in which Frankie, ironically, finds his "proper" place as a withdrawn nonparticipant, a vulnerable alien, "a freak," a "victim," "like someone in a wheel chair or on crutches — just asking for it" (pp. 190, 189) — set apart by, among other things, his knowledge and intelligence, made into a "Miracle" (p. 205); a story in which he learns that ". . . something dreadful could suddenly cut him down without warning," "without defense," and that life is "unsafe" and ". . . for all his caution . . . he was the one who carried the scars" (p. 194); a story in which he acquires "all the proof he would ever need — that nothing secret and remote was ever lost in the world, was ever perfectly private" (p. 206); a story in which he learns "that both things existed, the unnameable fish and the thing that had eaten it," "the worst thing in the world" (p. 210); a story in which he learns about the vileness of humanity and is symbolically stoned as an outcast; and, finally, a story in which being on the move, unsettled, living in hotel rooms, ironically becomes the norm. The story ends in Jersey City, "the end of the world" (p. 226), with the horrifying, mad incident of Frankie's hanging himself in effigy, an emblematic image that brings us around full circle to the beginning of the story and Frankie's mock suicide by rat poisoning. And there is a sense in which Frankie is indeed dead, for he does not know who he really is.

Tribal Justice, Blaise's second book of short fiction, may be considered an extension or amplification of the thematic and metaphoric world of *A North American Education*, a world of alienation, dislocation, rootlessness, and failure. Blaise subtly establishes a sense of narrative continuity between the two books

by beginning *Tribal Justice* with the story of "Broward Dowdy,"
a character who figures, albeit in a minor way, in "Snow
People." The title *Tribal Justice*, as Blaise has said,[43] is both
specific and metaphoric, and because all the stories in the book
implicitly pivot around the notion of the tribal and/or justice,
any story in the book could be fittingly entitled "Tribal Justice."
North America, the book suggests, is composed of a large
number of tribal entities based on ethnic, geographical, religious,
or other types of cultural differences — Redneck, Cracker,
Yankee, Black, Jew, English Canadian, French Canadian. Blaise's
central characters in these stories, all of them proto-artists or
outsiders with an impaired sense of self, must try to live in such a
culturally disparate world, must find the means to survive when
they deliberately or inadvertently penetrate another tribal world.
Tribal justice is a code by which one may suffer and be punished
just as certainly as one may by legal codes. But although we are
forever encountering other people's tribal gods or taboos, we
usually do not know what the codes of these tribes are. In
defence, we often formulate new tribes, sometimes by resur-
recting discarded tribal gods, and we bring our sense of the tribe
with us wherever we go.

The stories in *Tribal Justice* are organized according to
phases of the tragic vision into three groups of five, four, and
three stories, respectively — a descent motif being deliberately
suggested as the stories move from innocence to experience, from
childhood through adolescence and youth to adulthood, from
the unqualified hope of "Broward Dowdy" to the utter pessimism of "Among the Dead," the final story of the book. Life
becomes increasingly more complicated morally for Blaise's
protagonists as the stories move from hope and the possibility of
acting to a consideration of the choices one must make to the
results of those choices, and there is less and less a sense of
control, of being able to effect resolutions, and more and more a
sense of vulnerable helplessness. Consider, for example, the
meaning of the final image of "Among the Dead" and of the
book:

> I know suddenly that I'm in danger. As though I'd been
> speeding up steadily, unconsciously, on a sheet of ice,
> simply because it was smooth and the tires were quiet. I

have faith enough in omens to know too late that the truck is a pirate on the streets, out purely to cut and damage. I'm already pulling back, looking for a break in the walls of snow to turn off, when half a cinder block bursts loose from the mounds above me and I helplessly slide in position to receive it. It burrows across the hood like a meteorite, bounces once indecisively, hanging in front of the windshield as I swerve, then skids harmlessly off the fender into the gutter snow. By the time I straighten out, the truck's red lights have already receded. Other cars take my place, in cautious pursuit, rushing to embrace the city. (p. 224).

Like so many of Blaise's stories, "Broward Dowdy" establishes a continuity between the physical and the moral in its rich texture of details and skilful use of nuanced dialogue. A "war story," a "story of a separate peace," "Broward Dowdy" gives us a glimpse of not the other side but the underside. It is a story about a boy trying to understand dislocation in the world and in his own personal life through the social adjustments he must make when he enters the, at first "nauseating," world of the Dowdys, significantly a family of migrants. (Blaise thus establishes early in the book a migrant motif that runs throughout the stories, reinforced here by the detail that the narrator and his mother, dislocated, live in a trailer, a "mobile home.") Blaise himself has commented on this story:

"Broward Dowdy" contrasts the squalor, intolerance, poverty, and brutishness of central Florida with a certain nobility of character, humility, and fundamental human decency. Two boys confront each other over the gulf of literacy and the all-important determinant of class. The narrator's family has temporarily fallen (due to the War), and that fall enables the narrator to glimpse at a life he would otherwise have dismissed. The War — an event that Broward knows nothing about, can know nothing about — has brought them together. Squalor and dignity can co-exist; the war is not confined to unnamed islands in the Pacific — the last image in the story conveys strongly the possibility that Broward Dowdy will also be a casualty.[44]

"Relief," a story, according to Blaise (Cameron, pp. 6–7), very much in the mode of Faulkner (compare the first paragraph with that of Faulkner's "That Evening Sun"), concerns the narrator's "years on a promontory threatened by swamps" (p. 26), metaphorically stranded, balancing, between civilization and the primitive. "The Fabulous Eddie Brewster," a story written, Blaise says (Cameron, p. 7), according to *The New Yorker* formula, is about a man's ironic ability to adapt and survive, a story that explores the various meanings of the words *collaboration* and *assimilation*. Blaise has also commented on this story:

> It assumes a certain similarity between central Florida of the 40's and Vichy (Nazi-occupied) France during World War II. A man of many disguises who could prosper during one régime should do well under the other. And Etienne-Eddie manages very well. But I was also, consciously, talking about Canada and the French-English conflict, about losers and survivors, those who hang back (from moral scruples), those who dream but can't really act, and finally, those who can take the Big Plunge, no matter what the consequences. I rather like the character of Eddie Brewster — sure he's a hustler and a cheat and a collaborator — he's not terribly admirable, but he's also around to establish a dynasty in his second, perhaps even his third, country. The *story* is about an immigrant hustler with a blot on his record; the *mold*, however (to me at least), is about extending oneself, from never leaving Regina, to never leaving the French-speaking ghettos of New England, to not taking the final plunge (in backing the brother with a little money), to plowing ahead like some force of nature, starting over rather than yielding to bitterness, envy, or self-pity. Resistance, semi-transformation, and utter collaboration are all under scrutiny in this story. . . .[45]

Yet both Etienne-Eddie and Louis, the narrator's father, are ultimately repudiated, I think, in the moral stance implied in the mother's apparent divorcing of the father, about which we learn strategically in the final paragraph, forcing us to reevaluate the narrative in light of this moral perspective.

A story about the bewilderment of adolescence, "Grids and Doglegs" is thematically an important story in Blaise's canon. It explores the fundamental dualities and antitheses that always converge in Blaise's fictional world, particularly those dramatized in *Lunar Attractions*: arrogance and humility, pride and shame, dreams and reality; the desire or need of "the orderly intellect to lay out patterns" (grids), on the one hand, and the "recalcitrant body and physical world" ("kinky" doglegs), on the other (Cameron, p. 8). The dialectic is epitomized towards the end of the story when the narrator (who, metaphorically, wishes to dance but not be noticed) has his illusory sense of order shattered, for the second time in one evening, by his date's remark about wanting to use the bathroom, and he responds in terms of "doglegs":

> We came to the car; I opened Cyndy's door and she got in. "Normie?" she said, as she smoothed her skirt before I closed the door, "could we hurry? I've got to use the bathroom."
> I held the door open a second. *How dare she*, I thought, that's not what she's supposed to say. This is a date; you're a queen, my own queen. I looked at the sidewalk, a few feet ahead of us, then said suddenly, bitterly, "There's a hydrant up there. Why don't you use it?" (p. 60)

For the second time in one evening, however, an illusion of order is reestablished in the final scene as both the narrator (who is, incidentally, Norman Dyer of "The Montreal Stories") and his date, Cyndy, play their assigned roles:

> *Years of this*, I thought: slapping headlights, kicking tables, wanting to scream a memory out of existence, wanting to shrink back into the stars, the quarries, the right-field stands — things that could no longer contain me. A smiling older man from the table across the aisle snapped his fingers and pointed to his cheek, then to mine, and winked. "Lipstick!" he finally whispered, no longer smiling. I had begun to wet the napkin when I saw Cyndy and the hostess approaching — and the excitement that followed in Cyndy's wake. I stood to meet her. She was the Queen, freshly

beautiful, and as I walked to her she took a hanky from her purse and pressed it to her lips. Then in front of everyone, she touched the moistened hanky to my cheek, and we turned to take our places. (pp. 60–61)

Many of the motifs in this story are picked up and developed more fully in *Lunar Attractions*: alienation, '50s Americana, baseball, astronomy and chess as metaphors,[46] a consciousness of fiction in the narrator's artistic development from the "primitive fiction of gaps and clusters, grids and doglegs" (p. 47), to "story," as well as the dualities explored in the story.

"I'm Dreaming of Rocket Richard," the last story in Part I, in which, interestingly, the narrator is French-Canadian, explores the intense and perverse pain of humiliation and tribal alienation through a characteristic Blaisian series of antithetical images: Montreal and Florida, English and French, American and Canadian, the Bruins and Les Canadiens. "The Seizure," the first story in the second group, continues the motif of cultural and ethnic alienation, although the focus of the story is really elsewhere. In its portrayal of the vileness of humanity very much in a Célinesque mode, it is a story about a sensitive young man, Judd-Justin (suggesting justice),[47] who must come to terms with crudeness and violence in the world:

To be twenty years old and still not have the answer to anything, to have no one to turn to except the Negro at your side whom you respect and fear, and who, you suspect, hates your guts. The whole world was winking behind his back. (p. 87)

Although Judd does not want to take part in the repossession of the Szafranskys' furniture, he must take responsibility for the despicableness of such action because he is "the boss's son": " 'I don't make the rules,' said the deputy. *I do*, thought Judd. *God help me*" (p. 84). The story ends with Blaise making a telling reference to Céline's *Mort à crédit* (*Death on the Instalment Plan*), the title of which is brilliantly appropriate to the story given the seizure of furniture for a failure to meet credit payments and given that we are metaphorically witnessing the death of humanity on the instalment plan. Blaise implicitly throws the question back to the reader. "What, finally, is the right response?" (Cameron, p. 8):

> Over the whining and clatter of gears, Judd began to speak, then to shout: "It's not what I'm reading. It's not just a single book. Reading this book is like going to the Szafranskys day after day—are you listening, Delman? Can you hear me over the motor? It's like confronting something purer than your own situation, you know? This book happens in Paris fifty years ago, but it's today, it's me, it's you. Delman, listen: Haven't you ever seen something so close that it frightened you—or disgusted you? So much so that you had to turn away from it, thankful that it wasn't your situation? Haven't you ever felt that at last you've seen something *final*, the end of something, some definitive corruption, only to return to your own little world and see that it's just slightly less pure, less corrupt, less crystalline? Only slightly? Haven't you? That's how I feel about myself and about the store. That's how I feel about those poor fucking people we took the furniture from. As though everything that I can understand is radiating out from this little book, embracing more and more things that I can't understand, and I want to look away from all of it. Delman"—and now he was shouting, slapping the dashboard so that Delman would at least look his way and quit smirking for just a second—"I feel like it's drowning me. I feel like *we've all died a little bit today* [emphasis mine]. Delman, do you understand?" (pp. 88–89)

The universal quality of the incident we have just witnessed is conveyed through Blaise's use of a shifting third-person point of view by which we see into both Judd's and Delman's minds, by the initial use of a first-person plural, a collective voice, and by the strategic use of a second-person point of view: "You've seen him a thousand times in clothing stores, used-car lots, hotels. Cigars, rings on pinky, gold watch band gleaming on a hairy wrist" (p. 75); "Mrs. Simmons: you've seen her too" (p. 78). The ambiguous geographical and cultural setting of the story — "Where are we? North? East? Midwest? You cannot say" (p. 75) — the references to the American Civil War, and Delman's two haunting visions of the vileness of humanity from *Life* magazine, which suggest that those scenes are analogous to the American Civil War and are being typologically reenacted in the story, all reinforce the sense that this is a universal human story.

"Notes Beyond a History" is a densely textured, richly descriptive story that explores "the other side" of Florida, of history, through a dialectic between the primitive and the civilized, memory and history, myth and fact. The story of Theodora Rourke, as Sutherland the narrator intuitively knows, is beyond history, residing somewhere in the realm of myth, legend, mystery, magic, and fear. It cannot be accommodated by the discipline of history, only by memory. The narrator's discovery of the grotesque tribe of black-white, French-English Catholics in the Florida jungle in 1932 has, paradoxically, both compelled him to become a historian, a wish to order, to make sense of, the past, of experience, and, because of its effect on his imagination, prevented him "from becoming a good one" (p. 104) — even as the trauma of the experience, the narrator implies, drove his brother, in his subsequent vocational interest in rockets and the moon, away from this world altogether.

"How I Became a Jew," the following story, is set firmly in history — "Cincinnati, September, 1950" — and it deals openly, strongly, with the motifs of tribal justice and alienation. Gerald Gordon, precocious and Georgian, must learn "to live with them" (p. 106) — the blacks, Jews, and Northerners of the heterogeneous world of his high school. It is, however, no more prejudiced and dangerous than the Georgian world from which he has come. The story closes pathetically with the perverse mythic concentration of Gerald's first day of school into a dream of socialism:

"Israel," I said aloud, letting it buzz; "Israel," and it replaced Mozambique as my favorite word; *Israel, Israel, Israel,* and the dread of the days to come lifted, the days I would learn once and for all if Israel could be really real. (p. 119)

The last story in Part II, and the longest in the book, "The March," is about "the ways in which we fool ourselves," about choices. It depends for its ironic effect on the firmness of its setting in place and, especially, in time:

My story is bound, in time and place, to the spring and
summer of 1963, to a quadrant of North America that
knows no borders, and to a mood that has vanished as
surely as the spring snows of a dozen years ago. A determinist romance where transcendence lives a microsecond
before it dims into nothing new. I am moved by that in art,
in life; by the slow revelation of a larger design, the way we
live one detail at a time and never know the depth and
extent — the meaning — of what we have made. Every life a
universe unrevealed, as well as a simple, repetitive design. I
am more patient with design now than I was ten years ago.
(p. 121)

Writing retrospectively in 1973 with a sense of historical irony,
with "design," the narrator actually does know the meaning of
what he has made of his life — that is, a "determinist romance" —
by his choices in the spring and summer of 1963.

Pierre-Hector Desjardins, French Canadian from Manchester,
New Hampshire, comes ultimately from a family which has left
"basseville" (lower town), Quebec City, a family for whom
". . . nothing we had ever believed and no place that we had ever
lived had truly been our choice" (p. 124). Returning to his ancestral past, to Quebec City, to confront his tribe and its collective
indignation (which he interprets reproachfully as a "single whine
of resentment" [p. 145]), he is given the opportunity to rectify
that situation by freely choosing his future. It is really a choice,
however, between parts of himself: either his "real future" or his
"historical future," either Linda (his Jewish-American girlfriend)
or Kiki (his Canadian-Métis girlfriend), either the United States
or Quebec, either the civil rights movement or the Quebec
nationalist movement, either Dreiser or Wolfe, either necessity
or flux.

Although he shares neither Québécois bitterness nor American
guilt, Pierre rejects his genuine tribal identity in his decision to
return to Linda and the civil rights march on Washington, ironically thinking that he is going to embrace a larger movement, a
larger identity. In rejecting Kiki, he has rejected his historical
future in ironic favour of his real future. For the historical future
of 1973 tells us that the civil rights movement was eventually
taken over by the blacks themselves and that the nationalist

movement, the Québécois sense of identity, grew and flourished. Pierre has failed to understand fully a dictum which he has offered to the Québécois: "that revolution was rooted in personal transformation, that the most entrenched enemies of change were the patterns of accommodation inside ourselves" (p. 140). Still, given the horror and pathos of Linda's letter, how limited his choice was. Ultimately, however, as implied in the first paragraph, quoted earlier, he does learn that ". . . no gesture in the universe is truly empty" (p. 167).

"At the Lake," the first of the stories in Part III, carries us firmly into the bleak final phase of Blaise's tragic vision in *Tribal Justice*: the consequences of our choices. The story revolves around the related metaphoric notions of being suckered, being hooked, and being invaded, as we watch the narrator's "dream of a northern retreat" (p. 200) disintegrate into "rage and disillusionment" (p. 208). Blaise himself has commented on the coordinating metaphor of the story:

> There it all is from the very first page, I say, "I was suckered into it." I use the name "Lac Sangsue" and I specifically say that the name of the lake does *not* refer to the bugs or the leeches, but rather to the shape of the lake. I specifically said of Lac Sangsue (meaning bloodsucker) that it's named for its leech-like shape, not its fauna. You see, the metaphor is of *naming* things, not *doing* things. My character places his faith, like many academics, in the names of things, in aesthetics. He wants to drain off the "health" of nature, he dreams of transforming himself simply by lying in the sun on his dock in "immemorial torpor." All of it is a denial of reality, all of it is a desire to place faith in names rather than in reality, so that eventually reality comes, eventually what happens to him is that he is forced to pay the price for his preference to live in a world of aesthetics rather than realities so he ends up with bloodsuckers around his body. (Hancock, p. 56)

Between the first and the final moments of the story, the narrator refers to being suckered twice (pp. 201, 202) and hooked once (p. 203), and he discovers that the lake has carp, otherwise known as "suckers" (p. 203). Here is the final 'bloodsucking' scene of the invasion of self after he learns of the "invasion" of his cabin:

What finally happened to me that day is still happening. . . . Feeling reckless, swimsuit dripping heavily — *plop*, *plop* — almost thickly, on the floor. I spooned in the coffee, poured the water. . . . I must have turned about then, coffee in hand, taken a step or two toward the door. Barefoot, I felt something in the puddle of water at my feet. Water was still rolling down my legs. Thinking only of broken glass, I then glanced down at my feet.

In the puddle that had formed as I was making my coffee, three long brown leeches were rolling and twisting, one attached to the side of my foot and the other ones half on the tiles, slithering away. Another *plop* and a fourth dropped from my trunks, onto my foot, and into the wetness. I dropped the coffee, perhaps I deliberately poured it over my feet — I don't remember. I don't remember much of the next few minutes except that I screamed, ran, clawed at my trunks and pulled them off. And I could see the leeches, though I tried not to look, hanging from my waist like a cartridge belt. I swatted and they dropped in various corners of the cabin. I heard them dropping and I heard myself screaming, and I was also somewhere outside the man with leeches, screaming; I watched, I pitied, I screamed and cried.

Even later, when I was dressed and searching the cabin for the dark, shriveled worms, scooping them up with a coffee spoon and dropping them in the flames of a roaring fire in the stove, my body was shaking with rage and disillusionment. I watched the man with the blistered back sit in his wretched little cabin, burning leeches. After an hour, losing interest, I turned away. I haven't been back since. (pp. 207–08)

A story "about the rights of a victim and consumer," "about the arrogance of providers, the frailty of identity" (p. 214), "He Raises Me Up," contrary to the ironic movement suggested in the title, is a further descent, a further loss of control, for the narrator. Stranded in his broken-down car on a cloverleaf in the middle of the night, the narrator begins to see his situation metaphorically, paradigmatically (reinforced by Blaise's strategic use of the second person), as man's absurd existential condition in the world, just as he identified himself early in the story with the comic heroes of silent film:

> Comic because of the way I'm dressed, the five dollars (babysitting money) in my pocket, the faith I'd placed in advertising, the simplicity of my dream of merely getting home in a well-groomed car . . . like the great comic heroes of the silent films, a simple man oddly dressed with a modest aim of, say, crossing a street. Wind blows his bowler, his skimmer, into what — a woman's purse? Fresh concrete? A baby carriage? Guileless but guilty, before he crosses that street a city will learn to cringe. Some enormous frailty will be exposed: technology, wealth, politics, marriage, whatever organizing idiocy that binds us all together will come flying apart, for the moment. Not funny for the clown, of course; his features remain dead-pan, as grim as mine wondering if I should try to start the engine one last time, for heat. (pp. 209–10)

Even though he has somehow blissfully maintained his "posture in the universe" (p. 212) for some seven months, this assault, like that on his teeth, was inevitable: "His car, his teeth. Inescapable indices of the inner man" (p. 213). A metaphoric victim of "gypsies," he has no choice but to "surrender" (p. 215).

I have already alluded to the ultimate sense of defeat implied in the final story of *Tribal Justice*, "Among the Dead." It is a story about all the living dead of Montreal, including the French-Canadian journalist who is the narrator, not just the prisoners of Saint-Vincent-de-Paul Penitentiary, where he voluntarily leads discussions. The narrator's own sense of helplessness and vulnerability is epitomized in the final paragraph quoted earlier, but the sense of the world in which he lives — our world, too, metaphorically — is suggested in such remarks as these:

> Despite its reputation, its tourist bureaus, most of the island of Montreal will break your heart. Most of us live with broken hearts, thumping little fists constricting our throats. (p. 217)

It is a society based totally in the present — the future has
been legislated out and the past is irrelevant. . . . It is a
society based on a single premise satisfactory to all: that
from nine months before they were born until three days
after they die, they will have passed an abbreviated life
without ever having been wanted by a single soul. They
never had a childhood, nor did they ever grow up.
(pp. 219–20)

To say the least, a bleak tragic vision of the world.

Days and Nights in Calcutta grows out of Blaise's experience in India during 1973–74, and it is, as Geoff Hancock has
noted, less a collaboration between Blaise and his wife, Bharati
Mukherjee, than "two separate books written without consulta-
tion aside from the simple agreement that Clark would 'deal with
external reality and she would talk about emotional and inner
memory' " (Hancock, p. 46). It is an exploration and analysis of
the Bengali presence in each of their lives and in their marriage.
As in Blaise's overt fiction, everything in *Days and Nights* is voice
and texture too — in some ways even more effective than the
straightforward fiction in these terms. Blaise speaks of why the
book is more important to him in some ways than his other
work:

The importance of *Days and Nights* was first of all technical — I had to integrate a narrative and a set of feelings
and responses and build up a series of characters, plus I had
to read and manipulate a lot of factual materials. In other
words, it was a novel for me, very much a non-fiction
novel, with a clear sense of myself-as-character, making me
a little more naive than I was, a little more priggish than I
am, in order to, I hope, create a believable transformation
of character by the end. I didn't want to be a Vedantist from
the beginning — I wanted to respect my considerable reser-
vations about India, and show that I went to India not from
prior vulnerabilities, but under the compulsion to understand my wife and myself. Writing that book showed me
that I could do a book-length study and that I could disci-

pline my prose to be non-fictional and that I could string together a few thousand sentences with the injunction that they be continuously wonderous (as Dunstan Ramsay might say), meaning that they show people back home who share none of my problems or my autobiography the simplicity of some very complicated situations.

Secondly, the book informed me of my own feelings: through writing it and the discipline of preparing myself to write it (while still living it, in India), I learned that I have . . . a "shadow" that India touched. I endured more in India than I could have elsewhere, and I also resisted and fought back and demonstrated more vociferously than I have since. In other words, it taught me something of life-as-theatre; it brought something out of me, an affectionate side, that one must repress (for the most part) in North America. It did all those things for me that India is supposed to do, in other words — dented me, even smashed through. I haven't known such freedom, emotional freedom, since.

It is by far the most important book to me — it freed me, for I started with two advantages that I can never have in my fiction: 1) I'm an absolute amateur here, and know *nothing* about this place and will *never* know anything but the most superficial claptrap about it; 2) Everything about the place is fresh, fascinating and of absolute interest, and all I have to do is find a voice, a distance (a vantage point), and let my eyes do the writing. You can see that these two conditions are precisely opposed in my fiction, where I labor under the burden of being an expert in *myself* and the further burden of having *nothing* fascinating to be dealing with. (Cameron, pp. 23–24)

Blaise is far too modest when he speaks of having nothing fascinating to deal with when he uses himself as the material of his fiction, as *Lunar Attractions*, what Blaise sees as the "final work" of his "personal quest for identity,"[48] attests — "a novel about the total development of an individual. How he comes about his individuality, his sexuality, his politics, his profession, and his identity."[49] More specifically, Blaise sees the novel in retrospect as a conscious attempt "to create the portrait of the

authentically Jungian or even Freudian whole mind,"[50] which is
"hermaphroditic,"[51] "solipsistic," and "cosmogenic": ". . . it
sees every aspect of the natural and historical world being played
out in its own imagination, and it literally creates the world that
it sees . . ." (Letter, 16 Nov. 1981). The novel leads to the
inevitable intrusion of the real, mundane world, "the world
of postal inspectors and teachers and gold-diggers," upon
the solipsistic, cosmogenic "world of image and fantasy and
dream": "the rupturing of that perfect lunar wholeness, its love
of dead systems, stuffed animals, vanished civilizations, etc. . . .
by the invasion of the sun-god, the disruptive, vegetative,
chaotic, sexual, etc. at the end" (Letter, 16 Nov. 1981).

Blaise is clearly working in the tradition of the *Bildungsroman*
(novel of formation) or *Erziehungsroman* (novel of education),
and because his emphasis is on the development of the protagonist, David Greenwood (Boisvert), as an artist figure — for
Blaise, a symbol of "unifier and synthesizer, questor and ques-
tioner" (Cameron, p. 9), ultimately visionary — technically the
novel is a subspecies of the *Bildungsroman*, a *Künstlerroman* (an
artist's novel). That is to say, the psycho-sexual development of
the protagonist towards wholeness, self-realization, and selfhood is expressed by his growth as an artist, particularly in terms
of artistic vision and the quality of that vision. David moves
through successive displaced forms of art ("approaches to art"[52])
— digging in the Florida mud, combing his father's hair, perusing
the outdated British atlas, creating fantasy maps, going to baseball games and museums, exploring Palestra, keeping his book of
bizarre correspondence, and being interested in chess, archae-
ology, and stamp-collecting — to fiction-writing. In Freudian
terms, this movement through forms of art is a sublimated form
of sexuality openly and consciously identified as such by the end
of the novel. David comes to understand the equivalence of body
("the ultimate mystery" [p. 154]) and art, body and self, crea-
tivity and sexuality, as he lies passively, femininely, waiting to
have his innocent lunar membrane shattered by the experienced
sun-art god, Apollo. He waits, prepared, for the world to invade
mind, chaos to enter the world of imagination, for body and
spirit to commingle.

In a way that I cannot begin to convey here, *Lunar Attractions*,
more intricately, more richly, than any of Blaise's other work,

reveals Blaise's intense awareness of the infinite and insolent strangeness of the world, "of the sinister and of duplicities and dualities" — "the 'other side' of the familiar surface" (Hancock, pp. 54, 52), the other side of the moon, a world of mystery and madness. Both narrator and protagonist, David looks back on his childhood in Florida during the 1940s and his adolescence in a Midwestern American city modelled on Pittsburgh (which he calls Palestra — "wrestling school," place of struggle) during the 1950s. Because of the abundant details about Americana, there is a sense in which the novel may be viewed as a compressed social history of America during those two decades. This is one way in which David's experiences acquire a paradigmatic quality. But he is deliberately choosing and structuring, "inventing," details from his memory in order to create a self-portrait of the artist, what he calls an autobiographical "proto-fiction." It is a process that ultimately allows for revelation of a larger design, of meaning, in his past. The motives for fiction are complementary: to shape experience in order to give it meaning and to stave off "chaos and randomness and senselessness" (Cameron, p. 9). Implicit in the process is the notion of fiction as a means of discovering, inventing, identity, even as all the successive displaced forms of fiction in the novel are. Although it has other meaning, the final moment of the novel, David's anticipating the imminent invasion of the masculine muse, Apollo, constitutes the decision to create the "proto-fiction," the "lunar wholeness," which is the novel itself.

As David moves from ages five to seventeen, "from being master and creator of a coherent world to being simple player in the real world" (Letter, 16 Nov. 1981), we see him in a series of moral, social, and psychological contexts. In each we glimpse the gradual "seasoning of the green wood" (Letter, 16 Nov. 1981): his relationship to his parents, to fellow students and friends, and to girls and women; the books he reads and the ways in which the entertainment world of radio, television, and movies has shaped his view of himself and of "America"; and, of course, his participation in the various displaced forms of art. The attitude towards self in the novel is intensely self-deprecating — freakishness, left-handedness (sinister and obscene), and alienness are prominent metaphors of the eccentricity or abnormalcy of self. We might be tempted to respond to such a figure negatively or pathetically, but, as Michael Dixon points out, Blaise (through his narrator) obviates such a response by giving the protagonist paradigmatic status. His isolation as the only child of "aliens," for instance, makes him acutely aware of "the universal need for a defined place in an ordered world," for identity, and his obsessive hoarding of facts ultimately makes him aware "that a 'fact' without context is 'meaning-less,' "[53] that there is, as he learns from A. King Gordon, the stamp dealer, a significant difference between mere "gathering" and "collecting." For one thing, the latter is a "sacred" activity.

Convergence is a major thematic and structural principle in the novel that works in terms of an intricate pattern of imagistic and thematic polarities or dualities which are sometimes complementary and sometimes antithetical but which forever impinge on each other or converge, for "all affinities must somehow converge" (p. 134): life and art, art and science, artistry and vision, fact and imagination, experience and fiction, actuality and fantasy (reality and dreams), art and sexuality, the body and art, logic and analogy, gathering and collecting, chaos and order, sanity and madness, past and present, intellect and personality, extroverted and introverted, faith and reason, arrogance and humility (pride and shame), lust and hate, love and lust, the primitive and the civilized, Europe and America, America and Canada, English and French, hearing and seeing, the colourful and the pale, sex and money, day and night, life and death, caterpillars and butterflies, buzzards and storks, whippoorwills and eagles, dinosaurs and airplanes, Chesterfields and Luckies, left-handed and right-handed, surface and depth, mother and father, brother and sister, male and female, homosexuality and lesbianism, Apollo and Diana.

All of these are subsumed in the main controlling metaphors of the novel, the sun and the moon, solar and lunar principles; and besides those already mentioned (wholeness and "image and fantasy and dream"), the lunar-moon motif has several conventional and unconventional, sometimes conflicting, connotations: change;[54] lunacy or madness; the irrational, unnatural, or aberrant; the instinctual, Jungian shadow; the dominating power of the feminine; lesbianism; and of course Diana.[55] The polarities or dualities manifest themselves most obviously in the *Doppelgänger* or alter ego motif in which characters are subtly identified (sometimes ironically) with each other, in the relationship among the several Jungian anima figures in the novel, and in other structural relationships between characters, all of whom converge in David to take on meaning in his personal mythology. The most obvious are his solar father and lunar mother (both displaced types of the artist); Wesley Duivylbuis (who is clearly David's alter ego) and Irving Melnick; Blackthorne and Virginia Pritchett (McQuade);[56] Judith Freisilber and Sheila Roberts; Paul Gaylord and Paul Lachance; and, of course, the most startling convergence of all, Laurel Zywotko, who is her brother Larry Zywotko, who is Paul Lachance.

Although the novel has a three-part structure, marking periods of David's chronological life, there are five — four of them major — emblematic pictures that reveal and epitomize the stages of David's psychological life. The first is the detailed picture of David's mind at age five that begins the novel, a lunar vision of the shadowy world that others (from the solar world) fail to see and "a microcosm of the whole, but in a way that only the whole can reveal" ("To Begin, to Begin," p. 22). Because of its descriptive power, it is worth quoting in its entirety:

> He stands at the rear of the rowboat casting toward a green rubbery beach of lily pads thirty feet away. The sun is low: watermelon pink as it hangs behind the cypress. The sky is a pale, scratched green, verging to peach; it is never blue in my memories of Florida. Trees are black and skies are white or purple, when not an unearthly pastel. The lake that day was glossy olive and thick as molten glass. We were anchored over submerged grasses, each stalk spotted with snails and larvae, the whole growth dense with bluegill. My hand had been in the warm brown water so long that the air itself seemed thin and cold. I could imagine myself breathing in that water. Birds could rise from the grass and mosquitoes hum through the water to settle on my hand and bite it. Nothing would surprise me. It seemed impossible that every cast did not produce a fish.
> Then the grasses lurched, pushed apart by an urgent underwater current, and in the middle of a bald spot over the sandy floor I saw a tiny alligator, motionless but for the mild twitching of its tail. Like a lizard near a light bulb, it

lay glued to the water, snapping at tadpoles with a shudder of its body as they twisted by.

Suddenly the boat shivered.

"Hey, hey, sonny boy!" My father's call was nearly a song. "Look at this!" The tip of the pole was doubled, and the line sliced the water like fine wire. I reached for the net; then I froze. He couldn't see it (he would never see it), and I have never completely rid it from my memory; it is the chord my imagination obsessively plays. Rising behind him nearly as tall and thick as a tree trunk, hung for just an instant the gnarled, stony tail of a full-grown alligator. Then the tail impacted the water, smashing its surface with a sonic boom. I was blinded and pushed backward by an airborne wave of water. My father, in the luckiest fall of his life, was knocked forward over the middle seat and on top of me. Had he slipped backwards he would have been lost. Like most habitual fishermen I have known, my father could not swim a stroke.

He still held the rod, and the line still cut the water in spasms that practically hummed. He was on his knees, face glistening, shirt plastered to his back. We were sloshing in six inches of water. "What in the Jesus hell?" he muttered. He'd skinned his knees, and the boat was rocking madly. I could smell the layers of tobacco, coffee, and toothpaste on his breath, and I saw too much white in his eyes. Nothing is more terrifying to a child than sensing the fear of his invincible father.

It was up to me to save us. In my own panic I thought the giant alligator and whatever was on the line were somehow related. Maddened mother and threatened cub, like grizzlies. I reached for the small knife he kept for snagged hooks. He was still too shocked and too slow to stop me. We were dead anyway, I thought: the gator must have been just under us. I snapped the fishline with a touch of my blade. My father was over me in an instant shouting, "Good God, no, no!" and beating the metal handle of the now-limp rod against the side of the boat. He beat the rod until he snapped it, and then he threw the stump, reel and all, over the lily pads toward the shore. In his rage he nearly fell overboard. His face was the darkest red I'd ever seen. His anger, for the moment, was directed at the water and sky, but he had seen me cut the line.

I held the lantern as he rowed back to the boat-landing deep in the cove near our cottage. A few stars were out by then, the full moon blazed like a spotlight, and I could feel shadows under us as we rowed home in our normal silence. The gator had been after my hand. That's what had caused the sudden parting of the grass. And the grass itself now seemed carnivorous, the brown spots little mouths full of piranha teeth. My father refused to believe what I had seen. Fishing was his purest love. For him, boat-sized alligators in the water he had to trust would mean the end of everything. He believed instead in something larger: a land-locked tarpon, a marlin; his imagination was as wild as mine. He'd buy new equipment, stronger line, and he'd be out again next Sunday. Only, he'd be there alone. He'd never take me with him again.

The shadow and the silence never lifted. A picture of my mind, age five. (pp. 3–5)

David's "sensing the fear of his invincible father" and his cutting of the fishing line resulting finally in his father's "now-limp rod" are a Freudian image of power and impotence with obvious sexual connotations, and it is an image that anticipates the final scene of the novel when son ironically replaces father, and sexuality, power, and impotence recur as motifs.

David spends most of his next five years, as he has his first five, "between life — the sweaty, sunshiny experience that I imagined most of my classmates knew — and a long lunar night that I alone inhabited, and that anyone else, I was sure, would call death" (p. 55). The second emblematic picture is a replica of David's lunar mind at age ten in the baked crayons, David's "caught vision,"[57] that of an embryonic artist as he creates his proto-work of art, "a beautiful pattern, a dazzling accidental map," "a thick, textured, multicolored pizza of wax, a Persian carpet" (pp. 88, 89):

"What is it, David?" she asked, and I couldn't answer, for I was lost in its reds — the blood of my dead sister, I kept thinking — and the multifariousness of black; every color

was tending to black, but I had caught them before they
yielded up their essential green, or blue. I saw in them the
elusive shimmer of things still moist but dying — birds'
wings, fishes' backs; I still remember it, it is — or was — a
replica of my mind at the age of ten, a repository of facts
and textures and colors. And as I stared, I grew frightened
of it, as though I were staring at my own disembodied
brain. A voice whispered to me, *this is crazy; you've done
something crazy. You're loony, that's what.* (p. 89)

The third major emblem is a recurring image that takes on
increasing universal meaning for David with each recurrence, the
nightmare *tableau vivant* of *Nubian Lion*, *Attacking Bedouin
and Camel*:

"It's a *nightmare*, Judy. You know how in a nightmare, if
you're dressed in a suit of armor that has only one little hole
it it, some arrow or something is going to find it, right?" . . .
"Something improbable just begins to chase you. It's
usually something you're confident you can beat. That's
why you let it get closer and closer. Maybe twenty impossible things had to go wrong for something like this to
happen and he's thinking about every one of them. And so
am I. Everything else in here is a picture of the normal way
things happen, right? But this thing — sure, it's corny — but
look at my hands!"
. . . .
    "Whenever I look at this, I can imagine all kinds of things
that could sneak up on me." (pp. 224–25)

And I thought of the Bedouin with his jammed rifle, his
leg raked by the lion's claw, the camel's anguished neck
twisted in a way that would never straighten, and I knew
again why that undead assemblage (Hannes Fischer, 1883)
had moved me to tears that first day. Not for the camel or
for the Bedouin, but for us all: Hannes Fischer and my
mother and the Freisilbers, and my father and the lions and
finally, always, for me. All of us caught smiling and innocent and confident under a blue Hapsburg sky on broad

lawns behind high fences, while out there on the street raged madness and final destruction. . . . That *tableau vivant* of Bedouin, camel and lion stands for me even now as a picture of my adolescent mind as binding as that first one of my father, his broken rod and the alligator had been at five. (p. 246)

The fourth emblem is David's "file," or *"book,"* of bizarre correspondence, a picture of his mind at age seventeen (pp. 250–55). And the last emblem is David's final, mysterious, converging vision of Sheila Roberts which fuses together dream and reality, art and experience, the past and the present, male and female principles, violence and love, love and lust, art and sexuality, art and the body, hearing and seeing, victory and defeat, power and impotence, gun and rod,[58] father and son:

"What in the hell do you *mean* — not losing it? What makes you think you've got it?"

I was standing close to her now, five steps away, and my breath was short, arms trembling, hands still clenched.

"One thing," she said.

"What?"

"Want me to show you?"

I didn't answer. Perhaps I expected a gun, something she could hold and point and threaten me with. But of course that wasn't it. The bracelets tinkled violently even before I saw her move, and in an instant I was confronting a lady with her skirt held high and nothing on underneath, and as in a dream I was advancing, my hands open and ice cold, advancing not for the throat but on that vision: oh, I knew so suddenly *everything*, how the parts and the passions fitted and I swear it was a moment of love — unashamed and inviolate and heedless of consequence. Then my own small pistol went off in a loud report, doubling me over as she dropped her skirt the moment my fingers touched her there and she was gone and the music came back louder than ever and I found myself clutching the same door frame for support until the spasms passed and then I ran far from the parked cars to lie in the grass under the sun and to wait for the god to invade my blood.[59] (p. 305)

The detail of the door frame in the passage reminds us of the anguish of David's father over Joe Whitehouse (Giuseppe Casabianca, with whom Sheila Roberts is thus identified as a power agent) and of the haunting vision of Laurel "against the door frame" (p. 167). In its sexual context, it is a scene that should be implicitly compared with the other sexual moments in the novel between David and Judy as well as David and Laurel / Larry. Virginia McQuade's erotic poems, "Lunar Attractions" and "Apollo," are also invoked here. What we are witnessing is the symbolic death of the innocent David Greenwood — it is implied that it is suicide — and his need to be reborn, to be transformed. And so the novel ends with the narrator lying passively in a female position waiting for the penetration of the life-giving Apollo, and the Freudian motifs here at the end and throughout the whole scene bring us back full circle to the beginning of the novel. David's final understanding about Laurel / Larry and about Wesley's inability to accept the equation or equivalence of opposites prepares him to understand, to balance, if not resolve, the contradictions between lunar and solar principles in his own self.[60] An astoundingly rich book, *Lunar Attractions* deserves a book-length commentary, but I hope that I have suggested in these probing, rather than comprehensive, remarks some of its power. It is a book that deserves to be much better known.

One can make only tentative assessments of living writers, of course, and Clark Blaise is no exception. With only four books,[61] his canon is relatively small, but, as I have been trying to show, the extraordinary richness and intensity of these books, the sheer consistency of good writing, suggests that on qualitative grounds Blaise might be considered a major Canadian writer of fiction. He is at a turning point in his career with his move back to the United States and his writing beginning to take a new turn. It remains to be seen where these changes will lead. In the meantime, Blaise has given us, in my judgement, some of the most rewarding books of fiction ever produced in Canada.

NOTES

[1]Geoff Hancock, "An Interview with Clark Blaise," *Canadian Fiction Magazine*, Nos. 34–35 (1980), pp. 46, 48. In all further references, this work is abbreviated as "Hancock."

[2]Blaise's parents divorced some twenty years later, and his mother returned to Winnipeg. In 1978 his father, who had remained in the United States, died in Florida, while Blaise was writing his novel *Lunar Attractions*. According to Blaise, that novel is indirectly dedicated to his father.

[3]Leesburg, Florida, where Blaise lived for a time, is the fictional Hartley of several of his stories.

[4]John Metcalf, "Interview: Clark Blaise," *Journal of Canadian Fiction*, 2, No. 4 (Fall 1973), 77. In all further references, this work is abbreviated as "Metcalf."

[5]In another interview with Hancock, Blaise says, "The Florida I knew as a child was very wild and untamed, full of nature, poverty, illness, violence, and terror for me" ("Interview," *Books in Canada*, March 1979, p. 30).

[6]Pittsburgh is the fictional Palestra of *Lunar Attractions*.

[7]Sandra Martin, "The Book That Changed My Life," *Saturday Night*, May 1976, pp. 34–35. In all further references, this work is abbreviated as "Martin."

[8]Malamud's *The Assistant* affected Blaise as offering "a fresh way of telling a story" (Martin, p. 35), and *Lunar Attractions* is dedicated to Malamud and his wife.

[9]Among other Canadian writers who have attended the Iowa Writers' Workshop are Dave Godfrey, W. D. Valgardson, Rudy Wiebe, and Kent Thompson.

[10]Bharati Mukherjee, "An Invisible Woman," *Saturday Night*, March 1981, p. 36.

[11]Blaise's move to the United States is a complicated issue, but some of the reasons are suggested in his wife's essay cited above. In a letter to me, he says, "I want to go into an eccentric orbit around Canada for the next few years, wobbling in, and out, of focus . . ." (Letter received from Clark Blaise, 9 June 1980).

[12]Douglas Rollins, "The Montreal Storytellers," *Journal of Canadian Fiction*, 1, No. 2 (Spring 1972), 5.

[13]Rollins, p. 5.

[14]Only Hood and Smith have remained in Montreal. Blaise continued his association with Metcalf by coediting Oberon's annual anthology *Best Canadian Stories* from 1978 to 1980, and he also coedited with Metcalf an anthology of short stories for classroom use, *Here and Now* (Ottawa: Oberon, 1977).

[15]One of Blaise's most recently published fictions, "Man and His World" (*Fiction International*, No. 12 [1980], pp. 80–90), written in the third person, is a significant stylistic departure from his previous fiction, and another story, "Prying" (*Toronto Life*, March 1982, pp. 38, 87–92), has a woman as its central character and is also in the third person.

[16]One story in *Tribal Justice*, "The Fabulous Eddie Brewster," originally entitled "The Mayor," had won the University of Western Ontario's President's Medal on first publication in *The Tamarack Review* in 1967.

[17]Blaise was justifiably disturbed by the *Books in Canada* judges' grudging recognition of the merits of *Lunar Attractions*. (See *Books in Canada*, April 1980, pp. 3–4.) Their apparent "passionate embrace of mediocrity" and "distrust of an admittedly professional and (just possibly) a distinguished, or at least accomplished, novel" Blaise sees as a symptom of a larger cultural malaise in Canada:

> The deeper forces hurt anyone who writes seriously in this country, be he or she honored or forgotten. The enemy out there is (to be kind) the amateur spirit, which translates to a love of mediocrity. And I mean as well its necessary corollary: a fear of ambition, an embarrassment with excellence. Layton would have called it constipated and masturbatory; I'd call it a decayed gentility, others might excuse it as neo-colonialism. The point is, no one escapes it. ("The Truth Is: We Are All Laytons," *The Globe and Mail*, 3 May 1980, p. 6)

[18]*A North American Education: A Book of Short Fiction* (Toronto: Doubleday, 1973), p. 131. All further references to this work are indicated by page numbers in parentheses.

[19]"Author's Introduction," in *New Canadian Writing, 1968: Stories by David Lewis Stein, Clark Blaise and Dave Godfrey* (Toronto: Clarke, Irwin, 1968), p. 67.

[20]"Author's Introduction," in *New Canadian Writing, 1968*, p. 68.

[21]Barry Cameron, "A Conversation with Clark Blaise," *Essays on*

Canadian Writing, No. 23 (Spring 1982), p. 14. All further references to this work (Cameron) appear in the text.

[22]See Jack Kerouac, *The Dharma Bums* (New York: Viking, 1958).

[23]There are other affinities between Blaise and Malamud: both, for example, focus on alienated protagonists and the unfulfilled life.

[24]*Days and Nights in Calcutta* (Garden City, N.Y.: Doubleday, 1977), p. 18.

[25]See Wayne Booth, *The Rhetoric of Fiction* (Chicago: Univ. of Chicago Press, 1961).

[26]Clark Blaise, "To Begin, to Begin," in *The Narrative Voice: Short Stories and Reflections by Canadian Authors*, ed. John Metcalf (Toronto: McGraw-Hill Ryerson, 1972), p. 26. All further references to this work appear in the text.

[27]Michael Dixon's review of *Lunar Attractions*, in *Queen's Quarterly*, 86 (Winter 1979–80), 722–23, is a significant exception.

[28]Robert Lecker's probing essay "Murals Deep in Nature: The Short Fiction of Clark Blaise" (*Essays on Canadian Writing*, No. 23 [Spring 1982], pp. 26–67; rpt. in his *On the Line: Readings in the Short Fiction of Clark Blaise, John Metcalf, and Hugh Hood* [Downsview, Ont.: ECW, 1982], pp. 17–58) appeared subsequent to my writing of this essay. Ann Mandel has written intelligently about Blaise, especially *Days and Nights in Calcutta*, in a forthcoming book that deals with Alice Munro as well as Blaise. Mandel's brief comments on Blaise in an essay in *The Ontario Review*, "Useful Fictions: Legends of the Self in Roth, Blaise, Kroetsch, and Nowlan" (No. 3 [Fall 1975–Winter 1976], pp. 26, 30, 27), are certainly tantalizing: *A North American Education* explores, she suggests, "that borderline area between autobiography and fiction . . . between the teller and the tale — that borderline space where the useful fictions are born and thrive"; the book is a manifestation of "the self writing about itself and its life, creating its own masks through the assumption of style"; and "a rich presence of place and physicality of imagery becomes possible when the self is freed again and again from one story to the next, to see itself *there*, and then *here*, when each story is imagined *again*."

[29]See W. H. New, "Fiction," in *Literary History of Canada: Canadian Literature in English*, 2nd ed., gen. ed. and introd. Carl F. Klinck (Toronto: Univ. of Toronto Press, 1976), III, 259–60.

[30]*Sex and Violence in the Canadian Novel: The Ancestral Present* (Toronto: McClelland and Stewart, 1977), pp. 49–52.

[31]Russell M. Brown, "The Insolent Infinity," rev. of *A North Amer-*

ican Education, Canadian Literature, No. 58 (Autumn 1973), pp. 114–16. All further references to this work appear in the text.

[32]*Tribal Justice* (Toronto: Doubleday, 1974), p. 47. All further references to this work appear in the text.

[33]Frank Davey, "Clark Blaise," in *From There to Here: A Guide to English-Canadian Literature since 1960* (Erin, Ont.: Porcépic, 1974), pp. 55–57; "Impressionable Realism: The Stories of Clark Blaise," *Open Letter*, 3rd ser., No. 5 (Summer 1976), pp. 65–74.

[34]Davey, *From There to Here*, p. 56.

[35]Davey, "Impressionable Realism," pp. 72, 74.

[36]Davey, "Impressionable Realism," p. 72.

[37]As Blaise himself has said, ". . . the interchangableness of the various characters is not meant as a particularly well-disguised secret" (Metcalf, p. 79).

[38]"He was a walking violation of American law, clad shoes to scarf in Egyptian cottons, Polish leathers, and woolens from the People's Republic of China" (pp. 4–5). Clothing, of course, has long been a traditional symbol in literature for the appearance or illusion of identity. Consider, for example, the clothing motif in *King Lear*.

[39]Other instances of Dyer's patronizing attitude are the following: " 'It'll come, don't worry,' Dyer smiled. *Don't worry, my son*; he wanted to pat him on the arm" (p. 8); and " 'Ah, yes,' he said, smiling. French-Canadians were like children learning the language" (p. 10).

[40]In his fantasy, however, the dummies become torsos and naked bodies, diction that suggests a movement, once again, away from reality, a restoration of illusion.

[41]*Prism International*, 5, Nos. 3–4 (Winter 1965–Spring 1966), 27–42. The story also relies, excessively for Blaise, on dialogue, not in this extensive form one of Blaise's major strengths, as he himself admits: ". . . I don't have the ear to sustain a story through dialogue" (Metcalf, p. 79).

[42]Perhaps as a subtextual detail here we are meant to see Pascal's image or vision of man, of self, poised between the abyss of greatness and the abyss of wretchedness, a vision which Pascal apparently first experienced after an accident on the Pont de Neuilly, when his carriage hung halfway over the water until he was rescued. See Robert W. Gleason, S.J., Introd., *The Essential Pascal*, trans. G. F. Pullen (New York: New American Library, 1966), p. 10.

[43]In a radio interview with Bud Reilly, *Metro Journal*, *CJRT*, Toronto, 1974.

[44]"Author's Commentary: The Cast and the Mold," in *Stories Plus*, ed. John Metcalf (Toronto: McGraw-Hill Ryerson, 1979), p. 28.

[45]"Author's Commentary: The Cast and the Mold," pp. 28-29.

[46]"I think of those [chess and astronomy] as anxiety-ridden. Chess! I used to play competitive chess and I never knew a more ego-destructive and tossing-and-turning-all-night-long type of occupation than chess-playing. You'd replay endlessly your mistakes. I think of chess as the epitome of sickly pursuits, something worthy of Thomas Mann or Nabokov — it's really out of that tradition. And astronomy too, is the most humbling of sciences. The concepts of astronomy are so humbling to human ambition and to the human frame, to the human context, that I look on it as an apprenticeship either to humility, or to cynicism. . . . So I would dispute the idea of either of those things being mind-improving or healthy. They're metaphors" (Hancock, p. 57).

[47]Blaise also uses names elsewhere for their symbolic significance — in *Lunar Attractions*, for example.

[48]Hancock, "Interview," *Books in Canada*, p. 30.

[49]Hancock, "Interview," *Books in Canada*, p. 30.

[50]Letter received from Clark Blaise, 16 Nov. 1981. In all further references, this letter is abbreviated "Letter, 16 Nov. 1981."

[51]Aristophanes speaks in Plato's *Symposium* of a mythological notion relevant to the novel. He says that there were originally three sexes — man, woman, and the union of the two: ". . . the man was originally the child of the sun, the woman of the earth, and the man-woman of the moon, which is made up of sun and earth . . ." (in *The Dialogues of Plato*, ed. R. M. Hare and D. A. Russell, trans. Benjamin Jowett [London: Sphere Books, 1970], 189a–190c, II, 203).

[52]*Lunar Attractions* (Toronto: Doubleday, 1979), p. 154. All further references to this work are indicated by page numbers in parentheses.

[53]Dixon, rev. of *Lunar Attractions*, p. 722.

[54]In the Ptolemaic astronomical system, the world above the moon is unfallen, stable; the sublunary world is subject to eccentricity. The world above is a world of spirit, and the world below is one of sense, as in Donne's "A Valediction: Forbidding Mourning."

[55]The goddess of not only the moon, but also forests, animals, and women in childbirth, though also honoured as the virgin goddess and patroness of women in general and worshipped as an earth goddess associated with fertility rites and "the great mother of the gods." Another mythic trace in the novel is the story of Apollo's pursuit of

Daphne, who turns into a "laurel" tree (greenwood), which becomes sacred to him as a god of poetry.

[56]She is one of the many name-changers in the novel—all the names of characters seem to have symbolic significance — a motif that suggests identity problems and dissatisfaction with, perhaps an outright repudiation of, one's past and an urge to transcend origins.

[57]A term from Michael Ondaatje's well-known poem " 'The Gate in His Head.' "

[58]Compare the detail of the fishing pole in David's story of the two brothers (displaced versions of himself and his father), where it is again a symbol of both sexuality and power (p. 289).

[59]The absence of conventional punctuation (specifically commas) in this last sentence establishes a sense of swift continuity between David's successive actions.

[60]"Wesley Duivylbuis (Wesley + Devil). . . . Things in Wesley's world cannot both 'be' and 'not be' at the same time: Laurel / Larry is not permissible. . . . He cannot find a coded way of acting out his confusions, as David can" (Letter, 16 Nov. 1981).

[61]Blaise's fifth book, and second novel, *Lusts* (Garden City, N.Y.: Doubleday, 1983), was published subsequent to my writing this essay.

SELECTED BIBLIOGRAPHY

Primary Sources

Thesis

Blaise, Clark. "Thibidault et fils." M.F.A. Thesis Iowa 1964.

Books

Blaise, Clark. *A North American Education: A Book of Short Fiction.*
Toronto: Doubleday, 1973.
———. *Tribal Justice.* Toronto: Doubleday, 1974.
———, and Bharati Mukherjee. *Days and Nights in Calcutta.* Garden
City, N.Y.: Doubleday, 1977.
———. *Lunar Attractions.* Toronto: Doubleday, 1979.
———. *Lusts.* Garden City, N.Y.: Doubleday, 1983.

Contributions to Periodicals and Books

Blaise, Clark. "Thibidault et fils." *Prism International,* 5, Nos. 3–4
(Winter 1965–Spring 1966), 27–42.
———. "Stories by Clark Blaise." In *New Canadian Writing, 1968:
Stories by David Lewis Stein, Clark Blaise and Dave Godfrey.*
Toronto: Clarke, Irwin, 1968, pp. 65–134.
———. "To Begin, to Begin." In *The Narrative Voice: Short Stories
and Reflections by Canadian Authors.* Ed. John Metcalf. Toronto:
McGraw-Hill Ryerson, 1972, pp. 22–26.
———. "The Sense of an Ending." In *76: New Canadian Stories.* Ed.
Joan Harcourt and John Metcalf. Ottawa: Oberon, 1976, pp. 63–69.
———. "Writing Canadian Fiction." *Fiction International,* Nos. 6–7
(1976), pp. 5–11.
———, and John Metcalf, introd. *Here and Now.* Ed. Clark Blaise and
John Metcalf. Ottawa: Oberon, 1977, pp. 5–6.
———. "Author's Commentary: The Cast and the Mold." In *Stories*

Plus. Ed. John Metcalf. Toronto: McGraw-Hill Ryerson, 1979, pp. 27–29.

———. "The Truth Is: We Are All Laytons." *The Globe and Mail*, 3 May 1980, p. 6.

———. "The Important Things Begin Where the Game Leaves Off." *TV Guide*, 26 July–1 Aug. 1980, pp. 17–20.

———. "Man and His World." *Fiction International*, No. 12 (1980), pp. 80–90.

———. "A Writer's Forum on Moral Fiction." *Fiction International*, No. 12 (1980), pp. 7–8.

———. "Prying." *Toronto Life*, March 1982, pp. 38, 87–92.

———. "South." In *Small Wonders: New Stories by Twelve Distinguished Canadian Authors*. Ed. Robert Weaver. Toronto: Canadian Broadcasting Corporation, 1982, pp. 23–30.

———. "Memories of Unhousement, A Memoir." In *The Pushcart Prize VIII: Best of the Small Presses 1983–84 Edition*. Ed. Bill Henderson. Wainscott, N.Y.: Pushcart, 1983, pp. 121–44.

Secondary Sources

"Blaise of Glory." *Books in Canada*, April 1980, pp. 3–4.

Booth, Wayne. *The Rhetoric of Fiction*. Chicago: Univ. of Chicago Press, 1961.

Brown, Russell M. "The Insolent Infinity." Rev. of *A North American Education*. *Canadian Literature*, No. 58 (Autumn 1973), pp. 114–16.

Cameron, Barry. "A Conversation with Clark Blaise." *Essays on Canadian Writing*, No. 23 (Spring 1982), pp. 5–25.

Davey, Frank. "Clark Blaise." In *From There to Here: A Guide to English-Canadian Literature since 1960*. Erin, Ont.: Porcépic, 1974, pp. 55–57.

———. "Impressionable Realism: The Stories of Clark Blaise." *Open Letter*, 3rd ser., No. 5 (Summer 1976), pp. 65–74.

Dixon, Michael. Rev. of *Lunar Attractions*. *Queen's Quarterly*, 86 (Winter 1979–80), 722–23.

Gleason, Robert W., S.J., introd. *The Essential Pascal*. Trans. G.F. Pullen. New York: New American Library, 1966.

Hancock, Geoff. "Interview." *Books in Canada*, March 1979, pp. 30–31.

————. "An Interview with Clark Blaise." *Canadian Fiction Magazine*, Nos. 34–35 (1980), pp. 46–64.

Lecker, Robert. " Murals Deep in Nature: The Short Fiction of Clark Blaise." *Essays on Canadian Writing*, No. 23 (Spring 1982), pp. 26–67. Rpt. in his *On the Line: Readings in the Short Fiction of Clark Blaise, John Metcalf, and Hugh Hood*. Downsview, Ont.: ECW, 1982, pp. 17–58.

Mandel, Ann. "Useful Fictions: Legends of the Self in Roth, Blaise, Kroetsch, and Nowlan." *The Ontario Review*, No. 3 (Fall 1975–Winter 1976), pp. 26–32.

Martin, Sandra. "The Book That Changed My Life." *Saturday Night*, May 1976, pp. 34–35.

Metcalf, John. "Interview: Clark Blaise." *Journal of Canadian Fiction*, 2, No. 4 (Fall 1973), 77–79.

Moss, John. *Sex and Violence in the Canadian Novel: The Ancestral Present*. Toronto: McClelland and Stewart, 1977, pp. 49–52.

Mukherjee, Bharati. "An Invisible Woman." *Saturday Night*, March 1981, pp. 36–40.

New, W. H. "Fiction." In *Literary History of Canada: Canadian Literature in English*. 2nd ed. Gen. ed. and introd. Carl F. Klinck. Toronto: Univ. of Toronto Press, 1976, III, 259–60.

Rollins, Douglas. "The Montreal Storytellers." *Journal of Canadian Fiction*, 1, No. 2 (Spring 1972), 5–6.

Hugh Hood (1928–   )

KEITH GAREBIAN

Hugh Hood (1928–   )

KEITH GAREBIAN

Biography

HUGH JOHN BLAGDON HOOD was born of mixed ethnic ancestry in Toronto on 30 April 1928. He has strong historical connections to Quebec, eastern Ontario, Nova Scotia, and, more remotely, to Britain. His mother's grandmother, a Quebecker named Aubeline Lemieux, married a sea captain named Blagdon from Lévis. Hood's maternal grandfather, Alfred Esdras Blagdon, married Eugénie Sauriol from eastern Ontario and settled in Toronto. Hood's paternal grandfather, John, was born in Shelburne, Nova Scotia, and was a descendant of Admiral Samuel Hood, member of a famous naval family from Bridport, England. He married Katherine MacDonald from Antigonish and lived in Nova Scotia. It is therefore not surprising to find in Hood a sense of a single, yet bilingual, Canada. Hood remembers hearing French spoken around his home from earliest childhood.

He received all his own formal education in English, attending Catholic parish and high schools where he received his grounding in Catholic doctrine and liturgy, and in Scripture. He went on to obtain a Ph.D. from the University of Toronto in 1955 with a thesis on "Theories of Imagination in English Thinkers 1650–1790." After teaching in Hartford, Connecticut, for six years (1955–61), he settled in Montreal and has taught English literature ever since in the French milieu of the University of Montreal. He is fluently bilingual, and several of his books create a bicultural ambiance that bears witness to his perception of Canada as a dual nation in which a minority French culture still possesses a strong sense of itself.

Not by any means a Québécois nationalist, Hood is proud of Canadian biculturalism. In a letter to Naïm Kattan in *Le Devoir* in 1964, following the publication of his first novel, he articulated his aim to unite the whole of Canadian bilingual culture in his work, however imperfect the style of his written French or however vulnerable he would become to the charge of opportunism in his writing:

> J'ai l'ambition de devenir un romancier ni anglais ni français mais tout à fait et simplement canadien. Je veux réunir les consciences de mes parents en la mienne. Et je me propose à écrire dans mon français très imparfait des phrases et de temps en temps même des pages entières dans mes romans et nouvelles afin d'unir dans mon oeuvre la totalité de notre culture, la culture la plus intéressante du monde.[1]

Hood is not material for sensationalism. He lives with his wife, the artist Noreen Mallory, and their two sons and two daughters in Notre Dame de Grace (N.D.G.), a quiet, aging section of Montreal, and though he has a circle of artist-friends (such as painters Seymour Segal and Louise Scott, photographer Sam Tata, and writer John Metcalf), he is not a social creature given to gossip or glittering trivia around the cocktail circuit.

After numerous short stories and two false starts as a novelist, he set aside his unpublished manuscripts ("God Rest You Merry" in 1958, and "Hungry Generations" in 1960) to produce a collection of short fiction, *Flying a Red Kite*, in 1962. This brought him an award of two hundred dollars from the Toronto Women's Canada Club in 1963. His short fiction continued to appear in numerous journals such as *Esquire*, *The Tamarack Review*, *The Canadian Forum*, *Prism*, *The Fiddlehead*, *Queen's Quarterly*, *The Montrealer*, and *Saturday Night*, while he was exercising his scope and style in the 1960s with novels such as *White Figure, White Ground* (1964), *The Camera Always Lies* (1967), and an urban pastoral, *Around the Mountain: Scenes from Montreal Life* (1967). Citations came in "The Yearbook of the American Short Story" and "Distinctive Short Stories in American Magazines" in 1961 and 1967.[2] Moreover, Hood twice won the President's Medal from the University of Western Ontario: in 1963 in the short story category for "The End of It"; and in 1968 for a general article, "It's a Small World." *White Figure* won the Beta Sigma Phi Award in 1965 for the best first novel by a Canadian.

The 1970s bore five new novels: *A Game of Touch* (1970); *You Cant Get There From Here* (1972); *The Swing in the Garden* (1975); *A New Athens* (1977); and *Reservoir Ravine* (1979). The last three, together with his latest novel, *Black and White Keys* (1982), comprise the first third of Hood's serial epic The New Age / Le nouveau siècle, which is designed as a twelve-part philosophical fiction that will use all the materials of Hood's life in order to tell a massive story of Canada's "ranges of behaviour" or "moral possibilities."[3] *The Swing in the Garden* won the City of Toronto Book Award for 1975 and was much touted to win the Governor General's Award that year, though it failed to do so.

More of Hood's short stories were collected in *The Fruit Man, The Meat Man & The Manager* (1971), *Dark Glasses* (1976), *Selected Stories* (1978), and *None Genuine Without This Signature* (1980). Hood remained a virtuoso, turning briefly to sports biography with *Strength Down Centre: The Jean Béliveau Story* (1970), essays with *The Governor's Bridge Is Closed* (1973), a commentary on Seymour Segal's painting in *Scoring: Seymour Segal's Art of Hockey* (1979), and more essays with *Trusting the Tale* (1983).

His prodigious production will, no doubt, continue. With so much material to his credit, Hood is anything but that familiar Canadian phenomenon — the one-shot success. If destiny permits, Hood aims to complete his millennial New Age series by the year 2000.

Tradition and Milieu

George Woodcock calls Hood "the great Balzacian."[4] Some other critics think of him as a Canadian Proust, possibly because of Hood's own comments on his attempt to write a Proustian novel about Canada.[5] But Hood, who invites critics to make comparisons between his work and that of great literary predecessors, says there have been no major literary influences on his work.[6] He does point, however, to certain writers who have helped him articulate his preoccupations. From Dante he has derived a mode of allegory which is both Roman and Catholic and which provides a way of linking visible and invisible worlds. Hood has always preferred Dantean allegory to Spenserian because it is "very much more able to save this world, and to preserve this world, than Spenserian" (*BF*, p. 49). Hood finds Spenser dualistic, Platonic, and not possessed of a very substantial awareness of "the fleshly solidity of things." Hood's own work has always thrived on physicality, but it has sought, like Blake's (though without idiosyncratic symbolism or ideology), to make connections between matter and spirit, and to treat literature as a secular analogy of Scripture (*BF*, p. 32).

Hood, who describes himself as "through and through a Catholic novelist" (*BF*, p. 81), is most strongly steeped in Scriptural tradition. In his autobiographical essay "Before the Flood" (*BF*, pp. 5–20), he recalls that among the very first books of his childhood were Butler's *Catechism* and the Benziger Brothers' *Bible History* — an "Old Testament Made Easy" (*BF*, p. 5) — with its fascinating steel engravings, maps of the Holy Land, and stories "that you...turned over in your head with no power whatsoever to banish them from the imagination" (*BF*, p. 7). Hood's Catholic upbringing also ensured that the Bible entered by ear as well as by eye. At church, he heard the New Testament read fifty-two Sundays a year, plus feast days and holy days of obligation. Almost the whole of the sacred text was read to him in the course of a few years. The parables and longer sacred narratives rubbed against his miscellaneous readings of children's literature — especially British adventure stories about young heroes and heroines — and he became dimly aware of "some allegiance of heroes with innocence and virtue" (*BF*, p. 12), one of the central themes in his fiction today.

But even as his allegorical imagination was being exercised, his sensory exhilaration was being provided great range. The liturgical rituals and emblems of a practised Catholicism were accompanied by his exposure to vivid secular emblems in such things as *The Wonder Book of Motors* with its automobile badges whose colours "were those of chivalric blazonry, bright, unambiguous, specific, nothing to do with good taste, hierarchical, permanent, even liturgical" (*BF*, p. 14). These emblems were precise ornamental forms that had heraldic grace and power, and they were precursors of the literary emblems he was to find in Dante, Chaucer, Spenser, Donne, and Shakespeare.

From the beginning, then, Hood's sensibility was emblematic, and it tempered a classical sense of order and form with a romantic sense of mystery and wonder. His "sportive play of imagination" (*BF*, p.31) today ensures that his allegory is not restricted to sombre tones and moods. Like Wordsworth, he makes long associative chains, "bringing vast quantities of material together, and synthesizing them and comparing them and adjusting them minutely in their relationships" (*BF*, p.30). The most emphatic example of this power emerges from the pastoral *The Swing in the Garden*, which is an encyclopaedia of Canadian history, politics, economics, and sociology, a map of a section of Ontario, a vast catalogue of objects in daily Canadian life, and an experiment with Wordsworthian "spots of time."

Wordsworth has always been a felt presence in Hood's writing, particularly in the diction and concepts which appear throughout *Flying a Red Kite* (and most explicitly in "Fallings from Us, Vanishings"), the long excursion and the vision of the New Jerusalem in *A New Athens*, the lakeside setting of *Reservoir Ravine*, and the philosophical meditations in all his major works. Hood puts a discussion of "spots of time" in the second chapter of *Around the Mountain* and admits to having tried to imitate *The Prelude*, especially with reference to the idea that "there are significant moments in our experience which can be spread out over all the rest of our experience and give form" (*BF*, p.62).

In common with most of the great English Romantics, Hood is "very much concerned with the structure of the imagination, and its relationship to the observable world and to the invisible world, and imaginative knowing as a mode of knowing — perhaps the most important mode of knowing, certainly more important than rational inferential thought" (*BF*, pp.21–22). His doctoral thesis was concerned with "the psychology of the imagination, particularly in the seventeenth and eighteenth century [sic], and the views of the imagination which evolved in that period towards the mature thinking of Wordsworth and Coleridge" (*BF*, p.22). It was, as he also remarked in his fascinating interview with Tim Struthers, a propaedeutic to Romantic poetics—particularly those of Wordsworth and Coleridge—and it argued that the mediaeval view of modes of knowing was very much like the poetic psychology of Wordsworth and Coleridge, especially where moral and artistic valuation are concerned.

The thesis is carried forward in his novels, which, for all their

splendid emblematic narratives, make an effort to comprehend
the nature of the imagination and its relationship to the visible
world. Like Coleridge, who is his "great model in English literature for the union of intellect and the poetic gift" (*BF*, pp. 62–63),
Hood is meditative, and though he does not share Coleridge's
pantisocratic passion or Godwinian ideology, he has wide ranges
of reference which slowly reveal networks of ideas. The New Age
series is really a single, enormous synthetic span, in which the
first book is a massive repository of ideas and emblems that link
up complexly as the series progresses.

The aesthetic complex and synthesis are achieved through a
deeply religious approach to life. Here again Coleridge serves as
a model, for as Robert Lecker has observed in his essay "A Spirit
of Communion: *The Swing in the Garden*" (*BF*, pp. 187–210),
"Hood sees God in the Coleridgean sense, as the embodiment of
a Trinitarian view which resolves dualities through the creation
of a synthesizing Holy Third" (*BF*, p. 188). The most obvious
example of the Trinitarian view is in the title story of *The Fruit
Man*, in which, to quote Hood himself,

> the Fruit Man is God proffering the apple, and the Meat
> Man is Christ incarnate, and the Manager is the Holy Spirit
> moving the world. The Manager manages the world, the
> Meat Man offers himself for us to eat, and the Fruit Man
> places the knowledge of good and evil in the middle of para-
> dise and tells us not to strive too high for it. (*BF*, p. 38)

The Trinitarian view, which is fundamentally Catholic rather
than purely Coleridgean, dominates Hood's moral vision. There
are numerous examples of the synthesizing third in his structures, characters, emblems, and themes. It is not at all surprising
to find a three-part division in both *You Cant Get There From
Here* and *The Camera Always Lies*, or a romantic triangle in
White Figure, White Ground, or a triptych at the beginning of
The Fruit Man. Hood seems to be arguing that "unity and trinity
are built into existence," and that "life is shot through with Trinitarian structures" (*BF*, pp. 40–41).

Hood does not invite comparison with Canadian literary
predecessors or contemporaries, but this is not because of any
colonial romanticism or vain self-aggrandizement. It is simply

because he does not believe that there has been any Canadian writer good enough to have served as an influence. Stephen Leacock he admires more for his "agreeable tenuousness" in *Sunshine Sketches* than for a full shape (*BF*, p. 52), and Morley Callaghan more for his pioneering work and some of the theological questions his work raises, than for sheer artistry (*BF*, p. 26).

It is to foreign masters that we should turn for correspondences. *The Swing* seems to be modelled in certain ways after Proust, whom Hood regards as the greatest novelist of our century for having written "the modern epic of the individual consciousness which aims at the discovery of the fundamental laws governing the human mind."[7] But to say that Hood patterns certain things in his fiction after Proust is not necessarily to assert that Hood is the equal of his model. As Hood himself admits, he does not understand humans the way Proust did, and he does not rival Proust in his psychological analysis. However, there are certain powers of Proust that Hood does rival: intellectual analysis of the nature of history and the metaphor of time, for example (*BF*, p. 66). Like Proust, Hood sees our image-making faculty as a means both for grasping the world and for detaching ourselves from it, "the essentially double process of consciousness," as Roger Shattuck terms it.[8]

Comparisons have been made between Hood and Joyce in the matter of epiphany, and between Hood and Anthony Powell in the matter of social relationships over long periods of time. Joyce, for Hood, is the "master of the dictionary" and "the master of the meanings of words" (*BF*, p. 64). The Joyce who interests Hood is not the symbolist or Mallarméan, but the Joyce who compiles esoteric etymologies. And Hood, who thinks of himself as an encyclopaedist and maker of catalogues, naturally feels drawn to Joyce's massive assimilative synthesis. Then there are also Joyce's epiphanies with which Hood makes a connection, for the epiphany as a "sudden flashing forth of intelligibility" (*BF*, p. 71) serves as a focal point in Hood's anagogical method.

What Hood has learned from Anthony Powell have been techniques for moving around in a time span, looking at it "sometimes from the point of view of a man whose generation is coming to a close, but not in strict chronological order" (*BF*,

p. 70). Matt Goderich, the narrator in *The Swing*, is sometimes forty-five years old, and sometimes eight or seventeen. He is a reflection of his times and country as he grows up, and his story is not only about himself but the groups and subgroups that produced him. This sense of one small society in a larger one is what Hood finds in Powell, who can see a society "as an infinite series of social relations" (*BF*, p. 69).

But Hood finally transcends comparisons. In spite of the games he frequently plays with sly allusions, parodies, and cross-references to Proust and Powell, he makes imaginative leaps beyond all predecessors and contemporaries. In Canada, his fiction defies Margaret Atwood's puerile literary categories about victims,[9] or John Moss's analysis of patterns of isolation.[10] In terms of both American and European literature, which are largely concerned with the self in recoil from the world, Hood's work stands outside any tradition of pessimism, cynicism, or nihilism. Where other writers (such as J. D. Salinger, Norman Mailer, James Baldwin, Bernard Malamud, Günter Grass, V.S. Naipaul) discover absurdity in the liberal's idea of the victim, the conservative's idea of the pariah, or the radical's idea of the rebel, Hood discovers intelligence and form in man and the world. He is not sympathetic towards the modern distemper, and while locating man at critical junctures of history, he does not attest to alienation or nihilism. Where the persistent sense of modern fiction is that of cataclysm or corruption, Hood looks back to Eden and ahead to the millennium. And yet this mythic sense is never divorced from the mundane world; it is an encounter with the cosmos to which Hood joins civilization.

Hood gives attention to all the aspects of formal realism but is a critical assessor of his own realism, though he does not fall into Cartesian dualism, where conceptual reality becomes the only reality, or where there is a radical cleavage between mind and body. Hood is a monist who, like Aquinas, would describe the intellectual soul as the form of the body, which depends on the body for its sense knowledge. His monistic critical realism shows its philosophical underpinnings in his doctoral thesis. His Catholic education helped him to develop the view that imagination and abstraction (as Aristotle and Aquinas understood them) are really the same power of the soul, and that scholastic notions of abstraction were "penetrative and life-enhancing and vitalistic and not concerned to 'murder to dissect' but...to comprehend fully and to rejoice in the nature of the things they contemplated" (*BF*, pp. 22–23).

Critical Overview and Context

From the very outset of his literary career, Hood has experienced curious reactions from critics. While Ronald Sutherland and Robert Fulford rushed to proclaim him as part of the Canadian mainstream, Margaret Atwood and D. G. Jones ignored him altogether in their grids for Canadian literature. A. J. M. Smith lumped him together with Ross, Garner, Ludwig, Richler, and Munro for realism and a "peculiar amalgam of irony and sentiment,"[11] which is really quite a startling lump considering the many radical ways in which Hood differs from his contemporaries. Paul Denham tells us that Hood is concerned with "delineating states of individual consciousness,"[12] although Hood himself asserts that he is more interested in emblems and icons of redemption and atonement.[13] His anagogical method did not receive scrutiny until John Mills drew attention to it, explaining that Hood fashions "a sequence of emblems, *topoi* for meditation, in which nothing is dramatic, although almost everything is rendered vividly and in which the characters, though unbelievable in their serenity, are intensely alive."[14]

Without any guiding aesthetic by which to read and judge Hood's work, critics at first expressed provincial condescension. For *Flying a Red Kite*, his first book, Hood was praised for his "sound English,"[15] "chic Esquire style,"[16] and his very convincing Canadians in "specific Canadian situations."[17] Yet there was also a sense that he was somehow too Canadian. The newspaper reviews of the next book, *White Figure*, were stunning in their inability to understand his method and purpose. One reviewer found the novel "pseudo-sophisticated," which confirmed for him "how painfully provincial and amateur" most Canadian fiction was.[18] Another complained of the "oddly Canadian tone of morality," especially in the ending, in which the protagonist's French Canadian wife becomes pregnant and experiences "Victorian bliss."[19]

The academic critics were more perceptive, though no less

divided in their reactions. Philip Stratford, writing in *Saturday Night*, explained that the book was not simply about the shopworn theme of the artist, but was the story of "white on white, not one of marked contrasts and moral chaos, but one of subtle and satisfying variations within the limitations of the normal and possible."[20] Desmond Pacey in *The Fiddlehead* raised a negative view in interesting terms, faulting Hood for being indecisive, for not having fully made up his mind "whether to write a serious novel about the nature of the artistic experience or a romance about family feuds and ancestral guilt in rural Nova Scotia."[21] Nevertheless, Hood was regarded as a serious craftsman, and Ernest Buckler made Americans aware of Hood's talent in a *New York Times* review, which ended with a phosphorescent glow: "He has an incisive humor; he's not afraid of an honest sentiment; he can outwrite many an established novelist."[22]

It was Hood's second novel, *The Camera Always Lies*, that led to a cliché about his writing. After fulsome praise for his documentary sense and urban pastoralism in *Around the Mountain*, Hood was castigated for his solar romance set in Hollywood. William French was disappointed that Hood had turned to American content.[23] Phyllis Grosskurth saw the book as "unsubtly blatant" — a weak imitation of Scott Fitzgerald.[24] Others called it a "distorted rehash of real life"[25] and a "thoroughly bad novel."[26] But it was Robert Fulford who concocted the famous canard, commenting that almost everything Hood wrote in nonfiction had "a sharp, clear, truthful ring," whereas almost everything he wrote in fiction was "dull, flat and spiritless," when it wasn't simply "embarrassingly pretentious." Fulford found in Hood "a superior journalist" being "slowly strangled by an inferior novelist."[27]

Critics usually missed Hood's allegory beneath the documentary veneer. This led to bizarrely narrow misreadings. How else to explain the label of "pot-boiler" for *The Camera*,[28] an allegory of violence, or Dave Godfrey's incredible charge of "frippery" against the brilliant Grail story "Fallings from Us, Vanishings"?[29] Sometimes the critics' bemusement was outrageously risible, as in William French's case when he wondered if *A Game of Touch*, an allegorical exploration of human values, was "a comedy, a put-on, or a serious attempt at allegory."[30] The same novel was mislabelled by Fulford as the first of the Trudeau novels,[31] and by

Patricia Morley as a "modern version of the picaresque."[32]

But there was a cult forming. Alec Lucas praised Hood's short fiction for its ability to go beyond the particular, relate inner life to the external framework of society, and derive meaning from life rather than impose it.[33] And after three splendid books, *The Fruit Man*, *You Cant*, and *The Governor's Bridge*, Hood received special attention from William New, Frank Davey, John Moss, and Patricia Morley. In *From There to Here*, Davey saw Hood as a refreshingly romantic contrast to the gloomy anxieties of Margaret Atwood, Graeme Gibson, and Marian Engel. Though Davey placed Hood rather incongruously close to Mordecai Richler, he considered him to be "one of the most accomplished of his generation in the art of invisible craftsmanship" and felt that Hood's "total credibility" was "unexcelled in Canadian writing."[34] William New asserted that Hood strove for an "effect of surface reality which on examination proves to be masking much deeper truths."[35] John Moss seconded this view by arguing in *Sex and Violence in the Canadian Novel* that the primary intent of Hood's novels was "to comprehend the ultimate nature of reality, the ontology of being, on a scale that includes the spiritual without demeaning the mundane and ordinary."[36] Ignoring or overlooking the didactic, and emphasizing comic structure and technique, Morley, in the first book-length (or, more precisely, half book-length) study of Hood, argued that he, like Rudy Wiebe (the other half in her book), has an essentially comic vision and that his comedies involve all three types of integration mentioned by Northrop Frye: social, erotic, and individual (Morley, pp. 2–3).

Hood's applauders often helped to complicate matters by raising contradictory voices. *You Cant* was treated by New as a parable about *Canada's* cultural dilemma, while Morley treated it almost like propaganda for moral rearmament. New read Leofrica, Hood's imaginary African setting, as "a sort of Canada rewritten by the mind" (New, p. 264), whereas Morley suggested that the "controlling intellectual pattern is a vision of the brotherhood of man under the fatherhood of God and an ironic portrait of that brotherhood betrayed" (Morley, p. 52). Other critics, upset by the mixture of gravity and humour, and oblivious to Hood's religious allegory, griped over their copies of Conrad and Waugh.

However, more perceptive criticism was forming. Dennis Duffy argued that the "ultimate concern of Hood's fiction is the presence of grace," which provides a sense of "a larger backdrop against which everyday human activities, tragic and otherwise, are played."[37] Kent Thompson wrote of Hood's "expanding universe,"[38] and Pierre Cloutier suggested that "most of Hood's work up to now" had been "an allegory of salvation" and showed that *You Cant* could be interpreted in terms of *allegoresis* and *mystère littéraire*.[39]

The Swing started The New Age series and prompted some of the most stimulating and sophisticated literary debate in Canada. Everyone found much to praise in Hood's loving evocation of Toronto in the 1930s, and Fulford remarked that the book could be read as a history text (Fulford, p. 66). However, not everyone found the form illuminating. Brian Vintcent called the book a "rag-bag of random opinions and observations on the passing scene";[40] Peter Stevens, oppressed by the "ponderous piling up of realistic detail," wished that the narrator's memory would fail;[41] David Pryce-Jones in England rediscovered the famous law of diminishing returns, "whereby the more detail a novelist provides, the less composed his overall picture becomes";[42] and the present writer found the book "an inchoate drama" in which documentary detail swallowed the narrative.[43] John Mills charged that, despite the vigour and clarity of its prose, the novel appeared to lack form and contained no story in the conventional sense. Mills found that none of the changes in the pattern of the narrator's life was accompanied by any sense of crisis, and that drama did not seem to interest Hood very much. Mills concluded that Hood's bland Catholic optimism verged on Pelagianism and resulted in the vision of a Norman Rockwell in which nothing could disturb the narrator's tranquillity.[44]

Hood responded to Mills's charges, declaring in an epistolary exchange that he was not a post-Flaubertian psychological novelist but "an epic novelist, a maker of catalogues and encyclopedias and compendia of syntax-forms, and vocabularies of names and a story teller and etc." (Hood and Mills, p. 136). His strong declaration of aesthetic principles generated critical reassessment of his method, although not everyone approved of this method. Sam Solecki criticized it for being overly didactic, and for creating a form that falls "somewhere between fiction and history with none of the strengths of either."[45] But, after examining its form closely, I now found *The Swing* to be a Canadian pastoral in "its blameworthy after-the-Fall style that does not, however, shrink from new tensions that provoke our conventional understanding of relationships between the new and the old, the individual and society, man and God, knowledge and innocence."[46] Robert Lecker considered the book to be "an innovative high point in Canadian fiction" and explored its four aspects of communion: aesthetic, communal, communicative, and spiritual (*BF*, pp. 187–210).

When *A New Athens* and *Reservoir Ravine* appeared, I had to revise my earlier assessments of Hood as a novelist. Sensitive to Hood's purpose and method, I found *A New Athens* a "dream of a novel"[47] and *Reservoir Ravine* an emblematic witness to generation, nativity, and redemption.[48] Dennis Duffy saluted The New Age series as "a magnificent project, worthy of the highest genius."[49] Hood, it was becoming increasingly clear, was developing his own fictional species in which it was possible for him to be "*both* a realist and a transcendentalist allegorist" not bound by "the forms of ordinary realism" (Hood and Mills, p. 145).

In 1979, at a symposium in Hugh Hood's honour at Stong College, York University, several eminent critics celebrated his ascendancy in Canadian literature, and in November 1983, I published the first book of criticism entirely devoted to Hood.[50] My book discusses every novel in turn and deals with all the short-story and nonfiction collections up to 1981. It does not content itself with paraphrase or thematics. Now keenly aware of Hood's rich texture and subtlety, I focus on his emblematic method, and, in providing detailed analyses of a few short stories, I outline a significant new way of looking at Hood's craft. Because my argument — a sustained allegorical treatment of Hood's work — has been summarized in this essay, there is little reason to discuss the book at length. Suffice it to say, however, that I do argue that Hood is not a bland historian, memoirist, or moralist. The world comes alive in sport, politics, sociology, art, religion, commerce, banality. The sense of play and games merges quite naturally with the concept of holiness, and evil is relieved by a celebration of human purpose.

Hood's Works

Hood tells us that, when he first began writing fiction, he had no literary theory and belonged to no school. Instinctively he turned out to be "a moral realist, not a naturalist nor a surrealist... or *avant-garde* writer."[51] All his early writing deals with "credible characters in more or less credible situations" (*GB*, p. 127) and shows us human relationships in continually shifting phases. His fiction shows us where the human joins with the divine, and thus it is a series of diverse panels about human existence, shaped into a comedy of salvation. However, this salvation is not always attained. It sparkles as the optimum hope, but the paths to it are fraught with temptations that delay, interrupt, or end the pilgrimage.

The moral tone is high, though it avoids being injunctive or doctrinaire. Hood does not force issues or moral victories. By some special balance in his craft, he is always interpretive and never simply a passive documentarian. And sharpening this sense of significance is a strong physical form for the stories. Sometimes this sense of form leads to a game with numerologies. Most often, however, it is organic and crystallizes by the device of the emblem.

An emblem is distinct from a symbol. Both are iconic embodiments of thought and feeling, but whereas a symbol "at once reveals and conceals,"[52] an emblem is a visual design that is a speaking picture. An emblem and a symbol are both analogies for reality, but a symbol is a metaphor "one half of which remains unstated and indefinite" (Tindall, p. 12), whereas an emblem, deriving as it does from hieroglyphics, is always particular, though it can vary its power of identification from the explicit allegory of an Aesopian fable to the enigmatic subtlety of a metaphysical conceit in John Donne's poetry.

An emblem combines the beautiful with the didactic and externalizes the hidden. Hood uses it to express the divine signature in the world. As with Baudelaire (who in "Correspondances" makes the poet a seer who sees into the infinite), Hood practises a method in which the reader can participate.

Hood's emblems are numerous: a Halloween gorilla mask in "Going Out as a Ghost";[53] a mountain overlooking a bicultural metropolis in *Around the Mountain*; a sunken "ghost" ship in

A New Athens; an oil painting of white light in *White Figure*; a childhood swing in *The Swing in the Garden*; an Olympic stadium whose "O" shape is an analogy for existential nothingness in "Ghosts at Jarry."[54] The list could go on intriguingly, but it is sufficient to say that this iconography of the imagination produces an allegorical mode.

Hood's allegory in its full emblematic force is not a primitive species of ciphering. It is a convention by which *inner* drama of conscience or soul is revealed in a discursive narrative, and its very essence reconciles emblem with subjects of the fiction. In this way, it is expansive rather than narrow, and its deliberate didacticism in no way seeks to reveal by minute dissection. The narrative is always coherent, and the characters, even when they fail to express the dark side of human nature, are more or less complex in their lifelike effects, rather than lifeless abstractions of ideas, virtues, and vices. Therefore, Hood's allegory, by appealing both to the pictorial imagination and rational intellect, leads us into a totality of structure and meaning, and its multiplicity of intention renders it polysemous or of more senses than one — as in Dantean allegory.

Hood's emblems shape ideas and structures. The title story in *Flying a Red Kite* turns the human spirit into a sacramental which is no sham. It begins with signs of things gone awry — sometimes in comically grotesque images. The main character, Fred Calvert (whose surname forms an association with Calvary), is riding home on a bus one hot Saturday afternoon. The ride begins badly as Fred, encumbered by parcels, queues up for the wrong bus, which waddles up "like an indecent old cow" and stops "with an expiring moo."[55] Fred has to join another queue and wait under the "right sign." Fred and his wife, Naomi (another biblical association), had "thought of Montreal as a city of the Sub-Arctic and in the summers they would have leisure to repent the misjudgment" (*FRK*, p. 177). We learn of Fred's boyhood failures in fishing and hockey, and of how, as "one by one the wholesome outdoor sports and games had defeated him" (*FRK*, p. 178), he had transferred his belief in sports to his young daughter, Deedee.

The mood of frustration continues as he climbs onto a crowded bus. An Irish priest (one of two loud, vulgar revellers) mutters, "It's all a sham," as the bus passes a cemetery with its neat graves (*FRK*, p. 181). Fred's depression is not cured at home. A drink of Coke bloats him up and upsets his stomach; he regrets having bought a red kite for his daughter; the "spoiled priest" stays in his mind; and the weather is wrong for kite flying.

All the portents of wrongdoing or infelicity are linked to a sequence of passions. Fred and his daughter start up a mountain, and Fred makes a covenant with his daughter not to come down until they have flown the kite. The ascent makes him victim to a scourge of bugs, and he twice fails to launch the kite, his "natural symbol" of something holy (*FRK*, p. 178). He ascends higher — higher than he has ever been before — and the weather, now changed into dazzling sunshine, dry and clear, is perfect for his pastoral pastime. Deedee finds a wild raspberry bush and eats from it, relishing the fruit, which is not bitter. As trickles of dark juice run down her chin, Fred, on his third attempt, manages to loft the kite, which soars up and up. The flying kite and "the dark rich red of the pulp and juice of the crushed raspberries" (*FRK*, p. 188) become complementary natural symbols of grace or benediction as Fred realizes in a flash that the "spoiled priest," who claimed that life and monuments to souls were a sham, was wrong. The resurrection of the red kite — a tongue of fire, as it were, whose string burns his fingers (*FRK*, p. 188) — matches the resurrection of Fred's spirit.

The act of flying the kite becomes an analogy of faith for Fred because it sets up a proportion between his earlier depression and his new joy. Fred's various crises pass away at the moment of the kite's soaring, and this becomes the climactic epiphany in the story — a gift of the spirit that meets its challenges without yielding. The kite now is, indeed, something holy, for it joins heaven to earth via the ball of string and brings a feeling of accomplishment and peace to Fred, whose name, by the way, is etymologically related to "peace." The kite flying justifies Fred's belief in the "curative moral values" of sports and games and heals his discomfort over the "spoiled priest's" cynicism. As he and his daughter kneel and embrace in the dust and squint at "the flying red thing," his spiritual passion is relieved and he is regenerated, as it were, through signs of grace: faith, the Spirit (the kite is a cross in its wooden ribs), and sacramental water/blood (the red berry juice).

Most of the other stories in the book coalesce around two

complementary themes — various gifts of the spirit, and the alarming "doubleness" in life. The "doubleness" is of the nature of human existence itself and can produce a disturbing ambiguity as in "Nobody's Going Anywhere!" with a teasing image of black comedy (FRK, pp. 158–75); or it can give rise to a comedy of manners as in "He Just Adores Her!" (FRK, pp. 136–57), where the "doubleness" arises out of the bipartite structure and tension between two couples.

Hood's success in short stories obtains to a large extent from his attention to texture. The literal approach in "Recollections of the Works Department," a much anthologized story, yields a memoir of a youth's summer job without pushing to become a myth of the working class (FRK, pp. 63–98). In "Silver Bugles, Cymbals, Golden Silks," Hood uses documentary detail about a boys' band to create a pastoralism in decline (FRK, pp. 40–62). The opening, very much in the manner of the boyhood reminiscences later seen in The Swing, builds up credibility as the author describes all the rituals of summer camp, but the point is analogical rather than literal. As the band and its uniforms deteriorate, we are likely to remember Robert Frost's line "nothing gold can stay."[56] And yet there is a healing consolation. The narrator's tender nostalgia is genuine and affecting, for it offers us a lesson in the coming of age and in the gift of love.

Nowhere else in this book is Hood's sense of texture and structure so brilliantly in evidence, however, as in "Fallings from Us, Vanishings" (FRK, pp. 1–17). On the surface, this is a story of how a young man loves not only a girl but her mother and a whole host of memories as well. But it is more than a Wordsworthian lyrical exercise. Wordsworth, of course, gives it the title and some of its emblematic suggestions, but the piece is really a Grail story in which the Arthur figure is quite literally an Arthur who goes in quest of all the glory in things, past, present, and future.

The title comes from the "Intimations of Immortality" ode and suggests decline and evanescence — a ghostliness that somehow does not vitiate the material substantiality of experience. But more than Wordsworth, the story suggests mediaeval legend and emblem. It begins with the protagonist Arthur Merlin (questing king and magician are the mediaeval connotations of his name) "brandishing a cornucopia of daffodils, flowers for Gloria"

(*FRK*, p. 1). The cornucopia ("horn of plenty") is here a golden cup because it holds the bright yellow daffodils — Wordsworth's symbol of lyric exultation. In legend, a cornucopia is Jupiter's cup, and Hood fills his opening paragraph with emblems of Jupiter in the fertility and arboreal images. Hood also maintains the element of romance so that the mood helps to colour the deeper thematic underpinnings.

Gloria lets us remember Wordsworth's "clouds of glory" and "glory in the flower," especially when Merlin hands her the daffodils and watches her bury her face in the petals. She is "the daffodil girl, the primavera" (*FRK*, p. 7). She wears a "flowery robe" and daffodils are "her favourite flower" (*FRK*, p. 8), so that she is Merlin's golden one. But there is an illusion here — just as there was a ghostly one in the Grail legend. She is unattainable because she is a "ghost" who haunts Arthur, no less than she is haunted herself by the "ghosts" of the past. Indeed, her "ghost-liness" forms an important part of the central leitmotif in which time quivers without being forgotten or laid to rest in the mind or soul.

Gloria would prefer to forget the past because it holds too many tragic memories for her. Her father had died on a sinking ship, and she cannot accept Arthur's sacral association for water (*FRK*, p. 10). Nor does she wish to remember her mother's death in a car smashup because this meant that both her parents had disappeared and there was nothing left for her. Gloria would much rather live in the present and place her trust in the senses, which help her experience concrete particulars rather than abstract generalizations. "I only see what's there," she maintains once to Arthur (*FRK*, p. 11), and her state of being is frequently described in terms of senses of touch, taste, and sight.

In contrast, Arthur is tense with memory, but grateful for it. An historian, "builder of archives, ranker of green filing cabinets," he loves documents and relishes the past (*FRK*, p. 5). He does not censor experience or memory, and his sense of period provides the documentary relish in the story. He has the gift of triple vision in the sense of his mental presence in three levels of time.

On the allegorical level, the story is a version of time and feeling, and of Arthur's magical (Merlinesque) reconciliation of the two. As a boy, he had adored Gloria's mother, Mrs. Vere, "that golden widow" (*FRK*, p. 4), whose name etymologically means "the truth." But she is a part of his past, and his present involvement is with Gloria, his glory in the present, who cannot, or will not, connect the triple levels of time. She is haunted, "packed full of sensation" almost exclusively from time present, and he cannot exorcize her of her spiritual demons, although she appeals to the magician in him: "You exorcist! Just come and get me!" (*FRK*, p. 16). What to her is an unsettling possession, is to him a beneficent condition. Their dialogue here does sound melodramatic and arch at times, but it is Hood's way of signalling his didactic intent and of building to an emotional climax.

The final paragraph is quieter, lyrical, and poignant as Gloria disappears, merging with the twilight, wavering away — one of "a long file of daffodil girls marching out of the past and into the future" (*FRK*, p. 17). As the title shows, she vanishes, and by being one of "the descending heirs of Eve," she falls away from him (*FRK*, p. 17). His eyes lose her, just as King Arthur's eyes lost the Holy Grail, but Arthur Merlin does not lose his feeling for, or idea of, her. Although his setting is the image of a vast wasteland ("a sandy place"), he is content and blessed with his memories.

The pattern of light and darkness merges with the theme of decline. Arthur's yearning to see Gloria "illuminated by the sunset" occurs on "nearly the longest day of the year" (*FRK*, p. 5). All through their beach encounter, Arthur is very conscious of fading light and the oncoming twilight. The sun throws a shadow across them, and the sand under them grows black and loses its daytime warmth (*FRK*, p. 12). "The soul of the world turns in on itself and is quiet, just before the dark" (*FRK*, p. 13), and Arthur is ever conscious of the passing of time. Gloria's final merging with the twilight occurs after a phase of sexual yearning and seals the pattern of a ghost-ridden beauty "going out of the light through the twilight and into the dark" (*FRK*, p. 17). Her going, however, is a thing of beauty that quivers with a twinge of glory and is, therefore, reminiscent of Wordsworth's "cloud of glory."

Another story equally impressive in its synecdoche is "Three Halves of a House" (*FRK*, pp. 99–123), and this, too, is a version of ghostliness as it tells its tale of possession. It begins as a geographical documentary as Hood, with conversational ease, conducts us on a guided tour of the Thousand Islands at the east end of Lake Ontario and the beginning of the Saint Lawrence. The islands "sprout in and all around the ship channel, choking and diverting the immense river for forty amazing miles....A third of the continent leans pushing behind the lakes and the river..." (*FRK*, p.99). The images of a human body ("pulse, circulation, artery, and heart") all fortify the sense of palpable, living force.

Hood shifts his narrative voice frequently in the story, modulating the tone and strengthening the sense of aesthetic distance. Soon after his description of the islands comes a description of the ocean-going freighters, and then he brings in the theme of ruin and decline via third-person, objective narrative. This is virtually a Gothic story, quasi-Faulknerian in its sense of the haunting spirit of the land. It is a tale of ancestral conflicts and madness. The house of the title is occupied by Grover Haskell and his insane wife, Ellie, but Mrs. Boston insists that it belongs to her and her daughter, Maura.

Hood uses the image of eyes in order to emphasize the haunting spirit of ruin and dispossession. Ellie has violet eyes, which give her an "ineffable saint's gaze, visionary, violet, preoccupied" (*FRK*, p.107). She yearns for Maura to be her daughter figure, and though she seems near madness in her behaviour, she is considered a religious visionary who speaks in symbols and who has "second sight" (*FRK*, p.110). Only Maura can see the true pathos in the situation, for her mother's "agate eyes" are cold and unclear.

The ghost of Ellie's "terrible father" still hovers about the house, which has a spectral, icy form in winter. Ellie sees the ghost of an unborn daughter in Maura, and Mrs. Boston sees the ghost of her husband in the house, as the house itself becomes unearthly, taking possession of the neurotic relatives — even those who wish to be dispossessed of it.

Ellie, who believes the house is haunted, turns into something of a ghost herself, moving with "no footfall," passing soundlessly in Maura's memory (*FRK*, p.115). When Ellie embraces Maura, the latter can hardly feel her hug and thinks of her aunt as "an invisible tissue of air."

The most haunted figures are Ellie and her husband, Grover Haskell. Grover does not really want the house, which is killing him as surely as the river is strangling Stoverville. He actually pleads with Maura to accept the place from him (*FRK*, p. 122). For her part, Ellie is haunted by several things which have become the ghosts of her tormented conscience. Her unrequited passion for Wallace Phillips has made her covetous of the Phillips daughter, who is not hers. Her life in the house becomes a harrowing punishment decreed by the gods and the dead. She continues to see her dead father and to hear his command forbidding her to marry Grover.

Hood's narrative voice switches again in the final section to get inside Ellie's "milky brains." In her bedroom, which is a bizarre synthesis of virgin womb, nun's cloister, and tomb, she goes through the mimesis of a woman in childbirth. But what is born is not even a phantom child; it is an eternal now, carrying the story full circle with its images of water, ships, and sirens. The strong landscape, a frame for the story, is internalized within Ellie's disintegrating mind, and the conclusion reveals a special ghostliness — a voyage unto death, as the dying Ellie's dissolving mind flows like the river current of Anna Livia Plurabelle's in Joyce.

Only Maura survives the ghostly haunting and ruin, because she has succeeded in making a career for herself in Montreal and preventing a family pattern of destruction from repeating itself in her life. When Maura returns to Stoverville, it is only a temporary visit. She feels no fatal ties. She is not like Grover, who is "an outsider who's gotten stuck fast inside" (*FRK*, p. 113).

The stories analysed above are among Hood's earliest and show that from the first he has always been a finely textured, finished writer with an uncommon skill with allegory. But his facility with narrative develops from the exigencies of life. His documentary eye perceives textures, and his craft, by the slightest pressure or rearrangement, creates subtle patterns that would otherwise lie buried in the very fabric of existence.

Perhaps his penchant for documentary detail comes a little from his intellectual curiosity as a professor (in the Academy of Fact, as it were), but most of it obtains, surely, from his affection for the totality of the world. Like James T. Farrell, Dos Passos, and Theodore Dreiser, he tries to get the facts right, but his special talent enables him to amass a wealth of detail and yet not lose the subtle design.

Although he frequently writes about places from his past,

Hood has none of the arch candour of a confessional writer or
the mannered innocence of a latter-day romantic. His voice is
always sincere, and because he has a developed view of the world
in which he is creatively surprised, he does not sound self-
absorbed in his first-person accounts. His personality, unlike
Hemingway's or Mailer's at times, does not stand above his
work, and so he is able to renew his creative energy whether he is
writing leisurely autobiographical narratives or commissioned
pieces that require him to be a recording journalist. Hood's
participation as a character in his own journalism (for example,
when he steps on the ice with the legendary Jean Béliveau in
Chapter vi of *Strength Down Centre* for a difficult lesson in the
art of ice hockey) is graced by a wry humour that undercuts his
own pretensions while magnifying his true subject, which is
always someone or something other than himself.

Hood has not produced a vast amount of journalism, and
consequently there is no justification for placing him in the
company of such luminous literary journalists as Naipaul,
Mailer, and Diana Trilling; but the quality of his contributions is
such that, were he not such a superb writer of fiction, he could
turn to a profitable career as an art critic, a sports commentator,
or a columnist in *belles-lettres*. His journalism is an extension of
his fiction in the sense that it is often about the same themes and
landscapes that are developed in his fiction. The Ontario
countryside in "Innuit and Catawba" (*GB*, pp. 58–69) and the
ravines in "The Governor's Bridge Is Closed" (*GB*, pp. 8–20) are
personal heraldic elements that establish emotional and intellectual resonances that also echo in such novels as *A New Athens*
and *Reservoir Ravine*. His technique of evocation is identical
with that in his fiction, for he works up scenes in his imagination
by digging out "all the imaginative possibilities in a given
landscape" (*GB*, p. 8).

Many of his essays — especially in *Around the Mountain* — are
written as short stories. As such, then, he is a superb journalist
who can crystallize his perceptions and attitudes by craft, and he
is a crafty fiction-maker who grows in authenticity by virtue of
his information, which is never simply a pastiche of isolated facts
but an integral part of his "documentary fantasy" (Fulford,
p. 77). His accumulation of detail is an attempt to correlate and
authenticate his perspectives, and it is illuminated by his sense of

history and metaphysic. It usually produces a finely tuned coordination between individual consciousness and the setting in which history grows increasingly complex.

The only exception is curiously in *Strength Down Centre*, in which Hood, as both participating figure and detached recorder of the statistics and folklore of hockey, fails to cure the strain between fact and narrative voice. He tries to write a sports biography as an Arthurian romance, but he begins with such dull, dense reportage and stays so shockingly unaggressive as a participant (except for Chapter vi, where he becomes amusingly and intimately personal) that the startling misproportion between fact and romance is severe and crippling, and the book is robbed of exciting thrust.

Hood's journalism, just like his fiction, is pervaded by a high moral sense that shows how his whole imaginative life is connected with the perils and triumphs of reality. "The Governor's Bridge Is Closed" shows that Thomas Wolfe and Heraclitus were both wrong: you can go home again and again, and although reality changes in the flow of time, you can step into the same stream twice, or even more often. The synthesizing power of human imagination and its relationship to both a continuing cultural tradition and that tradition's implicit structure of morality make it possible for the individual to experience a significant sense of permanence.

More than this sense of permanence, however, Hood's journalism is energized by a philosophy that posits "the perfection of the essences of things — the formal realities that create things as they are in themselves" ("The Ontology of Super-Realism," in *GB*, p. 131). Using such examples as the artists Vermeer or Hopper, or composer Joseph Haydn, as his models, Hood tries to concentrate on knowable forms and the knowable principles in them. His journalism — whether it be an impression of Ontario ("Innuit and Catawba"), a study of a tremendous shift in taste ("Circuses and Bread" [*GB*, pp. 21–34]), or a formal study of theatre design ("Murray Laufer and the Art of Scenic Design" [*GB*, pp. 113–25]) — attempts to capture the "visionary gleam" in all things.

Now this is not to imply that Hood is a noncritical enthusiast of reality. His moral imagination cuts into the perplexing entanglements of Canadian history and defines our cultural deficiencies while remaining optimistic about the Canadian conscience ("Moral Imagination: Canadian Thing" [*GB*, pp. 87–102]). Hood believes that Canada is a society permeated by Judaeo-Christian values, and he enlarges this feeling in the essentially religious article "The Absolute Infant" (*GB*, pp. 136–44), which repeats Thales of Miletus' dictum "Everything is full of God" (*GB*, p. 137) and fortifies this with Blake's view that "everything that lives is holy" (*GB*, p. 144). The entire article reads in retrospect like a preparation for *Reservoir Ravine* because history and eternity are shown to be united in a nativity-redemption narrative which is *always* taking place.

The interplay between Hood's fictional and nonfictional work satisfies his need for a realistic base while releasing him for a superrealistic ontology which posits an inspiration from above that enlightens and illuminates art and other human endeavour. To project this harmony of realism and transcendentalism, Hood has perfected a metaphysical style which is frequently speculative and metaphorical, while being simultaneously precise and involved in fact. In his "own" voice, Hood projects himself as an accessible writer, the journalist of immediacy, not closed in some obscure or distant literary world, but exultant in his communion with common things that he magically illumines with uncommon light, particularly through emblems.

The interplay between fact and fiction is best seen in *Around the Mountain: Scenes from Montreal Life*, which fuses Hood's documentary talent with emblematic device in a perfect harmony of revelation. The very title and external structure make it abundantly clear that this is not mere literary journalism or a sketchbook. The mountain is a focus for epiphany. Many of the stories trace patterns of ascent and descent, and many, too, mention the qualities of vision and modes of knowing that are altered by geography. As the weather, colours, and locales alter, so do our insights. The stories begin on flat land in the northeast of Montreal, and they gradually make their way to higher altitude. In the June story, the narrator is atop the mountain, looking down from above, and this is the holiest story. Then the next story winds around the mountain and back down to the flat land, this time to the west. This forms a complete rotation (*BF*, p. 45).

There are calculations even in the narrative voice. It is

not always the same narrator. One story has no first-person pronouns, and it is a distanced third-person story. In some of the stories, the narrator is called Hugh. Some of the stories are autobiographical; others are not. But they are all suited to the narrator's condition at the time of telling (BF, pp. 44–45).

The twelve stories form a year's cycle, though not every chapter is set in a single month. In some instances, months overlap, but at the end we return to mid-December from where we began. The overall design is somewhat along the lines of Spenser's *Shepheardes Calender* or a mediaeval Book of Hours (BF, p. 44). The cycle makes a clever mythology of urban pastoral, and Hood's warm humanism glows throughout.

The winter stories move from a bleak vision of political intrigue and sadism ("Predictions of Ice"[57]) to a climactic revelation in the final story of the book, "The River behind Things" (AM, pp. 167–75). The "solitary black figure" with a long black pole jabbing the ice becomes an emblem of death, as vapour wraps around him, and the scene composes its meaning for the narrator. It is the type of meditative emblem so mastered by Wordsworth — who expressed it in the leech gatherer, the daffodils, the solitary reaper — but in Hood's transforming art, it wipes away the city teeming with its thousands of stories and leaves us with solitary man making a single-minded effort to clear a place for himself near the river, under the mountain. The moment becomes purgatorial and the black figure a symbol of death.

At the other end of Hood's vision is a touchingly tender story, "Looking Down from Above" (AM, pp. 81–94), which begins with a grotesque old lady struggling up a steep city street and moves on to a family picnic in June on the mountain. One of the celebrants at the picnic is M. Bourbonnais, a janitor who is dying of cancer. The world view in this story, which reaches its apex atop the mountain, encompasses all human perspectives, including Bourbonnais's simple pleasures and the old lady's doggedness, and shows that "human purpose is inscrutable, but undeniable" (AM, p. 94).

Hood's urban pastoral mediates between Leacock's nostalgia and Brecht's infernal inversions. Hood's Montreal is never really hellish or purely innocent. It evinces both heaven and hell, but it balances its vision. "A Green Child" (AM, pp. 127–39), in which the narrator (infatuated by a beautiful girl with a green scarf) talks about the symbolic landscape of Antonioni's films of alienation, gives us the edge of the city, where huge, unfinished building constructions look colossally impersonal and apocalyptic. The narrator descends into a valley of shadows (rue Valdombre) in quest of his fleeting green child. But at the opposite end of this hellish view is the refreshingly innocent peace of the last story, in which the narrator and his young son drive out to the west island and find joyous experiences. This balancing of opposite views and feelings produces a single city, and though we see Wordsworthian "spots of time" in scenes that rotate in our imagination, we really have but one spacious vision that, without resorting to arid intellectualizing, allows connections to emerge.

Hood is the type of literary craftsman who believes in shaping all his work into a single piece. We do not need to be reminded that all his stories have a clear, simple moral — sometimes rather old-fashioned and orthodox — but we should bear in mind that his temperament as a moralist combines with his impulse as an historian to produce a unique memoirist's literature. Even in the rather peculiar essay collection *Trusting the Tale*, where Hood's impulse to offer us various pieces of his self sometimes gets the better of his literary judgement, he reveals that whatever his subject — photography, regional literature, fatherhood, male friendship, painting, hockey, short-story craft — he makes a consistent examination of moral posture. His loving portrait of photographer Sam Tata is completed with attention to Tata's "inner moral duality,"[58] and in drawing an affinity with Lloyd Person, a Prairie writer, Hood expresses his own benign tendency to memorialize past societies and adds a supreme qualification: "To write history, to tell a story of the way our forebears lived, is to perform an act of piety, a deeply moral act" ("Person's People," in *TT*, p. 43).

The Christian acquiescence and hope in the personal journalism of the book are of a piece with Hood's fiction, and it is possible to agree with his own self-commentary that "...there is always a very complicated pattern of cross-reference between all kinds of matters, like a big pile of small crocodiles, which oozes into his work and is probably of much greater importance in the art of the thing than the moral lessons which lie on top like woollen blankets over soft sexy silk sheets" ("Faces in the Mirror," in *TT*, p. 37).

There are a few duds in *Trusting the Tale*; there are also brilliant jewels. But whatever our assessment of this book's quality, the fact remains that all of Hood's writing makes a single pattern. Just as his nonfiction often has qualities of good fiction, so it also leads to another link — that between his short and long fiction. For Hood, stories and novels are "slices off the same ham" (Hood and Mills, p. 136), and although his literary reputation in certain quarters has been made chiefly on his short stories, he makes no distinction in importance between his long and short fiction, suggesting that all his books make up "one huge novel anyway, the one bright book of the redemption and atonement" (Hood and Mills, p. 137). It is not that he repeats the same stories or that he is technically limited. It is simply that his themes and essential style have not changed radically, although there have been widenings, focal alterations, and varnishings of form. As *Flying a Red Kite* shows, he has never had to learn to wipe his feet before entering the salon of superior fiction-makers, and each new collection of stories simply consolidates his style. His view is that "underlying everything there is some kind of intelligible and meaningful unity," and he expresses this unity in stories that tend to coalesce in groups or assimilate themselves into larger fictions (*BF*, p. 43).

In his third collection of stories, Hood dovetails his major theme of penance with ideas of love, holiness, and guilt, and his sharp focus gives *The Fruit Man, The Meat Man & The Manager* a moral cohesiveness. The Trinitarian title is an analogy for the Trinitarian aspect of God in Catholic theology and suggests one of Hood's favourite numerals.

The economy of grace is a theme even in the first three stories, "a deliberately-related triptych" in which "human art and love are models of immortality."[59] But it is especially strong in the title story, where Manager Znaimer's goodness offers a spiritual consolation to others (*FM*, pp. 188–97). Znaimer is one of three partners who run Greenwood Groceteria, a small store that cannot compete against supermarkets. But Znaimer's fatherly look and business manner attract customers. A turning point is reached when the store is forced to close because the nearby university buys out the land for a new sports centre. The gentle atmosphere changes, and Znaimer feels that "nothing holy" is left in his life (*FM*, p. 197). He disappears and surfaces only a year later with a gesture of charity to one of his favourite customers, Mrs. Cummings. This small charity is a permanent habitude and signifies grace, what Catholic theology describes as a "permanent hold of God in man's very being."[60]

Holy men appear with surprising frequency in this book, although the holiness is sometimes false or severely misleading. In "Cura Pastoralis" (*FM*, pp. 173–87), a young Catholic priest is accused of molesting a seven-year-old girl and suffers qualms of conscience over this. A comic "holy" man appears in "Who's Paying for This Call" (*FM*, pp. 198–207), Hood's satire of pop legend, in which a folksinger (a parody of Bob Dylan) becomes a legend revered by desperate hordes of youth ever in need of a spiritual "fix." However, he fails at the end to administer solace to a dying devotee, and the only message he can give is like the air escaping through a pinhole in his blue kazoo.

Hood is the most meditative writer in Canada. In *Dark Glasses*, using as his guiding text a quotation from Saint Paul to the Corinthians, he deals with the problems of seeing into the nature and truth of reality. The twelve stories—how he loves the epical number twelve!—derive most of their imagistic force from qualities of light and disguise, particularly in "Going Out as a Ghost" (*DG*, pp. 7–21), a Halloween story about conscience and responsibility, and in "Dark Glasses" (*DG*, pp. 119–29), a brilliant piece in which the narrator hides behind the dark glasses of self-righteousness, with dark light creating a mood of "fallenness" as in Milton's "darkness visible."

Reality is ambiguous, at least in its fluctuating phenomena, but Hood is able to find just the right form for each story, even though this sometimes makes a heavy demand on the reader. In "The Hole" (*DG*, pp. 110–18), Hood attempts to articulate via parody extremely difficult philosophical paradoxes about matter. Though it sometimes sounds like a compendium of metaphysics, epistemology, and rational psychology, "The Hole" is a satire on the overwrought contemplative mind of Professor Laidlaw, who does not recognize the impenetrability of certain realities.

Hood demands careful reading even in his apparently "innocent" stories, such as the much misunderstood "An Allegory of Man's Fate" (*DG*, pp. 130–43), which was once dismissed as a "trifle about a surburbanite named Bronson who puts together a do-it-yourself sailboat."[61] But this is no ordinary boat-building. This is a holy task — the building of an ark as a concrete representation of a man's faith in his own resources to deal with the many frustrations and failures in life.

The ark in this story points to another feature in Hood's aesthetic. As Tim Struthers has pointed out, Hood begins with an object and builds the universe or fictional world to which that object belongs (*BF*, p. 32). Hood has something of Alice Munro's density, but his fiction has a wider range than hers, and his materialism provides a sense of existence in which objects serve as structural elements. Cases in point are the old radio in "Where the Myth Touches Us" (*FRK*, pp. 189–217), the documentary movie in "The End of It" (*FRK*, pp. 218–39), and the picture of W. C. Fields in "Nobody's Going Anywhere!" (*FRK*, pp. 158–75). The details of objects, places, and characters are a transmission of the fullness of life, because particular realities are never merely themselves but are things that set off vibrant radiations about related things.

Hood's style and diction are admirably modulated according to the demands of a story, and this is really a matter of form emerging from the manifold activities of temperament and curiosity. A writer suggests Proteus rather than Procrustes, and when his style alters, the changes in technique represent what the writer has seen of reality. Though Hood is not an experimentalist in the sense of a John Barth or Alain Robbe-Grillet or even an Audrey Thomas, his experiments with technique are not negligible or slight. "Places I've Never Been" (*FM*, pp. 88–101) is a cinematic fantasy sequence, an hallucination that reads like a mixture of Graham Greene and James Joyce. "The Good Listener" (*NG*, pp. 134–44) is a montage of voices, unified by the largely silent but hypnotic figure of the "listener" — a mysterious, ghostly, yet palpable figure who makes no sound (except once) as he fades in and out "like a special effect in a film fantasy" (*NG*, p. 144) listening to various conversations of human distress. He appears to be the inverse of Coleridge's Ancient Mariner because of his compulsion to listen rather than to unburden himself. He might well be the Christ among us, taking on the sins and sufferings of the world, and he is certainly a compelling force in a story told purely in voices rather than in images.

Even more mannered, but much more substantial, is "Doubles"

(*NG*, pp. 167–89), which takes its time to announce its themes and strike its key chords, but which finally achieves its doubled patterns that spiral together in waves of haunting obsessiveness. The story is interested in mysteries of personality — in how different people are joined through the reflection of one man's eyes — but the compendium of enigma, analogy, and duplication makes for a very subtle form that suggests music. The narrator, in fact, is a musical composer who thrives on optimism, in spite of various vicissitudes of fortune, and even when his life twirls into disappointment, he never loses a fundamental benevolence. The doubles motif enters through a ghostly natural symbol — a sun inside the moon (*NG*, p. 171) — but is extended through the narrator's meditation on how one woman can be seen in the personality of another. The narrator loses his first love to another man but finds love a second time, and as his career prospers, he remains large-souled and healthy, rather than neurotic, and capable of seeing one form inside another. The story floats in and out of the mystery of the human person but, in so doing, gathers together various notes and measures that develop like a fugue into a suspended disclosure, a delayed resolution. Hood's tonal text has a gradual order of narrative that is similar to the order of melody.

When Hood fails in his experiments it is because he is too quirky. "Gone Three Days" (*NG*, pp. 98–117) is a case in point. It is divided mechanically into two parts — the first one being impressions of a severely retarded boy in a world whose brutality and rejection he fears; and the second being a male social worker's account of his attempt to rescue this boy from a life of animal suffering. Except for two or three lapses in diction, Hood manages — as well as Faulkner in *The Sound and the Fury* — to suggest the burdens of an inarticulate soul, but by dividing his story so mechanically and by placing the boy's impressions first, Hood tries his reader's patience and ends up telling the same story twice.

As a didactic writer, Hood has few equals anywhere. When he writes a rhetorical exercise in analogy, as in "The Woodcutter's Third Son" (*NG*, pp. 77–97), he does so with such wit that his spell of language and humour develops a parable which is close to fairy tale and yet is also a sophisticated transformation of life into a moral lesson. Even his playful satire "None Genuine

Without This Signature" (*NG*, pp. 145–66) can glint with different hues and values, as Hood pursues his interest in turning literature into a secular analogy for Scripture. He gives his tale something of the exotic intrigue of *The Arabian Nights* but never loses his grasp of the hard, underlying anagogical core.

Even in his long fiction, this neatly controlled balance between disparate elements is held with interesting efficiency. In *A Game of Touch*, realism predominates in the urban setting, characters, and action, but the novel is not constricted by its realism. It is a triptych, according to Hood, with a triple theme dealing with "sexual games, politics, and football, all of which are carried on along the two levels, the fantastic and the realistic" (Morley, pp. 42–43). Touch football is used to create a metaphor for contact and to exercise some of the tensions in the plot. Hood believes that "the metaphor of a game of touch applies perfectly to so much of Canadian life that most readers of the novel have responded to it at once."[62] The novel is really about various games people play and shows how these games (sex, politics, art, social life) are worth attention because we learn about different patterns of human nature and behaviour.

The surface of the book is very ordinary, beginning, as many of Hood's stories and novels do, with a hiker. This figure, Jake Price, heads for the city to "have a look around" and finds himself drawn into a pick-up game of touch in a park. Jake makes new friends, from whom he learns about people's places in a cosmopolitan society. From the hedonistic Marie-Ange (née Angela Robinson), he learns the oldest game of touch — free dalliance. From Roger Talbot, unfairly branded a *vendu* in Quebec, he learns the hazards of bicultural politics. Marie-Ange and Roger dovetail the themes of sex and politics and ensure, by their interesting personalities, that the commonplaces of men and women together at their games of sexual or political touch are not isolated but are turned into a calm investigation of characters in a troubled society.

A Game of Touch is an unusual piece of fiction for Hood in that its realism and satire are perhaps stronger than its allegory. But these former elements help give power to the generalities of allegory by their particulars. The realism helps to dramatize the conflicts compellingly and finds appropriate expression in the range of satiric incident; but it is the allegorical cast that gives the structure its weight and shape. In Hood, as in many of the greatest writers of the past (Spenser, Blake, Cervantes, Jonson, Marlowe, Bunyan, Pope, Fielding, Austen, Joyce), satire and realism are mixed into the allegory so that multiple meanings cohere within a single species of text.

Nevertheless, it is allegory that is Hood's true forte, especially when this is elevated into meditation, as it is in *White Figure, White Ground*, a spiritual parable. On the surface, a Maritime Gothic quest story in which a highly talented painter, Alex MacDonald, goes through a *crise de quarantaine*, this is really a story of spiritual crisis worked out through artistic contemplation. Alex goes with his French Canadian wife, Madeleine, to Barringford, Nova Scotia, to claim from his two old spinster aunts the house of his deceased father. These aunts, who control and warp the life of their niece Ellen, know the secret of their brother's tragic history, and Alex forces them to reveal it to him. But Alex's journey is not simply a psychological or domestic adventure. It is simultaneously a quest for his missing father and for a new type of art, an art that will find the source of light and, in a sense, the true Source of life and art. The novel works in dualities and is studded with Scriptural quotations. The most explicit association between art and religion occurs when Alex identifies with the great musical composer Haydn, who always signed his manuscripts *Laus Deo*. Alex comes to believe, "All art is religious if it's any good at all."[63]

The novel begins with a melodrama concerning Alex's two aunts and their shadowy ancestors, proceeds with satire on the art world and its hucksterism, and ends with a cocktail party that ridicules various "types" among the literati and cultural élite. But all this is surface colouring for the real comedy — a comedy of the soul as it is inspired by grace and redeems itself from the darkness of despair and chaos. In the search for his father and light (God), Alex, at the end, renounces both white and black as his emblematic colours and suggests that he is on the verge of entering a green period of optimistic hope. Alex overcomes his artistic block, and his final painting on the coast—sent as a gift to Ellen — is a dark comedy: a black picture with "wonderful, comical hints of green" (*WF*, p. 250). The aunts see only the most aggressive, violent blackness in the painting, which looks to them like "having what's outside inside," but Ellen knows that the picture could also be read "the other way around" (*WF*, p. 250).

The novel has its faults. There are, perhaps, too many stereo-types in the Maritime locale and characters — the sort that Desmond Pacey checked off in a review: "stiff-lipped old maiden aunts rocking on the veranda of a decaying old house by the sea," "a mysterious family feud," and "ancestral guilt" (Pacey, p. 71). There is also melodrama in the conflict between Alex and his aunts. Sometimes, especially in the sensual passages, there is a lush overripeness. And the greatest defect is, perhaps, the gap between Alex's folly and his eventual self-recognition. Alex at the end is essentially the same as Alex at the beginning — at least as far as Hood's rendition of him is concerned. He does not convince us of his despair, despite all his squirming on the beach in his period of spiritual devastation, and it is left to his wife, Madeleine, to explain his dilemma. In fact, the overuse of Madeleine as a foil for Alex and Ellen points up Hood's didacticism all too plainly.

Many of Hood's works can be summarized by, or linked to, biblical proverbs or references. *The Camera Always Lies* has often been misread as a romance about the fatal Hollywood star system, in which darlings of the gods are inevitably sacrificed to the monstrous appetites of the public and studio bosses. But the real significance of the book is its allegory of violence, which is founded on the dictum "They who live by the sword shall perish by the sword" (Matt. xxvi.52). The form is that of solar romance, recognizable in the movement from darkness to daylight in the tripartite division ("Down There," "Going Down," "Coming Up"), and in the movement from attempted death to renewed life, agony to transcendence. The cyclical movement in the world of phenomena carries us beyond base desires and instincts to higher aspirations. The pattern is espe-cially appropriate because the ascending lines of romance fit the solar myth embedded in the fiction. There are correspondences between Rose Leclair's story and the Orpheus-Eurydice myth: Orpheus (Jean-Pierre Fauré, *nouvelle-vague* director) crosses a wide body of water, descends into an underworld (Hollywood's dark studios and cinemas), and after suspending Eurydice's tortures of the damned (Rose's fall from stardom, mental breakup, and her disastrous performance in a new musical), returns the heroine to the upper world (Jean-Pierre and Rose jet off to Paris).

After Rose's *agon* in the motel, the flashback scene revives the story of Rose's crucial struggle against a violent system of exploitation and sacrifice. Part II expresses a classic pathos for Rose. It delves into the "hidden" world of deceit, betrayal, and violence and carries us into the gullet of Leviathan, the whole fallen world of sin and tyranny. Rose is the dying goddess, the former darling of the gods, who becomes the *pharmakos* or scapegoat. She has no legal recourse against her destruction by the studio bosses, but she is rescued by her own will to find justice and by the aegis of Jean-Pierre Fauré in Part III.

For all its merits, *The Camera* is a textbook romance. Everything about it is mechanically contrived, and although the documentary facts about movie-making are skilfully delivered, the novel never breathes on its own. Hood pumps the parable for all it is worth, scoring points like a diligent author who knows his literary conventions inside out, but his heroine (a mixture of Marilyn Monroe and Janet Leigh) is a passive figure, far less colourful than her sexy rival, Charity Ryan, and too good to be interesting in a story of calculated violence.

However, Rose Leclair's goodness and ultimately benign fate should not mislead us into thinking that Hood is unable to deal adequately with the challenges of evil, or to create a fiction of despair. *You Cant Get There From Here*, for all its rich satire and parody on a newly independent African republic, is an anatomy of human failure set in mythical Leofrica. A demonic satire on the corruptions of truth, justice, and love in the earthly city (Augustine's city of man whose citizens are vessels of wrath, greed, and misery), this novel implies man's failure to reach the heavenly city of nature redeemed by grace. Its texture is richly realistic in details of topography, economics, politics, sociology, and espionage, and it breathes the excitement of the thriller genre, but it offers an allegory of despair — a black world in total contrast to the predominantly white one of *White Figure, White Ground*.

Hood builds up a credible locale that seems particularly African while it is concomitantly a metaphor for the Shadow — the dark underside of our psyche that we often shrink from. Leofrica, a name that suggests Leo the MGM lion, the lion in Blake and Dante, and the British imperial lion, is given a geography and sociology of dualities, and the locale becomes an imaginative expression of Ulro or hell. Perpetual mists, a mud foundation, and the "constantly shifting bottom" of a river bring to mind Dante's Malbowges. The river and shore are emblems of deception and chaos, and the outskirts of Newport (which is a new port for salvation) suddenly become a treacherous swamp. The country "fools you,"[64] and the rocks, sand, and hot wind compound the infernal mood.

The key word in Hood's description of this geography is "shifting," which applies equally to the politics. Mass opinion shifts in the plot, as do the fortunes of several key characters. Even the title, at least in the original cover design by Michael Macklem, suggests uncertainties: "You can, you can't, get there, get here, from here" (Morley, p. 50). The words seem to organize themselves in multiple variations of meaning.

Ostensibly a political thriller about shifting alliances and neocolonial skulduggery, the story establishes correspondences between politics and religion and becomes a clever parable. Newport is meant to sound like a peaceable kingdom. The wandering Ugeti are like biblical nomads, and their stark rigours of survival like the Old Testament plagues on Egypt. Ugeti *rites de passage* are similar to "the Christian notion of the armour of righteousness" (*YC*, p. 12). Interfoods, the American conglomerate, is a secular Eucharist run by a people whose ambassador counsels the doctrine of the "invisible presence" in the body politic (*YC*, p. 38). The UN Articles of Charter serve as a universal scripture (*YC*, p. 22), but the country, subject to tribal mythology, adopts animals as its religious symbols — the cow for the totemic Ugeti, and the water-serpent for the Pineals. Native theology is a weird mixture of anthropology, sex, and religion, and the worship of Imine, the cow-goddess, and Abo, the serpent, are part of what Frye calls the psychology of the Fall — "a desire to prolong the helplessness of the perceiver and his dependence on the body of nature which surrounds him."[65]

In Hood's satire, dirt stains everything, as every major aspect of civilization is linked in a fundamental way to excrement or urine. The excremental vision, different in nature from Swift's, which assumes a universal debasement of nature, yields a special revelation. Money, a basis of commerce and, therefore, nation-

hood, becomes interchangeable with dung. A sturdy Pineal long-
shoreman, who needs to defecate, uses a fistful of ten dollar bills
for toilet paper and then allows these to "disappear into the
ambiguous estuary" (*YC*, p. 178).

This is the only novel in which Hood permits no release from
evil. Characters go to violent deaths — one is blown up by a
remote-control bomb; another is trampled on by an angry mob;
and Anthony Jedeb, the protagonist, dives to the bottom of the
river to escape the stones and bullets of his pursuers.

You Cant shows the futility of vanity. Jedeb's cabinet, like any
other political cabinet, is "a complete multi-modal account of
how you live in a society"; and very largely the dialectic is
worked out in terms of who are good and bad in the cabinet (*BF*,
p. 58). When we identify the cabinet with society, we also, by
extension, identify it with man's fate in the world. In this book,
that fate is horrible because, although Jedeb has a vision of
justice for the commonweal, it is an unclear vision that shreds.
Without solid vision, the country and its leader perish.

You Cant hardly prepares us for The New Age series, in which
Hood's fiction moves positively *backwards into the future*,
assured of apocalyptic insights into final reality. In The New Age
series, Hood is attempting to do as fully, powerfully, and multi-
modally as possible, what he is capable of doing in long
narrative. The series begins in Toronto in the 1930s, then
backtracks, but intends to catch up with the present decade,
before culminating in the millennium. It brings together various
periods of time in a single, wide focus, and without attempting to
be a psychological epic — like Proust's *Remembrance of Things
Past* — it presents "spots of time," long passages of discursive
rumination, and moments of the self, as it confronts inherited or
fresh experiences. The growth of group awareness in Canada is
reflected in the growth and development of Matt Goderich,
Hood's occasionally pompous and naïve protagonist, who is
fundamentally good-natured and intellectually curious.

Although certain of its devices come directly from Wordsworth, Coleridge, Proust, Joyce, and Powell, The New Age is a
new literary creation that constitutes a "documentary fantasy"
about the visibles and invisibles of existence. Its details of
geography, sociology, history, politics, economics, and family
and cultural life are thick with fact, rich in texture, and fasci-

nating in appeal. Yet its allegorical form illuminates these facts through images that glint from a single, slowly rotating crystal ball. We cannot as yet see the final images, but we know from Hood's various comments that his axis tilts away from Eden and then upwards to a beatific vision. Hood's most representative fiction is never the study of a passion, and his ultimate reality is not the heroic deed of a purely human being, but the magnetic force of a divinity that attracts goodness towards itself. Hood, like Dante, transforms literature into a salvific narrative in which the individual is raised to infinite heights.

On the face of it, *The Swing in the Garden* appears to mix documentary fact with fiction without telling a story in the conventional sense. The overall shape is determined implicitly by subtle emblems, and *The Swing* has the archetypal form of a quest in which characters seek a Promised Land. Matt Goderich seeks his own paradise of unity with fellow men in a world redeemed by love and justice. Although the book ends with signs of war and death, it shows largely a green world in which Hood's vision is pastoral — or, perhaps, what Shakespeare's Polonius might have called "historical pastoral" — and the mode encompasses realism, romance, and satire.

By setting his story in Toronto and by projecting his direct vision of life through Matt, who is all his different ages at once, Hood is able to exploit the tensions of pastoral through the fresh sincerity of a swain. Behind this, of course, lies the idea of innocence with which pastoral tends to merge into the myth of the golden age, an Arcadia or Eden of the mind where life enjoys a pristine purity. The swain, still untainted by major evils, is an ideal innocent whose growing perceptions, and conceptions, join the simplified to the complicated, so that Hood is able to keep contrasting ways of life in equilibrium. Matt is a normal, bewildered man, looking back on his childhood and adolescence and remembering the romance of youth through characters with romantic names, such as Alanna, Laetitia, Alysoun, Elaine, Amanda, Isabelle, and Roland. Hood's pastoral is highly sophisticated — an urban product, and, so, consistent with a primary condition of pastoral[66] — and its nostalgia, far from being primitive, is a Proustian yearning of memory that has an emotional function.

Matt is like his biblical namesake, a synoptic evangelist whose intellectual voracity engenders the interiorization of a period's manners. By observing himself and others as if they were all in some film brilliantly directed by himself, "objectified on the big screen of our imagination,"[67] Matt expresses changing social and cultural styles.

There is little humility in Matt, and certainly none of the sort traditionally associated with pastoral. His synchronous consciousness — the bringing into one picture of different parts of a story — has no time for conventional humility, and it is only his sense of social inferiority that crystallizes the delicacy of feeling inherent in the social aspect of pastoral.

Original Sin is a felt doctrine in the novel, and the allegorical undercurrent should come as no surprise to us. The very title is an intimation of the Fall in Eden, for the swing is an oscillation away from the paradise of childhood, as it were. There is a young Adam (Sinclair) in childhood's garden, and he is already envisaged as a scapegoat. There is a watchtower at a crossing, and its symbolism is a reminder of God's surveillance of man (SG, p. 10). But the pattern of a divinely human comedy is set by several images in the first chapter. The landscape beyond the Goderich garden is dominated by the Hill, which is viewed as a "promised land" (SG, pp. 6–7). And near the Hill is the Bridle Path or the Bridal Path, associated not so much with horses as with "the wedding march," or marriage — the fundamental end of old comedy (SG, p. 7).

Matt's expulsion from his infant's Eden is marked by a movement farther east — the symbolic direction of new mystery, knowledge, revelation, and life (SG, p. 32). The Edenic womb image is displaced by a demonic vacant lot where Matt almost drowns in a dark, water-filled hole (SG, p. 39). He later acquires a scar when he slips on a roller skate during his younger brother's christening; and the mark of his pain and disgrace is sometimes called, "not wholly jokingly," by his mother "the brand of Cain" (SG, p. 47).

In Chapter ii Matt's swing from innocence dips deeper into the darkness and frustration of the human heart. The cinema is a false paradise that lures by its one-cent candy, Flash Gordon serials, newsreels, cartoons, and trailers. The excruciating din of the assembled crowd, even from outside the theatre, sounds like Gehenna or Armageddon, "or the awakening of the Divine Beast in the Revelation to St. John on Patmos" (*SG*, p.56). Inside, Adam Sinclair becomes the victim of a mocking prank whereby he is cruelly de-panted in the dark (*SG*, pp.57–58).

Matt later acquires another scar. In what cannot be evaded as an aural pun, he is *scathed* by his unrequited love for Beatrice Skaithe, the *princesse lointaine* of the romantic satire in the plot. Beatrice remains the unattainable feminine ideal (like Dante's "blessed one") — an image of perfection, but in this case a Protestant one incompatible with Goderich Catholicism.

In the final three chapters, Matt's special penchant for cross-referencing (*SG*, p.116) is a symptom of his secular evangelism in that, by documenting the development of group manners and awareness in his society, he is a witness, like Saint Matthew, to the unfolding of a special destiny. Matthew supplements the Gospel, and his family name puts us in mind of the kingdom of God (*Godes rice*) that can be inherited by such grace. His moral imagination is helped by his parents: his mother, "the most sweetly reasonable person" he has known (*SG*, p.64), makes a dogma of the open mind, and of fairness and justice; while his father, a socialist philosopher, endows him with a habit of mind to see conflict between dialectical poles resolved (*SG*, p.68).

The Goderich family fortunes rise and fall; the country falls into political and socio-economic chaos; Matt's pride is lowered; and the "long fall" anticipated at the end of the book is a season of human degeneration as World War II erupts. As Matt scans pictures of war, the novel moves into the tomb of history and anticipates cataclysm. The "fires" of destruction dominate the final two chapters — Spitfires, machine-guns, buildings on fire, land-mine explosions — and the only positive "fire" is associated with the Goderiches, whose fortunes, though utterly burnt up in Jackson's Point, will raise themselves like "the fabulous phoenix" (*SG*, p.190).

The Swing is a quieter book than almost any other novel by Hood. Its pastoralism, however, is subtly complex, for it is structured so that the five chapters (five acts of a drama), "of about equal length, cover shorter and shorter periods of time and seem hurried and eventful as they go on" (Hood and Mills, p.137). The first human we see talking to baby Matt is the first to fall by enemy fire. The last line about "a long fall" suggests the widening arcs of human evil, so that a new age is "always before us, and always beginning," as Hood says, and life in youth is seen to be "a conspectus of possible great events that seem to widen out to infinity" (Fulford, p. 68). And this attitude of benevolent optimism graces the theme of innocence, for, like the dominant Adamic image in American literature of a hundred years ago, the most fruitful idea in Hood is that of an authentic wise innocent. However, Hood is not as vulnerable to moral delusion as the nineteenth-century American writers — de Crèvecoeur, Emerson, Thoreau, Hawthorne — for he creates an air of adventurousness and potential without asserting any dogma. The innocence of Matt Goderich is not that of prelapsarian Adam, whose moral position was "prior to experience."[68] However, like the biblical and American Adams, he finds the world and its history open before him once he is expelled from the Edenic womb of his infant environment. If the biblical Adam was a creator in his inventory of the world, then Matt is also a creator in his cross-referencing, ramifications, and annotations.

Hood's pastoral innocence is quite without the cheerless theology of nineteenth-century American literature, in which the "new man" or innocent Adam dissociates himself from the historical past. Though Matt quickly comes to realize the qualities of the fallen world about him, he is not like Emerson's Adam, split between the past and the future. For Matt, the synoptic witness to his time, the past is not an irremediable burden. He does not seek to escape it, or to burn it away according to Thoreau's injunction (Lewis, pp. 20–21), but to understand and use it as a guide to the present and future. Unlike the American Adam, who was "miraculously free of family and race, untouched by those dismal conditions which prior tragedies and entanglements monotonously prepared for the newborn European" (Lewis, p. 41), Hood's innocent has a past and present peopled by many tribes — including English, French, Scots, Protestants, Catholics, entrepreneurs, merchants, and others — all of whom are intensely human or nontranscendental in their potential for evil crises.

In constructing Matt Goderich's original relationship with the world, Hood digs into the Canadian landscape and finds referents for spiritual meaning in the physical scene, an outline of the ideal in the actual. Our understanding is drawn to those great writers before Hood who saw life as a human comedy, rife at times with violent tensions in the secular world but synthesized at the last by a transforming vision of the future. Hood's pastoralism begins with an innocence that does not go unchallenged or untransformed. It is tested by drama — even if, at times, only intellectual drama — and strong illuminations charge it, so that we grasp its special complexities, buoyant assurance, and encircling doubt about Canadian society growing up with Matt Goderich.

The Swing is a repository of ideas, characters, and emblems for The New Age series, and its density obscures its inner form. The two succeeding novels, however, clarify Hood's allegorical mode and draw unmistakable analogies with Scripture. *A New Athens* is Hood's Book of Revelation, which finds the "footpaths of the Divine"[69] in the "cunning corridors" (*NA*, p. 42) of human history. *Reservoir Ravine* is a Nativity-Redemption myth.

In *A New Athens*, Matt is a pilgrim who begins with an excursion across a "twinned Ontario trail," and as his mind composes relationships among the multiplicity of experiences, the human and the divine are connected through apocalyptic emblems that provide both aesthetic and intellectual intelligibility. Art historian that he is, with a degree in "Art 'n' Ark" (Art and Architecture) from the University of Toronto, Matt uses the "Janus-headed impulse of the historian" to lead us from the new Athens to a New Jerusalem, without diminishing the physical and visible world that art lives on.

Beginning with the observable world, Hood undulates into the divine so that the power of his documentary fantasy transforms facts into apocalyptic vision. Matt begins literally with the element of earth as he undertakes an excursion, digs into the lore of his setting, even goes underwater in one sense, and then, after experiencing a pentecostal spirit of fiery faith, ascends through Mrs. Codrington's visionary art to the New Jerusalem that is an allegory of his new Athens.

Everything connects in this book, for Matt's mind always seeks correspondences, sometimes by analogy, and the motif of doubled realities — a "twinned" Ontario trail for Matt's hiking, two fields, lake and river people, two close girl friends, two academic streams — is a suggestion that multiplicity of form does yield a single vision and meaning.

What helps Hood obtain this single meaning is epiphany,

which comes to have both secular and sacred contexts, perhaps most dramatically expressed in the final chapter, which carries the progression of sorrowful and glorious mysteries to an apocalyptic climax. The "wave of life" — the first epiphany — spends itself as Mrs. Codrington dies, but there is a new epiphany in the final revelation of Mrs. Codrington's legacy of sacred art. In her glorious triptych, the world of Stoverville is twinned with the world of spirit into a single nexus of atonement and redemption in which the damned are cast into perdition while the elect are gathered around the Godhead in the heavenly city (*NA*, pp. 211–16). The new Athens is thereby transfigured into the New Jerusalem, and Matt, who started out at the beginning of the book on the road of old Adam — "the Victoria Macadamized Road" (*NA*, p. 5) — finds himself composed into a vision of the heavenly city on top of an enormous height irradiated by the glory of the divine. The screws of the painting fix the vision to the wall, so that Mrs. Codrington's keys to the attic-studio bear a correspondence to the keys of David (Rev. iii.7–8), for they unlock what nobody can then close — the upper room with its revelation of the glorious mystery of redemption.

Matt Goderich serves as witness to various mysteries, and his analytical mind helps to clarify the procession and products of time while simultaneously provoking our exploration of the spiritual allegory. In *Reservoir Ravine*, Matt plays the role of Raphael, under the broad shadow of the *Book of Tobit*; he stirs the waters of memory, blessing his parents, as he recollects their wedding, his own nativity, and the general paradigm of redemption.

The ideas of contract and witness function importantly in the book, as they do in *Tobit*. The marriage contract of Andrew and Isabelle Goderich is an analogy for the contract between Christ and the Church, and there is also a metaphorical contract between Canada and Jerusalem (first made in the Hart House debate,[70] and later expanded by Andrew and his counsellor, Aaronsohn). Various witnesses attest to the history of the epoch — Hal Forbes from Winnipeg, Aaronsohn from Germany, Professor Brett, Colonel Jarvis, Miss Saint-Hilaire, among others — but the final human witness is Matt himself, already cast as one of the elect in *A New Athens*. In *The Swing* he makes history a vast repository into which he dips frequently; in *Athens* he is a

Janus-headed historian who follows the divine through the corridors of life; and in *Ravine* he looks on the reservoir as a form of memory (*RR*, p. 221). Matt finally becomes the "eyes" of his old blind mother, and it is his special mission to see for her and for all of us in order to discover a moral pattern in our national lives.

At the end of *Ravine*, the world has changed radically. Reports of German decadence (*RR*, p. 231) show how the grip of reason is breaking. There are omens of world catastrophe, and philosophy is losing its way. But Matt looks into his reservoir of memory and finds meaning. As a witness to his parents' story, as a critic of his own age, he is creator and redeemer: he gathers out of "the undifferentiated manifold of time of spouts, points, upwellings of persons" (*RR*, p. 193) a personal and national myth of Nativity, Fall, and Redemption.

Hood's Christian allegory, in the opinion of some of his critics, weakens his fiction. Sam Solecki, in a review of Canadian novels in English from 1960 to 1982, offers the comment that "... while Hood's commitment to an affirmative and religious vision is admirable (it's refreshing to read a contemporary writer who actually believes in something), his central characters, especially the pivotal Goderich, lack a shadow side and are usually almost too good to be true. Unlike other contemporary Christian novelists, Hood has not taken into account 'the evil facts which are a genuine portion of reality' (William James)."[71] Barbara Helen Pell, while recognizing Hood's achievement in The New Age series, as well as its technical virtuosity and fluid style, nonetheless finds a problem in Hood's religious vision: "His vision is Catholic and Christian, but in his epiphanies of God's grace he does not imaginatively embody man's fallen nature. His failure to dramatize the existential struggle against evil and despair in the limit-situations of life that we have seen in the work of Callaghan means that Hood's affirmations of God's grace are too simple and easy, untested and unearned."[72] However, Pell misses subtle nuances, and because her article was probably written long before the publication of Hood's latest novel, *Black and White Keys*, she is unable to confront what is Hood's most explicit engagement with the problem of evil, a work which would satisfy even Sam Solecki's desire for "a more profound sense of social relations and historical conflict than has so far been offered."[73]

Black and White Keys is a salvation history much in the way
the Bible is one. Created by a writer who sees history as "a recollection of Divine Being" (*TT*, p. 43), it narrates historical events
that are ordained to lead to moral salvation. Despite a turbulent,
tenebrous atmosphere for its black keys, it has a Messianic
pattern and provides synoptic witness to the problems and solution of "sin quantified."[74] Like *The Swing in the Garden*, it is
structured in five parts, but the narrative offers two voices —
Hood's third-person recounting, and the first-person participant
voice of Matt Goderich, the hero's son, whose discourses on
apparently vulgar mythologies of evil actually complete the
novel's radical vision of metaphysical evil.

In the first part, the predominant mood is dark, shadowy,
furtive, and wintry as the black and white design is set in the
opening pages. The initial setting is Ottawa, where a small clutch
of characters materializes in and out of shadow. Some of the
characters — Andrew Goderich and Charlie Pope, for instance —
deepen their relationships from the earlier novels. And later,
other characters from the preceding books also appear in a
Powellian set of interlocking harmonies. The first vivid emblem,
carved in relief over a doorway, is that of "Justice and her sister"
— "the two Canadas" (*BWK*, p. 3). However, the revelations of
monstrously obscene racial and religious persecution in Europe
make it seem that ". . . Justice is in hiding" (*BWK*, p. 4). Andrew
Goderich, now forty-two and out of his university position, is
commissioned by Ottawa to act as agent in a daring rescue of
renowned philosopher Georg Mandel from a Nazi concentration
camp. Despite Andrew's perplexity ("Why me?") and protesta-
tion ("I'm a frail vessel"), he is forced to bear "an heroic burden"
(*BWK*, p. 31), and in accepting this — however reluctantly or
humbly — he links Justice to the second emblem, Resurrection,
which appears for the first time as an altarpiece motif in a chapel
designed by Stanley Spencer (*BWK*, p. 57). The second emblem
crystallizes the transformation of World War II from "a sideshow
in the unfolding of modern history" into "the formative occurrence of the mid-century" (*BWK*, p. 48); and it prefigures
Mandel's own resurrection from the dead at Dachau.

The resurrection motif is enlarged by the appearance on Good
Friday of Samuel Aaronsohn, one who had been an important
moral and philosophical influence in Andrew's life in *Reservoir*

Ravine. Aaronsohn, once a witness to Andrew's marriage, now becomes a cowitness to Andrew's role of rescuing angel in a battle against the angel of death at Eastertide. The religious analogy is carefully worked out, as Andrew, the harrowing figure in the "snake-pit" of Ottawa and then the inferno of Dachau (*BWK*, pp. 5, 235), acquires in the course of his parachute-training a foot wound that is healed on Saint Patrick's Day. As in *You Cant Get There From Here*, Hood succeeds in deepening the plot with flurries of high-pitched action that are integrated with a moral pattern.

Chapter ii is Matt Goderich's counterpoint that repeats much of the texture and tone of *The Swing in the Garden*. Once again there is a leisurely recollection of a specific era in boyhood and adolescence. Once again there is a loving attention to minute particulars, but, again, there is deft control of what first appear to be gratuitous digressions on such discrete subjects as Nazi uniforms, Hollywood war films, pop singers, and freestyle wrestling. The Nazi movies and wrestling contests are analogies for evil, while the long essay on Crosby, Sinatra, Como, and pop music is shown (in Chapter iv) to be a key to the Proustian gestalt for it sketches how the liberation of memory and the "symmetrical poise" of popular culture pull together "the terrible stresses of those years" (*BWK*, p. 212).

Chapters iii and v carry us into the heart of sin and redemption. The Third Reich coils around events like a snake whose hiss is heard in the very sound of the *Reichssicherheitshauptamt* (*BWK*, p. 119). In places such as the "fog-shrouded castle of Dachau" (*BWK*, p. 125), there are such vicious experiments with evil that the New Age now becomes an euphemistic label for a century of race-murder. Yet there is a radiance that emanates from within the gloom of this infernal era. With Mandel's resurrection from the dead, there is a promise of universal witness from one who looks "as old as God" (*BWK*, p. 124), and Andrew Goderich's salvific mission is a fulfilment of Charlie Pope's prophecy of "the new Zion" in Canada because it is a Canadian who applies Christ's gospel for a Jew.

Hood's "sportive play of imagination" yields poignant patterns that, although parodic, are quickened by sensitivity to emotional and moral nuances. Mandel and Andrew, linked by leg wounds to the same foot, are also joined in charity. In a desperate attempt to revive the moribund Mandel in a hayloft, Andrew presses his body to the old man's "in a fearful parody of a wedding" (BWK, p. 154). This spousal union has a second level of parody because the true spouse behind the two figures is Christ: "...he and his beloved spouse in grace, the great mind, the lord of European thought, were robed in the protection of the Divine Love, in the presence of God" (BWK, p. 156).

Christological emblems multiply. At Ravensburg a Christ-clock stares down into the square, "an eternal reminder of last things signed with the mysterious and holy alpha and omega suggestive of a divine cycle of deaths and entrances" (BWK, p. 177). The dramatic contrast between the splendour of the country and its present horror chills the blood, and the catastrophe on the Bodensee (where Aaronsohn is machine-gunned to death) acquires the shock of an eerie Munch painting.

Andrew cannot get the Christian liturgy out of his head. Events resound like the Apocalypse, and he recalls Luke's gospel for the first Sunday of Advent (BWK, pp. 242–43). A Christ figure in his harrowing of hellish Dachau, a fisher of men over water and in the grave, he is stirred by Mandel's own earnest prayer to catch victims before they are sent east to their doom. Yet Andrew does not suffer from any kind of Messianism. He refuses the ultimate parody of Christ ("'He saved others, himself he cannot save' will never be said of me" [BWK, p. 244]), then falls into "a dazed and confused state of mind induced by months of paralysis of the will" (BWK, p. 256).

The final chapter solves the problem of evil. Andrew, who comes to see glorious parallels between himself and the biblical Andrew and between himself and Christ, the archetypal fisher of men, is reminded by a pastor that he has saved three unique witnesses to history. In the *metaphysic* of evil, numbers do not make a difference because a single testimony justifies the saving act (BWK, p. 269). The purely suspenseful elements of the narrative are given depth by the moral consequences, although in carrying the novel to its apocalyptic glorious climax, Hood permits fiction to overcome history. In reparation for the crime "which excises a history from history," which cuts a gaping wound "out of the book of life," Andrew writes his one great book on the axioms of sin. And now, with the black and white keys of his typewriter, he is able to emerge from his narcosis of self-doubt, disgust, and despair (*BWK*, pp. 291–92). But Hood, not content to leave virtue to its own reward, bestows the 1950 Nobel Prize for Peace on the character and, in a single arbitrary flourish, dispenses with historical reality. The motive is, of course, ennobling metahistory — the imperative to vindicate goodness or celebrate the salvific possibilities of history. But it is needlessly un-historical. Perhaps, however, it is Hood's way of doing justice to a just hero, who exhorts his Canadian countrymen to "go on in their peaceful way, in their search for just solution to desperate differences" (*BWK*, p. 298). The triumphant ending seals the Justice emblem. It also confirms the multiple connotations of Hood's title for the epical series. This is to be an allegorical epic about our own identity and redemption. Even in the heat and flare of the gas ovens, there are signs that sin and evil will run to their own ruin. Man is already redeemed, but he must retrace the stations of Christ's cross before ascending to his glorious destiny.

Hood's religious faith informs his most secular vision, and this fideism permits him to participate through literature in the enjoyment of an interior universe whose exploration is the theme of religious and mythological art of all ages. Beauty is established in the multitude and plenitude of being and is communicated supernally from the divine. Yet, Hood's emblematic imagination never becomes what Allen Tate has called the "angelic mind" — a mentality that, in its quest after direct knowledge of essences, denies man's involvement in the physical world and sets itself up in "quasi-divine independence."[75] What Tate perceives in Dante's symbolic imagination is what we can say of Hood's emblematic one:

> ...its fullest image is an action in the shapes of this world: it does not reject, it includes; it sees not only with but through the natural world, to what may lie beyond it. Its humility is witnessed by its modesty. It never begins at the top; it carries the bottom along with it, however high it may climb.[76]

Any summing-up of Hood's work as it now stands is incomplete because the meaning of The New Age series is yet to emerge as a totality. However, we can already see that the millennial *roman fleuve* will uncover a Canada, from the 1920s through the birth of the twenty-first century, that will become distance-less, visible, and immanent in the eternal world. Georg Lukács, in *The Theory of the Novel*, looks on Dante as "the only great example in which we see the architectural clearly conquering the organic," and therefore representing "a historico-philosophical transition from the pure epic to the novel."[77] Hood is somewhat like Dante translated into prose. In his work, the totality is a highly systematic mythology that transforms the separate parts of an epical *roman fleuve* into ordered, autonomous parts.

Just as Dante has a dual structure in which "the break between life and meaning is surpassed and cancelled by the coincidence of life and meaning in a present, actually experienced trans-cendence" (Lukács, p.68), so also Hood provides doubled realities, underscored by fulfilled postulates of Catholic philo-sophy. Hood, like Dante, does not endow his hero, Matt, with visible social superiority or with a heroic destiny that co-determines the destiny of the community. His hero's experience, however, does recapitulate human destiny in general by tracing the Nativity-Fall-Redemption myths.

The inner form of The New Age series recognizes the dangers that arise from the fundamentally abstract nature of the novel as outlined by Lukács: "the risk of overlapping into lyricism or drama, the risk of narrowing reality so that the work becomes an idyll, the risk of sinking to the level of mere entertainment literature" (Lukács, p.71). Hood triumphs over these risks by signalling clearly all that lies outside and beyond the particular confines of the world. In this sense, he is as much at odds with Balzacian period melodrama as he is with Robbe-Grillet's objectivity, two extremes of realist fiction.

In resisting the anxiety-neurosis of Canadian fiction and other negative attitudes that have coloured most of twentieth-century fiction, Hood expresses a confirmation of divine consonance that makes and remakes being as a perpetual process of generated beauty and wholeness. His resistance to the negative raises a question of the fullness of his epical vision, because we may well wonder if life can be truthfully rendered in art without a problematic individual. As Lukács poses the issue,

> The contingent world and the problematic individual are realities which mutually determine one another. If the indi-

vidual is unproblematic, then his aims are given to him with immediate obviousness, and the realisation of the world constructed by these given aims may involve hindrances and difficulties but never any serious threat to his interior life. (Lukács, p. 78)

Is this so with Matt Goderich? Only on the surface, for Matt's life is a series of examined, although largely unresolved, problems of being. He does not suffer the way Raskolnikov or Bloom or Biswas suffers, but this is only because he adapts the discrete, unlimited nature of the material of life to the infinity of God's meaning. His limitation as a character is his faith, which is really a paradox because, whereas his biography is subjective and constrained by his possible experiences, his faith permits larger possibilities outside his immediate world. It is a special paradox, a Dantean one, in which the beginning and end take place between two points in eternity: generation (and its chaos that he seeks to order) and the certainty of redemption. Hood's epical fiction is a reading of the Book of Life according to the Book of Divine Revelation. The world is a real one — not an illusion. Dense with detail, thick with fact, it is flawed but redeemable; and the epical hero, Matt Goderich, is far from lonely, for he is a bearer not only of his own destiny, but of a gospel for all mankind. Instead of romantic disillusionment, Hood offers us the superrealism of one who can see where God is to be found in a world that believes God is dead or indifferent. Hood is a Canadian original — the first and only meditative writer in our nation's fiction who, by his anagogical approach, conditions the novel towards the paramount significance of human experience as salvation-history.

NOTES

[1] Hugh Hood, Letter to Naïm Kattan, *Le Devoir*, 12 Dec. 1964, p. 15.

[2] Martha Foley and David Burnett, eds., *The Best American Short Stories 1962* (Boston: Houghton Mifflin, 1962), p. 428; and Martha Foley and David Burnett, eds., *The Best American Short Stories 1968* (Boston: Houghton Mifflin, 1968), pp. 354, 359.

[3] Geoff Hancock, "Hugh Hood's Celebration of the Millennium's End," *Quill & Quire*, Nov. 1980, p. 40.

⁴George Woodcock, "Literary Echoes," *Books in Canada*, March 1980, p. 8.

⁵Robert Fulford, "An Interview with Hugh Hood," *The Tamarack Review*, No. 66 (June 1975), pp. 69–70. All further references to this work (Fulford) appear in the text.

⁶J. R. (Tim) Struthers, "An Interview with Hugh Hood," in *Before the Flood: Our Exagmination round His Factification for Incamination of Hugh Hood's Work in Progress*, ed. J. R. (Tim) Struthers (Downsview, Ont.: ECW, 1979), p. 25. All further references to this work (*BF*) appear in the text.

⁷Pierre Cloutier, "An Interview with Hugh Hood," *Journal of Canadian Fiction*, 2, No. 1 (Winter 1973), 52.

⁸Roger Shattuck, *Proust's Binoculars: A Study of Memory, Time, and Recognition in à la recherche du temps perdu* (New York: Vintage, 1967), p. 21.

⁹Margaret Atwood, *Survival: A Thematic Guide To Canadian Literature* (Toronto: House of Anansi, 1972), pp. 31–41.

¹⁰John Moss, *Patterns of Isolation in English Canadian Fiction* (Toronto: McClelland and Stewart, 1974), pp. 7–10.

¹¹A. J. M. Smith, ed., *The Canadian Century: English-Canadian Writing since Confederation* (Toronto: Gage, 1973), p. xviii.

¹²Paul Denham, ed., *The Evolution of Canadian Literature in English 1945–1970* (Toronto: Holt, Rinehart and Winston, 1973), p. 191.

¹³"Hugh Hood and John Mills in Epistolary Conversation," *The Fiddlehead*, No. 116 (Winter 1978), p. 137. All further references to this work (Hood and Mills) appear in the text.

¹⁴John Mills, "The Bloody Horse," rev. of *Close to the Sun Again*, by Morley Callaghan, *The Doctor's Wife*, by Brian Moore, and *A New Athens*, by Hugh Hood, *Queen's Quarterly*, 85 (Spring 1978), 64.

¹⁵Rev. of *Flying a Red Kite*, *St. Catharines Standard*, 26 Jan. 1963.

¹⁶Donald Stainsby, "Hugh Hood's Glitter Pure Gold after All," rev. of *Flying a Red Kite*, *The Vancouver Sun*, 7 Dec. 1962, Leisure Sec., p. 5.

¹⁷Munro Beattie, "A New Canadian Writer of Fine Short Stories," rev. of *Flying a Red Kite*, *The Citizen* [Ottawa], 5 Jan. 1963, p. 22.

¹⁸Percy Rowe, rev. of *White Figure, White Ground*, *The Telegram* [Toronto], 22 Aug. 1964, p. 19.

¹⁹H. M. R., rev. of *White Figure, White Ground*, *Winnipeg Tribune*, Aug. 1964.

²⁰Philip Stratford, "The Artist's Life," rev. of *White Figure, White Ground*, by Hugh Hood, and *Bright Day, Dark Runner*, by George Cuomo, *Saturday Night*, Oct. 1964, p. 30.

[21] Desmond Pacey, "A First Novel," rev. of *White Figure, White Ground, The Fiddlehead*, No. 63 (Winter 1965), pp. 70–71. All further references to this work (Pacey) appear in the text.

[22] Ernest Buckler, "Anti-Paintings of What Wasn't There," rev. of *White Figure, White Ground, The New York Times Book Review*, 16 Aug. 1964, p. 5.

[23] William French, "Hollywood? Who Needs It?" rev. of *The Camera Always Lies, The Globe Magazine*, 30 Sept. 1967, p. 26.

[24] Phyllis Grosskurth, "New Canadian Novels," rev. of *The Camera Always Lies*, and four other books, *Saturday Night*, Nov. 1967, p. 55.

[25] Chris Redmond, "A Distorted Rehash of Real Life," rev. of *The Camera Always Lies, Queen's Journal*, 27 Oct. 1967.

[26] John Cowan, "Thoroughly Bad Novel," rev. of *The Camera Always Lies, Sherbrooke Daily Record*, 24 Feb. 1968.

[27] Robert Fulford, "Hugh Hood's Misused Talent," rev. of *The Camera Always Lies* and *Around the Mountain, Toronto Daily Star*, 11 Oct. 1967, p. 43.

[28] Michael Gordon, radio rev. of *The Camera Always Lies*, CBC National Network, 4 March 1968.

[29] Dave Godfrey, "Turning New Leaves," rev. of *Flying a Red Kite, The Canadian Forum*, Jan. 1963, pp. 229–30.

[30] William French, "Scrambled Scrimmage, Fumbled Ball," rev. of *A Game of Touch, The Globe Magazine*, 24 Oct. 1970, p. 36.

[31] Robert Fulford, "Captain Canada," rev. of *A Game of Touch, Saturday Night*, Nov. 1970, p. 47.

[32] Patricia Morley, *The Comedians: Hugh Hood and Rudy Wiebe* (Toronto: Clarke, Irwin, 1977), p. 39. All further references to this work (Morley) appear in the text.

[33] Alec Lucas, ed., *Great Canadian Short Stories: An Anthology* (New York: Dell, 1971), p. 350.

[34] Frank Davey, "Hugh Hood," in *From There to Here: A Guide to English-Canadian Literature since 1960* (Erin, Ont.: Porcépic, 1974), p. 140.

[35] William New, "Fiction," in *Literary History of Canada: Canadian Literature in English*, 2nd ed., gen. ed. and introd. Carl F. Klinck (Toronto: Univ. of Toronto Press, 1976), III, 264. All further references to this work (New) appear in the text.

[36] John Moss, *Sex and Violence in the Canadian Novel: The Ancestral Present* (Toronto: McClelland and Stewart, 1977), p. 235.

[37] Dennis Duffy, "Grace: The Novels of Hugh Hood," *Canadian Literature*, No. 47 (Winter 1971), pp. 10–25; rpt. in *The Canadian*

Novel in the Twentieth Century: Essays from Canadian Literature, ed. and introd. George Woodcock (Toronto: McClelland and Stewart, 1975), p. 242.

[38] Kent Thompson, "Hugh Hood and His Expanding Universe," *Journal of Canadian Fiction*, 3, No. 1 (Winter 1974), 55–59.

[39] Pierre Cloutier, "All in All in Africa," rev. of *You Cant Get There From Here*, *Books in Canada*, Nov.–Dec. 1972, p. 26.

[40] Brian Vintcent, "One Novel Down 11 to Go," rev. of *The Swing in the Garden*, *The Toronto Star*, 4 Oct. 1975, Sec. H, p. 7.

[41] Peter Stevens, "Another 'Great Canadian Novel'... in Twelve Volumes," rev. of *The Swing in the Garden*, *The Windsor Star*, 3 Jan. 1976, p. 39.

[42] David Pryce-Jones, "The Week's Novels," rev. of *The Swing in the Garden*, *The Sunday Times* [London], 20 June 1976, p. 38.

[43] Keith Garebian, "Hood Has Detail, Not Emotion," rev. of *The Swing in the Garden*, *The Gazette* [Montreal], 8 Nov. 1975, p. 49.

[44] John Mills, rev. of *The Swing in the Garden*, by Hugh Hood, and *Two Stories: The Drubbing of Nesterenko & First Loves*, by Hanford Woods, *The Fiddlehead*, No. 112 (Winter 1977), pp. 143–46.

[45] Sam Solecki, "Metafiction or Metahistory?" rev. of *A New Athens*, *The Canadian Forum*, Dec. 1977–Jan. 1978, pp. 37–38.

[46] Keith Garebian, "*The Swing in the Garden*: Hugh Hood's Pastoral," The Commonwealth in Canada Conference, Concordia Univ., Montreal, 19 Oct. 1978.

[47] Keith Garebian, "Classic Condition," rev. of *A New Athens*, *The Montreal Star*, 15 Oct. 1977, Sec. D, p. 3.

[48] Keith Garebian, "A Reappraisal of the Mind through the Time Machine," rev. of *Reservoir Ravine*, *The Montreal Star*, 25 Aug. 1979, Sec. D, p. 3.

[49] Dennis Duffy, "A New Athens, the New Jerusalem, a New Atlantis," rev. of *A New Athens*, *The Fiddlehead*, No. 117 (Spring 1978), p. 107.

[50] Keith Garebian, *Hugh Hood*, Twayne's World Authors Series, No. 709 (Boston: Twayne, 1983).

[51] Hugh Hood, "The Ontology of Super-Realism," in *The Governor's Bridge Is Closed* (Ottawa: Oberon, 1973), p. 127. All further references to this work (*GB*) appear in the text.

[52] William York Tindall, *The Literary Symbol* (Bloomington: Indiana Univ. Press, 1955), p. 12. All further references to this work (Tindall) appear in the text.

[53] In *Dark Glasses* (Ottawa: Oberon, 1976), p. 8. All further references to this work (*DG*) appear in the text.

[54] In *None Genuine Without This Signature* (Downsview, Ont.: ECW, 1980), pp. 44–56. All further references to this work (*NG*) appear in the text.

[55] *Flying a Red Kite* (Toronto: Ryerson, 1962), p. 176. All further references to this work (*FRK*) appear in the text.

[56] Robert Frost, "Nothing Gold Can Stay," in *Robert Frost's Poems*, introd. Louis Untermeyer (New York: Washington Square, 1960), p. 227.

[57] In *Around the Mountain: Scenes from Montreal Life* (Toronto: Peter Martin, 1967), pp. 155–66. All further references to this work (*AM*) appear in the text.

[58] Hugh Hood, "A Few Kind Words from Mavis," in *Trusting the Tale* (Downsview, Ont.: ECW, 1983), p. 34. All further references to this work (*TT*) appear in the text.

[59] Introductory note, in *The Fruit Man, The Meat Man & The Manager* (Ottawa: Oberon, 1971), [p. 6]. All further references to this work (*FM*) appear in the text.

[60] E. M. Burke, "Grace," *New Catholic Encyclopedia*, 1967 ed., VI, 662.

[61] Wayne Grady, "Fiction Chronicle," *The Tamarack Review*, Nos. 77–78 (Summer 1979), p. 100.

[62] Hugh Hood, *Scoring: Seymour Segal's Art of Hockey*, illus. Seymour Segal (Ottawa: Oberon, 1979), n. pag.

[63] *White Figure, White Ground* (Toronto: Ryerson, 1964), p. 209. All further references to this work (*WF*) appear in the text.

[64] *You Cant Get There From Here* (Ottawa: Oberon, 1972), p. 99. All further references to this work (*YC*) appear in the text.

[65] Northrop Frye, *Fearful Symmetry: A Study of William Blake* (Princeton: Princeton Univ. Press, 1947), p. 75.

[66] Frank Kermode, ed., *English Pastoral Poetry from the Beginnings to Marvell* (London: George G. Harrap, 1952), p. 14.

[67] *The Swing in the Garden*, Pt. I of The New Age / Le nouveau siècle (Ottawa: Oberon, 1975), p. 133. All further reference to this work (*SG*) appear in the Text.

[68] R. W. B. Lewis, *The American Adam: Innocence, Tragedy, and Tradition in the Nineteenth Century* (Chicago: Univ. of Chicago Press, 1966), p. 5. All further references to this work (Lewis) appear in the text.

[69] *A New Athens*, Pt. II of The New Age / Le nouveau siècle (Ottawa:

Oberon, 1977), p. 11. All further references to this work (*NA*) appear in the text.

[70] *Reservoir Ravine*, Pt. III of The New Age / Le nouveau siècle (Ottawa: Oberon, 1979), p. 55. All further references to this work (*RR*) appear in the text.

[71] Sam Solecki, "Novels in English 1960 to 1982," in *The Oxford Companion to Canadian Literature*, ed. William Toye (Toronto: Oxford Univ. Press, 1983), p. 583.

[72] Barbara Helen Pell, "Faith and Fiction: The Novels of Callaghan and Hood," *Journal of Canadian Studies*, 18, No. 2 (Summer 1983), 15.

[73] Solecki, "Novels in English 1960 to 1982," p. 583.

[74] *Black and White Keys*, Pt. IV of The New Age / Le nouveau siècle (Downsview, Ont.: ECW, 1982), p. 292. All further references to this work (*BWK*) appear in the text.

[75] Allen Tate, "The Symbolic Imagination," in *The Man of Letters in the Modern World: Selected Essays, 1928–1955* (New York: Meridian, 1955), p. 97.

[76] Tate, p. 112.

[77] Georg Lukács, *The Theory of the Novel*, trans. Anna Bostock (Cambridge, Mass.: M. I. T., 1971), p. 68. All further references to this work (Lukács) appear in the text.

SELECTED BIBLIOGRAPHY

Primary Sources

Hood, Hugh. "Theories of Imagination in English Thinkers 1650–1790." Diss. Toronto 1955.
———. *Flying a Red Kite*. Toronto: Ryerson, 1962.
———. *White Figure, White Ground*. Toronto: Ryerson, 1964.
———. *Around the Mountain: Scenes from Montreal Life*. Toronto: Peter Martin, 1967.
———. *The Camera Always Lies*. New York: Harcourt, Brace & World, 1967.
———. *A Game of Touch*. Don Mills, Ont.: Longman, 1970.
———. *Strength Down Centre: The Jean Béliveau Story*. Scarborough, Ont.: Prentice-Hall, 1970.
———. *The Fruit Man, The Meat Man & The Manager*. Ottawa: Oberon, 1971.
———. *You Cant Get There From Here*. Ottawa: Oberon, 1972.
———. *The Governor's Bridge Is Closed*. Ottawa: Oberon, 1973.
———. *The Swing in the Garden*. Pt. I of The New Age / Le nouveau siècle. Ottawa: Oberon, 1975.
———. *Dark Glasses*. Ottawa: Oberon, 1976.
———. *A New Athens*. Pt. II of The New Age / Le nouveau siècle. Ottawa: Oberon, 1977.
———. *Selected Stories*. Ottawa: Oberon, 1978.
———. "Before the Flood." In *Before the Flood: Our Exagmination round His Factification for Incamination of Hugh Hood's Work in Progress*. Ed. J. R. (Tim) Struthers. Downsview, Ont.: ECW, 1979, pp. 5–20.
———. *Reservoir Ravine*. Pt. III of The New Age / Le nouveau siècle. Ottawa: Oberon, 1979.
———. *Scoring: Seymour Segal's Art of Hockey*. Illus. Seymour Segal. Ottawa: Oberon, 1979.
———. *None Genuine Without This Signature*. Downsview, Ont.: ECW, 1980.
———. *Black and White Keys*. Pt. IV of The New Age / Le nouveau siècle. Downsview, Ont.: ECW, 1982.
———. *Trusting the Tale*. Downsview, Ont.: ECW, 1983.

Secondary Sources

Beattie, Munro. "A New Canadian Writer of Fine Short Stories." Rev. of *Flying a Red Kite*. *The Citizen* [Ottawa], 5 Jan. 1963, p. 22.

Buckler, Ernest. "Anti-Paintings of What Wasn't There." Rev. of *White Figure, White Ground*. *The New York Times Book Review*, 16 Aug. 1964, p. 5.

Cloutier, Pierre. "All in All in Africa." Rev. of *You Cant Get There From Here*. *Books in Canada*, Nov.–Dec. 1972, pp. 26–27.

———. "An Interview with Hugh Hood." *Journal of Canadian Fiction*, 2, No. 1 (Winter 1973), 49–52.

Cowan, John. "Thoroughly Bad Novel." Rev. of *The Camera Always Lies*. *Sherbrooke Daily Record*, 24 Feb. 1968.

Davey, Frank. "Hugh Hood." In *From There to Here: A Guide to English-Canadian Literature since 1960*. Erin, Ont.: Porcépic, 1974, pp. 138–42.

Denham, Paul, ed. and introd. *The Evolution of Canadian Literature in English 1945–1970*. Toronto: Holt, Rinehart and Winston, 1973, pp. 10, 11, 191, 286.

Duffy, Dennis. "Grace: The Novels of Hugh Hood." *Canadian Literature*, No. 47 (Winter 1971), pp. 10–25. Rpt. in *The Canadian Novel in the Twentieth Century: Essays from Canadian Literature*. Ed. and introd. George Woodcock. Toronto: McClelland and Stewart, 1975, pp. 242–57.

———. "A New Athens, the New Jerusalem, a New Atlantis." Rev. of *A New Athens*. *The Fiddlehead*, No. 117 (Spring 1978), pp. 101–08.

French, William. "Hollywood? Who Needs It?" Rev. of *The Camera Always Lies*. *The Globe Magazine*, 30 Sept. 1967, p. 26.

———. "Scrambled Scrimmage, Fumbled Ball." Rev. of *A Game of Touch*. *The Globe Magazine*, 24 Oct. 1974, p. 36.

Fulford, Robert. "Hugh Hood's Misused Talent." Rev. of *The Camera Always Lies* and *Around the Mountain*. *Toronto Daily Star*, 11 Oct. 1967, p. 43.

———. "Captain Canada." Rev. of *A Game of Touch*. *Saturday Night*, Nov. 1970, pp. 47, 49.

———. "An Interview with Hugh Hood." *The Tamarack Review*, No. 66 (June 1975), pp. 65–77.

Garebian, Keith. "Hood Has Detail, Not Emotion." Rev. of *The Swing in the Garden*. *The Gazette* [Montreal], 8 Nov. 1975, p. 49.

———. "Classic Condition." Rev. of *A New Athens*. *The Montreal Star*, 15 Oct. 1977, Sec. D, p. 3.

————. "*The Swing in the Garden:* Hugh Hood's Pastoral." The Commonwealth in Canada Conference, Concordia Univ., Montreal. 19 Oct. 1978.

————. "A Reappraisal of the Mind through the Time Machine." Rev. of *Reservoir Ravine. The Montreal Star*, 25 Aug. 1979, Sec. D, p. 3.

————. *Hugh Hood.* Twayne's World Authors Series, No. 709. Boston: Twayne, 1983.

Godfrey, Dave. "Turning New Leaves." Rev. of *Flying a Red Kite. The Canadian Forum*, Jan. 1963, pp. 229–30.

Gordon, Michael. Radio rev. of *The Camera Always Lies.* CBC National Network, 4 March 1968.

Grady, Wayne. "Fiction Chronicle." *The Tamarack Review*, Nos. 77–78 (Summer 1979), pp. 94–102.

Grosskurth, Phyllis. "New Canadian Novels." Rev. of *The Camera Always Lies*, and four other books. *Saturday Night*, Nov. 1967, p. 55.

Hancock, Geoff. "Hugh Hood's Celebration of the Millennium's End." *Quill & Quire*, Nov. 1980, p. 40.

Lecker, Robert. "A Spirit of Communion: *The Swing in the Garden.*" In *Before the Flood: Our Exagmination round His Factification for Incamination of Hugh Hood's Work in Progress.* Ed. J. R. (Tim) Struthers. Downsview, Ont.: ECW, 1979, pp. 187–210.

————. "Hugh Hood: Looking Down from Above." In *On the Line: Readings in the Short Fiction of Clark Blaise, John Metcalf, and Hugh Hood.* Downsview, Ont.: ECW, 1982, pp. 99–120.

Lewis, R. W. B. *The American Adam: Innocence, Tragedy, and Tradition in the Nineteenth Century.* Chicago: Univ. of Chicago Press, 1966.

Lucas, Alec, ed. *Great Canadian Short Stories: An Anthology.* New York: Dell, 1971, p. 350.

Lukács, Georg. *The Theory of the Novel.* Trans. Anna Bostock. Cambridge, Mass.: M.I.T., 1971.

Mills, John. Rev. of *The Swing in the Garden*, by Hugh Hood, and *Two Stories: The Drubbing of Nesterenko & First Loves*, by Hanford Woods. *The Fiddlehead*, No. 112 (Winter 1977), pp. 143–46.

————. "The Bloody Horse." Rev. of *Close to the Sun Again*, by Morley Callaghan, *The Doctor's Wife*, by Brian Moore, and *A New Athens*, by Hugh Hood. *Queen's Quarterly*, 85 (Spring 1978), 61, 63–65.

————, and Hugh Hood. "Hugh Hood and John Mills in Epistolary Conversation." *The Fiddlehead*, No. 116 (Winter 1978), pp. 133–46.

Morley, Patricia. *The Comedians: Hugh Hood and Rudy Wiebe.* Toronto: Clarke, Irwin, 1977.

Moss, John. *Patterns of Isolation in English Canadian Fiction.* Toronto: McClelland and Stewart, 1974, p. 110.

——. *Sex and Violence in the Canadian Novel: The Ancestral Present.* Toronto: McClelland and Stewart, 1977, pp. 96–102, 234–45.

New, William. "Fiction." In *Literary History of Canada: Canadian Literature in English.* 2nd ed. Gen. ed. and introd. Carl F. Klinck. Toronto: Univ. of Toronto Press, 1976. III, 257, 263–65.

Pacey, Desmond. "A First Novel." Rev. of *White Figure, White Ground. The Fiddlehead,* No. 63 (Winter 1965), pp. 70–71.

Pell, Barbara Helen. "Faith and Fiction: The Novels of Callaghan and Hood." *Journal of Canadian Studies,* 18, No. 2 (Summer 1983), 5–17.

Pryce-Jones, David. "The Week's Novels." Rev. of *The Swing in the Garden. The Sunday Times* [London], 20 June 1976, p. 38.

Redmond, Chris. "A Distorted Rehash of Real Life." Rev. of *The Camera Always Lies. Queen's Journal,* 27 Oct. 1967.

Rev. of *Flying a Red Kite. St. Catharines Standard,* 26 Jan. 1963.

Rowe, Percy. Rev. of *White Figure, White Ground. The Telegram* [Toronto], 22 Aug. 1964, p. 19.

Smith, A. J. M., ed. and introd. *The Canadian Century: English-Canadian Writing since Confederation.* Toronto: Gage, 1973, p. xviii.

Solecki, Sam. "Metafiction or Metahistory?" Rev. of *A New Athens. The Canadian Forum,* Dec. 1977–Jan. 1978, pp. 37–38.

——. "Novels in English 1960 to 1982." In *The Oxford Companion to Canadian Literature.* Ed. William Toye. Toronto: Oxford Univ. Press, 1983, pp. 576–87.

Stainsby, Donald. "Hugh Hood's Glitter Pure Gold after All." Rev. of *Flying a Red Kite. The Vancouver Sun,* 7 Dec. 1962, Leisure Sec., p. 5.

Stevens, Peter. "Another 'Great Canadian Novel'... in Twelve Volumes." Rev. of *The Swing in the Garden. The Windsor Star,* 3 Jan. 1976, p. 39.

Stratford, Philip. "The Artist's Life." Rev. of *White Figure, White Ground,* by Hugh Hood, and *Bright Day, Dark Runner,* by George Cuomo. *Saturday Night,* Oct. 1964, p. 30.

Struthers, J. R. (Tim), ed. *Before the Flood: Our Exagmination round His Factification for Incamination of Hugh Hood's Work in Progress.* Downsview, Ont.: ECW, 1979.

——. "An Interview with Hugh Hood." In *Before the Flood: Our*

Exagmination round His Factification for Incamination of Hugh Hood's Work in Progress. Ed. J. R. (Tim) Struthers. Downsview, Ont.: ECW, 1979, pp. 21–93.

––––––. "Hugh Hood: An Annotated Bibliography." In *The Annotated Bibliography of Canada's Major Authors.* Ed. Robert Lecker and Jack David. Vol v. Downsview, Ont.: ECW, 1984, 231–353.

Tate, Allen. "The Symbolic Imagination." In *The Man of Letters in the Modern World: Selected Essays, 1928–1955.* (New York: Meridian, 1955), pp. 93–112.

Thompson, Kent. "Hugh Hood and His Expanding Universe." *Journal of Canadian Fiction*, 3, No. 1 (Winter 1974), 55–59.

Vintcent, Brian. "One Novel Down 11 to Go." Rev. of *The Swing in the Garden. The Toronto Star*, 4 Oct. 1975, Sec. H, p. 7.

Woodcock, George. "Literary Echoes." *Books in Canada*, March 1980, pp. 6–8.

John Metcalf (1938–   )

DOUGLAS ROLLINS

John Metcalf (1938–   )

DOUGLAS ROLLINS

Biography

JOHN WESLEY METCALF was born in the northern English city of
Carlisle on 12 November 1938, son of a former schoolteacher
and a Methodist minister. His father's profession required
frequent relocations, and Metcalf spent his childhood in York-
shire, the resort city of Bournemouth, and the London dormitory
suburb of Beckenham. He spent part of the war and many subsequent holidays on his uncle's farm in County Cumberland.
During his academic career, Metcalf was in the shadow of his
older brother Michael, now a distinguished mediaeval scholar
and lecturer at both Cambridge and Oxford, where he is a
Keeper at the Ashmolean Museum. Rejected by Cambridge,
Metcalf was awarded a scholarship to the University of Bristol in
1957; he read English and theology under such scholars as L. C.
Knights and Basil Cottle but was more interested in "friendships,
sex, drink, rock-climbing, travel in Europe, and being generally
disreputable."[1]

Always a voracious reader, Metcalf expanded his knowledge
of modern literature, which was not taught at the university. His
passion for the writing of Ernest Hemingway led him to an
interest in bullfighting and, on two occasions, to Pamplona for
the fiesta, where he had a chance meeting with Hemingway
himself. Metcalf's taste for travel had been whetted in his early
teens when he had accompanied his brother on a research trip to
Yugoslavia and Greece. During university vacations, he either
travelled (scruffy and penniless, he once had to be repatriated
from Calais at British government expense) or worked, once in a
Leicester bakery, once as an agricultural worker on the island of
Jersey, more often in restaurants. Awarded a B.A. in 1960 and a
Certificate in Education in 1961, Metcalf taught at a secondary
modern school in Bristol and later in a boys' reformatory. Before

being fired from his Borstal position, Metcalf became friendly with James Gaite, now an eminent educational psychologist and university administrator, who persuaded Metcalf to join him in his application to the Protestant School Board of Greater Montreal. The pair arrived in Canada in the summer of 1962, and Metcalf soon found himself at Rosemount High School teaching English and, to his dismay, Canadian history.

Metcalf first began writing for publication after a student showed him an advertisement for a CBC short-story competition. His first effort, "Early Morning Rabbits," won a 1963 prize of $100 and was broadcast on the CBC. Initial success was followed by disappointing rejections; however, in 1964 Earle Birney, then editor of the quarterly *Prism International*, recognized Metcalf's potential and made the unusual decision to publish eight of his stories over two issues.[2] That year Metcalf returned to England briefly for his father's funeral. Partly to save money to finance full-time writing and partly to escape a troubled love affair, Metcalf took a teaching position at the remote and aptly named RCAF base of Cold Lake, Alberta. A very British enthusiasm for classic blues and traditional jazz led him from Montreal to Alberta via New Orleans. Metcalf found the military atmosphere at Cold Lake extremely uncongenial, and his time there was lonely and difficult. Encouraged by the publication of one of his stories in *The Canadian Forum*, he worked on a novel (later scrapped) and produced more stories, all of which were rejected. However, he could state confidently, "I'm quite pleased with the writing. . . . I think its [sic] getting better even if the whole publishing continent of North America declares otherwise."[3] That Easter holiday he returned to Montreal and the relationship he had hoped to end. In August 1965 he married Gale Courey, a student he had met at Rosemount; they left for England the day after their wedding.

Metcalf's plan was to spend at least a year exclusively at writing, but his savings were soon exhausted and he took a job at a Catholic comprehensive school. His intention to settle permanently in England was also revised; his second decision to live in Canada was much more considered than his first. "England irritated me all the time," he has written. "Its class attitudes, after the easiness of Canada, seemed more rigid than ever. It was inefficient and parochial in its attitudes and made me feel very cramped."[4]

Shortly after Metcalf's return to Montreal in 1966, his work appeared in book form for the first time when two of the *Prism* stories were included in the Ryerson anthology *Modern Canadian Stories* (1966). Ryerson Press's fiction editor, Earle Toppings, became a valuable source of advice and encouragement. Metcalf lasted two years with the Montreal school board; he then worked part-time in a private school and marked essays to finance his writing. Publication in Canadian literary magazines increased, and Metcalf received a Canada Council arts grant in 1968, and was awarded the President's Medal of the University of Western Ontario for "The Estuary," judged the best short story published in Canada in 1968. Metcalf's daughter Elizabeth was born in 1969, and five of his stories appeared in *New Canadian Writing, 1969: Stories by John Metcalf, D. O. Spettigue and C. J. Newman*. His first book, *The Lady Who Sold Furniture*, containing a novella and five stories, appeared in 1970. He taught part-time at McGill University and Loyola College, now part of Concordia University. With the aim of creating a wider audience and promoting the cause of Canadian writing, Metcalf initiated the formation of the Montreal Storytellers Fiction Performance Group,[5] and with fellow members Hugh Hood, Ray Smith, Clark Blaise, and Ray Fraser read to high-school, college, and university audiences in Quebec and the Maritimes. By 1971 Metcalf had won a third Canada Council grant and was completing his first published novel, *Going Down Slow*,[6] when his marriage suddenly and unexpectedly broke up. In the academic year 1972–73, he took up his first writer-in-residence appointment at the University of New Brunswick in Fredericton. Although his literary output was relatively small, he was already recognized as an important writer and as an editor of taste and intelligence.

Metcalf taught at Loyola during 1973–74 and then at Vanier College in Montreal. He was awarded his first senior Canada Council arts grant in 1974. A collection of stories, *The Teeth of My Father*, appeared in 1975; the next academic year was divided into stints as writer-in-residence at the University of Ottawa, and Loyola. Metcalf married Myrna Teitelbaum in 1975, received a second senior Canada Council grant in 1976, and moved with his wife and stepson to an old fieldstone house outside the village of Delta, Ontario. He supported himself writing, editing, and doing literary assignments for various publishers and government arts councils and with a senior grant in 1978 and a short-term grant in 1980. He published two novellas under the collective title *Girl in Gingham* in 1978 and his second novel, *General Ludd*, in 1980. He taught creative writing and served as writer-in-residence at Concordia University during 1980–81.

Metcalf's determination to promote modern Canadian literature in the schools has resulted in his editing of poetry texts and anthologies of Canadian short stories, the most innovative of which, *Sixteen by Twelve* (1970), *The Narrative Voice* (1972), *Stories Plus* (1979), and *Making It New* (1982), allow contemporary Canadian writers to comment on their own work. His concern for deserving lesser known and younger writers is particularly demonstrated in his initiating and editing a series of anthologies (*First Impressions* [1980] and *Second Impressions* [1981]) designed to introduce them to a wider audience. He coedited the series of annual anthologies *Best Canadian Stories* during 1976–82, and, with Clark Blaise, the anthology *Here and Now* (1977). In June 1981 the Metcalfs, with two adopted children from southern India, moved to Ottawa. A book of essays, *Kicking Against the Pricks*, appeared in 1982, as did Metcalf's *Selected Stories*.

Tradition and Milieu

Metcalf has expressed annoyance at attempts to artificially ascribe Canadian influences to his work:

> Writing is an international business. There is no such thing as a national literature. . . . The influences are from whoever is good and whoever is being innovative anywhere. No culture is indigenous. The English language is not bound by national frontiers. I think that most Canadian criticism is just an unfounded and nonsensical extension of Canadian nationalism.[7]

Metcalf and Clark Blaise, in an introduction clearly designed in anticipation of some hostile responses to their editorial choices for a collection of short stories entitled *Here and Now* (1977), stated:

There is no intrinsic reason why Canadian literature cannot satisfy our literary aspirations. If the literature is mature, it will provide all the references Canadians need to know the world, and, incidentally, all the images and personalities the world needs to understand Canada.

If it is mature. . . . For fiction-writers, there is no . . . domestic tradition. We need foreign models . . . foreign standards. That is the reason we have not sought to define a tradition . . . . We have not defined a literature because the literature is still defining itself.[8]

The models which influenced Metcalf are clear. He has said that in his early work he was probably trying to employ the imagistic technique of "a five-line H.D. lyric transferred to a 3000-word story but muddied by Hemingway mannerisms and totally contradicted by gobs of Dylan Thomas."[9] The original version of Metcalf's first written and first published story, "Early Morning Rabbits," was "conceived as a pure Dylan Thomas short story" (Cameron, p. 411). After a number of years and many revisions, the story was published again, trimmed of many of its adjectives and adverbs, but Metcalf still found it "too lush" for his later taste (Cameron, p. 411).

Metcalf has stated that Cyril Connolly is "one critic who has influenced [him] more than anybody else, and not only influenced but also directly helped in [his] own writing and molded [his] taste" (Cameron, p. 407). Metcalf believes that it was not until he was in his late twenties, when he first read the criticism of Connolly, that he really understood how mannered and artificial Hemingway was in his use of language and in his structure. In a piece of his own criticism, a review of a story collection by Norman Levine, Metcalf expressed his rejection of much of the Hemingway influence when he complained that Levine "was trapped in a delicate but out-moded form": "One is always aware of Hemingway's looming bulk and sadly aware that such stories in 1971 are a cliché; the pattern of their rhetoric is predictable. I know; I've written them myself."[10]

Katherine Mansfield's influence led Metcalf "in the direction of being able to escape from plot" (Cameron, p. 411), but it is the early Joyce who set an enduring standard. Metcalf has stated:

The stories that I want to write I think of as chamber music and "high art" in the sense that the leftist critics use the term. I want to write elitist art. It's the austere that appeals to me more than anything else in art. I think that some, not all, of the stories in *Dubliners* are austere, cold, sculpted pieces of work that are brilliant and beautiful. That kind of austerity is what I'm aiming for. (Cameron, pp. 411–12)

For Metcalf himself, however, prolonged or unrelieved exposure to such austerity is not possible. He may watch Bergman or Fellini films and listen to Bach's cello suites or Bessie Smith's blues out of a sense of both duty and appreciation, but it is not high art which he loves emotionally. He says that the type of art which nourishes him is found in the stories of W. W. Jacobs and H. E. Bates and in the comic stories of Kipling, which are "so wonderfully vulgar and funny that I could never write them" (Cameron, p. 412). With Hugh Hood, Metcalf shares a love of P. G. Wodehouse — "one of the world's great writers, although I could never write his inanities because there is a more somber side to my nature, but if I could cut loose with language, Wodehouse is the man that I would admire more than any other" (Cameron, p. 412). Metcalf is an avid reader of detective thrillers and especially admires the work of Raymond Chandler.

He claims to have only recently realized "how large a part radio and the spoken word played in forming the way [he] write[s] and wish[es] to write" (*KAP*, p. 68). From listening to two of his father's "full-blown, non-conformist" sermons every Sunday, he, even as a small child, "developed a grasp of rhetorical structures" (*KAP*, p. 68). His radio listening began with BBC children's programs and later turned to "all the fine comedy programmes which culminated in the most entrancing radio programme ever produced — *The Goon Show*. The Goons created worlds in which I have never ceased to believe . . ." (*KAP*, p. 69). The influence of the rough-and-ready surrealism of the English music-hall performers and their descendants can be found in much of Metcalf's writing. Other examples of radio and stage comedians in "the great tradition of low farce" to whom he was devoted were Frankie Howerd, Benny Hill, Jimmy Edwards, and Tony Hancock. That the affection is still alive can be seen in the use of a line from a Howerd routine "pinched" for *General Ludd* (*KAP*, p. 69).

Metcalf's writing of dialogue, which some critics have admired for its "naturalness," is actually achieved through a highly skilled and literary manipulation which reflects his acknowledged debt to "P. G. [Wodehouse], Firbank, Waugh and Amis" (*KAP*, p. 67). Metcalf often uses dialogue rather than description to convey character and move action forward, employing a technique which can be traced back through Anthony Powell and Waugh to Firbank.

The influence of Amis can be detected in "The Lady Who Sold Furniture" and is undisguised in *Going Down Slow*. But the comedy in Metcalf's first novel was already darker than that in *Lucky Jim*, and in a 1979 interview he indicated a direction in which he has been developing for the last decade:

> I want to move into a blacker kind of humour, a more farcical kind of humour, because I think the times are demanding it. Stylistically speaking, my favourite writer in the world in [sic] Evelyn Waugh. . . . I want to try and write, if I am spared, a few sentences, a few scenes as viciously funny as those that Evelyn Waugh wrote. I also happen to think, of course, that funny books are the most serious ones that there are. [11]

Because of his work as an editor of contemporary Canadian writing, Metcalf is unusually familiar with the work of both the established and newer writers in this country, and he has expressed an admiration for many of them; however, the only Canadian writers he has acknowledged as influences on his own work were his fellow members of the "Montreal Story Tellers." Metcalf's early attempts at Imagism under the often astringent doctrines of Pound and T. E. Hulme had, by his own account, "induced literary constipation" (*KAP*, p. 79). Hugh Hood's influence had the dual effect of reassuring Metcalf "of the *respectability* of writing openly about a moral world — and of writing openly" (*KAP*, p. 78). Hood provided not a stylistic model but proof that relaxation in style was possible while maintaining artistic integrity. The "constructional and rhetorical ideas" that Clark Blaise presented "haven't worked themselves out in open or obvious ways," but Metcalf cites stories like "The Teeth of My Father," "Private Parts: A Memoir," and the recent "The Eastmill Reception Centre" as having grown from seeds planted by Blaise in earth prepared by Ray Smith (*KAP*, p. 79). ". . . the first-person voice that speaks in [these stories] owes much to Hugh. And much in them is also my own. And Waugh's. And Roger Longrigg's. And Richard Yates's. . . . Influence does not work in obvious ways and it's probably impossible to trace unless one person has consciously copied another" (*KAP*, p. 79). Close personal relationships with other serious writers were important for Metcalf during the Montreal Story Tellers period (1971–76) because it coincided with the last phase of his apprenticeship. The full expression of the effects of this period on Metcalf's writing is probably yet to appear.

Critical Overview and Context

The first critical notice of Metcalf's work appeared in *Saturday Night*, where he was heralded as "a discovery" for his contribution to *New Canadian Writing, 1969*. The reviewer declared Metcalf "as brilliant a master of the short story form as Maugham or Chekhov or Erskine Caldwell" and stated that of all the stories published in the two-year history of the New Canadian Writing Series, ". . . none . . . was as gem-like as any of Metcalf's."[12] The handful of other reviewers were considerably more cautious; however, all but one[13] were markedly enthusiastic. Most observed that while Metcalf's stories were traditional, they were superior examples of the genre in their "cogency" and careful control. Kent Thompson judged Metcalf "the best writer in the book" and "The Estuary," which had won Metcalf the 1969 University of Western Ontario President's Medal for fiction, the best story. In praising Metcalf's attention to the "craft" of short-story writing, Thompson used what has become a catchword in Metcalf criticism.[14]

Metcalf's first book, *The Lady Who Sold Furniture* (1970), was very positively received but with varying degrees of perception. Comments on Metcalf's "Englishness," "gift for characterization,"[15] "delicate facility,"[16] "neat, polished, controlled prose," and "disciplined handling of the short story form"[17] were typical. Kent Thompson found "The Lady Who Sold Furniture" the "most impressive piece of work in the collection" but allowed that Metcalf's short stories "come by way of James

Joyce and Chekhov, and . . . employ the familiar Joycean device of the epiphany."[18] Leo Simpson saw "a writer of admirable talent . . . making the crossing from the literary short story — the form in a pure state, but perhaps insulated, and certainly a mild test of a writer's power and range — to the tough disciplines, and complexities, of mature work."[19]

Only five of over thirty reviews of *Going Down Slow* (1972) were negative, and over half were highly positive. Patricia Morley published essentially the same review in *Canadian Literature*, the *Ottawa Journal*, and *Queen's Quarterly*;[20] the spelling of Metcalf's name was consistently correct in the last publication. If Isaac Bickerstaff had paid as much attention to accurate detail in his reading of the novel as he did to the amusing cartoon he drew for *Books in Canada*, his laudatory review would have been less slipshod.[21] A Montreal reviewer stated that "once shed of a sort of sophomoric wit, not to mention a fixation with gutter expletives, the author should be able to produce fiction of a challenging character."[22]

Many critics noted echoes of *Lucky Jim* in Metcalf's novel, but while Kenneth Gibson's cautionary review complained that Metcalf paid up his debts to Amis "so honestly that one winces,"[23] Robert Weaver pointed out that a comparison with the early novels by Amis, John Wain, and John Braine was not entirely fair, for *Going Down Slow* was "more sophisticated and more contemporary than their books were, even when they seemed to be bringing something modern into postwar English fiction."[24]

"It's unusual to find a Canadian novel that manages to be trenchantly funny while making a devastating attack on a prominent element of our social structure. But *Going Down Slow*, a highly polished first novel . . . does just that," wrote William French.[25] Douglas Barbour agreed that it was "a very funny, genuinely comic novel" and placed it within the picaresque tradition.[26] J. R. Leitold also thought that the novel's episodic structure was effective and suitable; he saw an angry and mordant satire that contained "a brief but subtle scrutiny of compromise and betrayal."[27] David Helwig, in his wide-ranging and penetrating examination, found that "a major part of John Metcalf's inspiration is an angry dislike of much of what touches him."[28]

Aside from the usual references to Metcalf's fine craftsmanship, the most commonly used word to describe the collection of eight short stories entitled *The Teeth of My Father* (1975) was "disappointing," with reviews in this vein usually lamenting Metcalf's evident lack of development[29] and failure "to deliver the material he once promised to produce."[30] Kerry McSweeney found "a distinct amount of sentimentality in the presentation of the central male characters" as opposed to the depiction of other characters in the stories.[31] Brian Vintcent found "little evidence that [Metcalf] has come to terms with his anger" and sensed "a watershed in his writing career" in that he had not yet "extract[ed] any really significant and integrated meaning" from the "bits and pieces of experience" he had so well recorded;[32] however, Anthony Brennan welcomed Metcalf's "response to the imperfect world" and felt that, since perfection did not seem imminent, ". . . we can look forward to many years of Metcalf's brilliant observations of particular life."[33]

"Gentle as Flowers Make the Stones" was most often hailed as a triumph and the best piece in the collection — it "deserves anthologized immortality . . . [as] a definitive statement of both the artist's mentality and human isolation."[34] Opinion was widely divided on the merits of the other stories. Barry Cameron provided, in both an extended study and its condensed version, a detailed examination of "a thematic and stylistic departure for Metcalf" in five stories dealing with different aspects of "the relationship between the artist and society or the relationship between the artist's execution or performance of his craft and his own personal life."[35] In his longer essay, Cameron provided a close scrutiny of the sequence to support his contention that Metcalf's stories are "an approximation of poetry."[36]

The novella "Private Parts: A Memoir," which was awarded the *Canadian Fiction Magazine*'s "Annual Contributor's Prize" for 1977, was published in *Girl in Gingham* (1978) together with the title piece, also previously published. Although critics of the book were divided over the relative merits of the two novellas, praise was generally very high with only two or three totally negative reviews. Wayne Grady used an out-of-context quote from a *Books in Canada* interview to equate Metcalf with the narrator of "Private Parts," who, according to Grady, exchanged the boyhood "joys and sorrows of self abuse . . . for the joys and sorrows of being a minor writer." Having conjured

Metcalf's work as literary masturbation, Grady wrote of *Girl in Gingham*, "Since neither story is really *about* anything of consequence (an occupational hazard among urban writers) their interest relies mainly on their style . . ," a style which Grady implied pandered to the debased values of "the times."[37]

Comparisons were frequently made between "Private Parts" and *Portnoy's Complaint* with a reviewer in *Canadian Literature* going so far as to say the novella "uses the techniques of Jewish humour to explore the sexual difficulties of a Gentile world."[38] John Mills judged the piece far superior to Roth's novel: ". . . its comedy is in part created by a spare, understated, classical style beyond Roth."[39] In his analysis, Robert Lecker wrote that "by the end of the story we realize that the 'private parts' referred to are not only sexual but spiritual, social, and aesthetic . . . ."[40] Many reviewers, such as William French[41] and Ken Adachi,[42] differed with Lecker's favourable assessment of the skill with which Metcalf managed the conclusion of "Girl in Gingham," while joining in the general approbation of Metcalf's comic and narrative skills. Lee Briscoe Thompson wrote an important critique of *Girl in Gingham*,[43] and, for a "Special John Metcalf Section" published in *The Fiddlehead*, Barry Cameron offered "some directions for the way in which [he thought the novella] *Girl in Gingham* should be read."[44] Metcalf's own "Notes on Writing a Story" in the same issue is not only a guide to the opening paragraphs of "Private Parts" but a condensed handbook on an approach to the reading of all Metcalf's work and by extension the work of any writer whose artistic concern is not "in raw timber but in carpentry."[45]

Metcalf's latest book of fiction, the satirical novel *General Ludd* (1980), has provoked more extreme division among the reviewers than any of his previous works, with some of the negative responses degenerating into personal attack on Metcalf himself. Cary Fagan moved from a survey of what were taken to be a number of the novel's weaknesses to an emotional objection to the use of a crippled Jew as "the central metaphor for all that [the narrator] sees as wrong in our society."[46] In a less personal expression of rampant special interest, a reviewer in *Quill & Quire* found it "unfortunate" that Metcalf's "ferocious cynicism suggest[ed] a distorted vision that almost destroys credibility," since Metcalf's creation "clarifies some serious problems in

Canadian publishing."[47] J. L. Granatstein's widely syndicated review stated that much of the success of this "splendid novel" was based on "Metcalf's rage at the ideology of Canadian life."[48] Notwithstanding his feeling that Metcalf's anger got the better of him at the novel's end, William French said that "Canadians should feel privileged to be scourged by such a talented scourge-master."[49] A wider perspective was evident in one of the few non-Canadian assessments of Metcalf's work: "Despite its bitterness, *General Ludd* hits the mark, with its comic, dramatic, stylistic, and philosophical felicities — especially for those who share John Metcalf's cultural views and Luddite tendencies."[50]

Metcalf's Works

John Metcalf has written that for him stories begin with the memory of images from his past or with particular words or phrases which seem to stick in his mind. Through a process which he regards as "basically magical," details gradually accumulate until he recognizes a general pattern; it is only then that he attempts to consciously manipulate the material which was "given" to him.[51] The success of the final work of art depends on his ability to capture in words his mental "pictures" and organize them into a meaningful pattern. Metcalf's position is that his writing attempts emotional autobiography rather than the faithful recording of actual events from his own life under the guise of fiction. He has cautioned readers that "to search for 'autobiography' is to be anti-literature; it is to avoid confrontation with the reality of the imagined world; it is to ignore the form, shape and purpose of the composed work in front of you" ("Author's Commentary," p.201). The impulses which move him to write are his "reactions to being alive. Anger, pleasure, the urge to record things before they are lost, the urge to celebrate, the desire to chart where [he has] been" ("Author's Commentary," p.199). Clearly the distinction and the interplay between fact and "the reality of the imagined world" are subtle and complex. By deliberately restricting most of his artistic exploration to his own interior landscape, Metcalf has defined one of his major tasks as a writer: to distance himself emotionally from his material while moving the reader to feel what he once felt. His past must be dispassionately examined and understood before being transmuted into an artistic expression which conveys the intensity of immediate experience. It is through the exercise of a highly developed technique that Metcalf attempts to mould his material to his artistic purpose.

Metcalf's early admiration of the Imagist poets and their principles established the base from which all his work has developed. His account of how his stories begin implies a natural affinity for the Imagist approach. Metcalf's concern for describing mental pictures and for writing prose that is "a progression, an accumulation, and a juxtaposition of images — a flow of imagery basically" (Cameron, p. 403) — reflects a regard for both the "ideogrammatic" method, which Ezra Pound adapted from his understanding of Chinese written characters and ancient oriental poetry, and the poetic principles of T. E. Hulme. Through the artistic realization of externals, the Imagists sought to express the modern sensibility as it experienced the commonplaces of life. The aim of their technique was to capture the essence of actual life. Abstract ideas were to be expressed only by the careful juxtaposition of concrete images, representations of particulars; if meaning emerged, it resulted from the accumulated and accurate rendering of particular objects and particular life.

Pound spoke for the Imagist group when he decreed: "1. Direct treatment of the 'thing,' whether subjective or objective. 2. To use absolutely no word that did not contribute to the presentation. 3. As regarding rhythm: to compose in sequence of the musical phrase . . . ." 4. To conform to the " 'Doctrine of the Image.' "[52] For Pound an image was "that which presents an intellectual and emotional complex in an instant of time."[53] Metcalf's rejection of abstraction (in an interview he echoed the cry "No ideas but in things" [Cameron, p. 422]), the precision and economy of his prose, and his sensitivity to the sound and rhythmic flow as well as the meaning of words illustrate the degree to which his practice squares with Imagist theory.

Language behaves differently in prose than it does in poetry; because Metcalf is a writer of prose who sees his mode of expression as primarily poetic, he must deal with these differences. If prose is a means whose end is the communication of meaning or idea, Metcalf attempts to shift the emphasis so that the selection of words, the manipulation of language, and the fusing of meaning and object become ends in themselves. Prose conventionally follows the order of logic; Metcalf's method is more directed to the isolation and illumination of moments, scenes, and episodes through the use of precise language and telling detail. His narrative frequently develops through the association of a series of "cinematic images" ("Author's Commentary," p. 202) and the use of montage. The result is a forward movement without the obvious use of connective material between the elements. While symbols may emerge from the separate images, it is the juxtaposition of these elements which implies much of the psychological and emotional significance of Metcalf's work.

His early stories also evinced a strong Dylan Thomas influence, the most profound and lasting aspect of which has been in the matter of theme. Most of Metcalf's writing can be divided into four broad, but not mutually exclusive, thematic categories. As his oeuvre grows, the individual works can be seen as parts of a coherent and developing pattern of vision and expression.

Thomas' influence can be clearly seen in the celebrations of childhood and nature and the laments for lost youth and innocence.

Explorations of human isolation and loneliness often reveal the sadness of seemingly insurmountable barriers to communication. Differences in age, race, class, education, and sensibility can shut people off from one another as can, paradoxically, the artist's dedication to his craft. Associated themes are the damaging effects of Puritanism (usually linked to a mother figure), failed love, and the loss of a child.

Authoritarianism in modern society is seen to be a threat to personal freedom, and it is the individual's moral responsibility to resist absolutely. Given present conditions, anarchistic and subversive personal opposition is the best course open. Failure to meet the challenge, through compromise or acquiescence, results in the betrayal of self and others, and spiritual death.

The tyranny of middle-class values and soft-headed liberalism have resulted in the eschewing of excellence and the mindless elevation of the third-rate. Governed by expedience and profit, contemporary life is mechanistic and shoddy. It is inimical to art and artists and generally antihuman.

The first story that Metcalf ever wrote, "Early Morning

Rabbits," was among his first eight stories published in *Prism International*. It became one of a series written over a number of years dealing with "youths and children and the process of growing up" ("Author's Commentary," p. 199). The central character's progress from dream to reality, illusion to disillusion, is commonplace, but Metcalf's control of mood and pacing is impressive, especially for an inexperienced writer. The creation of strong sensory detail underlines the boy's keen anticipation as he prepares to hunt rabbits and effectively conveys his feelings of revulsion at the ugliness and pain which results.

The boy expresses his identification with his uncle and his yearning for manhood by stabbing sacks of grain with his uncle's pig-slaughtering knife, but when he imagines his uncle killing the pig in the yard, he puts the knife back "because he fe[els] wrong."[54] This ambivalence is further revealed in the twinges of guilt the boy experiences after smashing a frightening (and phallic) eel into a pulp. Despite his emotional reaction to the death of animals, the boy is coldly deliberate in his preparations for the rabbit hunt. He ensures that he has a special knife "for skinning things," "string for tying through the legs to make them easier to carry," and "newspapers on the bottom of the bag to prevent blood from staining the canvas."[55] This careful orchestration of incident and detail prepares for the overwhelming horror and guilt the boy feels at the story's conclusion.

Metcalf reworked "Early Morning Rabbits" some twenty times between 1964 and 1970 and claimed to have rewritten it "every year as a sort of test-piece . . . to see how clean [he] could get." Although not satisfied with the 1970 version, he decided to publish it for "almost sentimental reasons and leave it at that"[56] in his first book, *The Lady Who Sold Furniture*.

A comparison of the two versions is instructive. Part of the development away from the more overt Dylan Thomas influence was Metcalf's cutting down of "all the lush verbiage . . . all the adjectives and adverbs that [he] used to plaster everything with."[57] The revised version reflects a growing confidence and control in allowing fewer or more particular words to convey the intent. Figurative and clichéd language is trimmed; point of view is used more effectively.

Metcalf's usual practice in writing stories of childhood, unlike that of Margaret Laurence or Alice Munro, requires the reader to supply most of the ironic perception. "Early Morning Rabbits" is not a story told by an adult viewing events in retrospect but one told by an omniscient voice which approximates the child's as closely as possible, shifting almost imperceptibly from time to time to provide, as in the story's third-to-last paragraph, the objective context the work demands:

> David stood staring. The seeping eye seemed to grow, spreading in a viscous pool, blotting out the fringe of trees and the stone wall and the crooked hawthorn tree, growing in its wounded brownness till it filled the world.[58]

The world being described is both inside and outside the boy's consciousness. The reader is taken from an external view in the first sentence into the boy's mind in the second. But while the reaction to the situation is highly subjective, the vocabulary (e.g., "viscous") and figurative constructions (e.g., "wounded brownness") are beyond the boy. The pain of the moment, which for the boy "filled the world," is subtly placed within a larger context for the reader. Other aspects of the revision also indicate the direction of much of Metcalf's development. As in most of his work, physical description is spare, characterization being achieved mainly through dialogue and action. The added richness in characterization and implication found in the revision is achieved despite the cutting of the story's original length by about a tenth. While the order of events remains essentially unchanged, an improved control of pacing and emphasis is accomplished by moving sentences within paragraphs and by dividing long paragraphs into shorter ones at the points of most tension and excitement. Although about a dozen words longer in total, the last *three* paragraphs of the original version become *seven* much shorter paragraphs, which gradually sharpen to the two one-sentence paragraphs that end the story on its point of climax:

> The squealing, the sound of chalk on board or scraping fingernails.
> And the running, running legs of the still body. (*LWSF*, p. 110)

The poetry of the lines concisely conveys both physical sensation and emotional response through the use of metaphor, onomatopoeia, and the repetition of harsh sibilants — "squealing . . . scraping"—and the apparent oxymoron—"running legs . . . still body." The lines paraphrase Blake's "Each outcry of the hunted hare / A fibre from the brain does tear"; they underline an aspect of the story's theme, Metcalf's belief that "we are a part of the land and its animals — the quality of our relationship is the touchstone of our state of grace" ("Author's Commentary," p. 202).

Two other stories published in *Prism*, "The Happiest Days" and "A Process of Time," became the first of Metcalf's work to appear in book form when they were reprinted in *Modern Canadian Stories*. Taken together the two stories contain in embryo many of the thematic concerns and technical devices which are found throughout Metcalf's later work. Both stories deal with teachers at odds with the realities of their profession.

In "The Happiest Days," a teacher who is alienated from his students and his colleagues daydreams regretfully about his lost youth and indulges in a masochistic fantasy with homosexual overtones. Told in the first person, the story is flawed by the clash of adopted and incompatible mannerisms; however, the many shifts of narrative focus from present to past to predictable future, from reality to imagination and fantasy, are smoothly handled and effective. The masterful control of an often complicated narrative focus is one of the hallmarks of Metcalf's narrative technique; it is well demonstrated in its early stage of development both here and in the companion story, "A Process of Time."

While the narrator of "The Happiest Days" yearns for the vanished ideal of Plato's Academy, Mr. Adams, the narrator of "A Process of Time," is bored with trying to teach poetry to unruly and uninterested students, most of whom would never "reach anything more complicated than 'Twinkle, Twinkle, Little Star.' "[59] Adams finds a kindred spirit in Tony, an intelligent and creative student who pursues his own interests and ignores most of what the school requires of him. When "the Gnome" (the principal) pays one of his terrorizing visits to Adams' class, the teacher at first tries to protect Tony and the rest of the class from the Gnome's bullying, but when his own position is endangered, Adams betrays Tony, leading to his final expulsion from an already worm-eaten Eden. The story concludes with Adams commenting ironically on the "process of time," the gradual erosion of his resolve and self-respect. He is guilty of the most serious kind of betrayal — that of his own conscience. His moral cowardice will ultimately lead to his becoming a part of the oppressive system he abhors.

"A Process of Time" is in many ways an early draft of *Going Down Slow*, Metcalf's first novel written almost a decade later. Throughout Metcalf's work, the modern school is seen as inimical to culture and real education. It stifles the best within students and teachers and misdirects their energies into mindless activities and struggles over discipline. A teacher at odds with the authoritarian and conventional values of the system is bound to be isolated and lonely. Acquiescence has its rewards, but the result of opting for security over principle can only lead to an unintelligent, subhuman existence (represented in "A Process of Time" by "Neanderthal" and "Peking Man"). In "The Happiest Days," the failure to resist results in self-loathing and a wish for punishment, "for there is no defence."[60]

Metcalf uses humour to leaven the serious subject matter in both stories, and the flippant tone of "A Process of Time" is found in much of his later writing. The latter is perhaps the most impressive of the early stories in its control and economy of expression.

The sequence of stories published in *Prism* revealed Metcalf as a writer of promise who, it is clear in retrospect, was already developing some of the themes and technical devices which have been most central to his subsequent work. However, it was a year before his next story, "I've Got It Made," was published.[61] Metcalf published no new material until 1967, but his work has appeared steadily ever since and all of his stories, subsequent to the strangely anomalous "One for Cupid,"[62] have eventually been published in book form.

New Canadian Writing, 1969 contained five stories by Metcalf. "The Children Green and Golden," its title acknowledging its shared spirit with Dylan Thomas' "Fern Hill," traces the activities of David and two playmates as they move on the hesitant but inexorable journey "out of grace." The story uses many of the central images of "Fern Hill" — sun, sea, song, swallows — as points of reference and organization, but it is not merely a prose paraphrase; the portrayal of childhood is less idealized, more complex and particularized.

The limited omniscient point of view, with David as the centre of consciousness, is used to reflect in language and attitudes the world of bright ten- or eleven-year-olds. The almost imperceptible shift to a slightly more elevated and objective narrative is marred only by an obtrusive Thomas echo ("rattling a careless stick,"[63]); the other derivative elements are effectively integrated. The pen which the boys smash as part of their rite of rejection is used here as a religious, sexual, and societal image; it is often used elsewhere in Metcalf's work for similar purposes.

It is not so much religion as the agents of religion that figure prominently in Metcalf's work. Uncle Michael and Auntie Mary might seem to be well meaning, but Metcalf shows that they are damaging in their treatment of the children whom they see as already burdened with "Sin." The boys escape back to nature, but the twice-repeated image of the high cliff and "the black shapes of the swallows flicker[ing] like the blink of an eyelash" (NCW, p. 20) recall Thomas' "swallow thronged loft" and indicate the brevity of childhood and the inevitable loss which comes with growth.

In its organic design, dramatic tension, and accomplished handling of the first-person narrative voice, "The Estuary" indicates a significant development over Metcalf's earlier work. The story opens with David, an intelligent and disturbed twenty-year-old, recounting the details of a recent session with his psychiatrist, Dr. Cottle. The court-enforced visits to Cottle are the result of David's suspected suicide attempt in Wales. Cottle's efforts to have David tell the full story and "acknowledge" his actions, as a means of entering into "a period of adjustment" (NCW, p. 52), are frustrated by his patient's pretended amnesia. What David refuses to reveal is that his walking into the sea was *not* an attempt at suicide but the result of his attempt to maintain contact with a pair of porpoises whose natural beauty and freedom contrasted to the civilized ugliness and boredom of his own life.

David's tone in addressing the reader is arch and flippant as he tells of how he cleverly read up on the nondirective method and turned it back on Cottle. David knows that the psychiatrist's aim is to make him accept that his "world is *necessarily* as it is" (NCW, p. 54), to make him accommodate himself to the reality he refuses to accept. And so David, who insists, "I'm always

happy *in myself*" (*NCW*, p. 51), protects his precious knowledge:
". . . behind my frank and honest eyes, quite safe from Dr.
Maximillian Cottle, I treasured the gleaming sweep of the
estuary; and louder than his questions the sound of the gulls"
(*NCW*, p. 59). Near the sea in Wales, he discovered that, like the
waters of the estuary, his life is united with the tides and primor-
dial forces of nature, though his passage too is marked by
barriers and "troubled water." His hysterical cry "Don't go!
Don't GO. You can't just leave me" (*NCW*, p. 59) was an attempt
to call back the porpoises, who had seemed to signal to him and
whom he believed he had instinctively understood. It was a
desperate attempt to preserve the moment when he had felt and
understood his oneness with nature and her creatures.

"The Estuary" is suffused with a rich complex of images,
symbols, and allusions which also function naturally as narrative
details and serve as organic links contributing to the unity of the
story's design. David's early assertion that his emotions are ". . .
partly seasonal. Like tides" (*NCW*, p. 50) seems frivolous in the
context but clearly relates to his crucial experience. The images
of sore and painful hands are part of David's perception of urban
life, and even the city pigeons, separated from nature, have
"horrid red feet—not pretty pink like coral—raw, red like sores.
Like the hands of the girl in the bus queue" (*NCW*, p. 56). The
steam-jetting train and its signal, symbols of mechanization, give
way to the porpoises and their "whistles" and "signals"; their
"warm huff and snort" are finally displaced by "people shouting
and a car-horn honking" (*NCW*, p. 63). Although entirely
Metcalf's own, the description of David's setting out at dawn in
the Welsh fishing village is reminiscent of the picture of "the still
sleeping town" in Dylan Thomas' "Poem in October"; and
David's epiphany is similar in spirit to Stephen Dedalus' coming
near to "the wild heart of life" on his seashore. David does not
see his experience in Christian terms—a "religious ecstasy and a
vision of Jesus in a white gown appearing over the bay to carry
[him] off in His arms" (*NCW*, p. 58) — but the account of his
epiphany is filled with Christian associations: the "pieces of
bread" David wants to feed the gulls and his taste of the "salt
gift" of the porpoises are both references to the communion
sacrament; other details, such as David's cut side and bleeding
hands and the role of the fishermen, underline the analogy and

the religious nature of his experience. Although not fully explicable in rational terms, or perhaps "basically too simple . . . to understand" (NCW, p. 51), David's pastoral vision expresses a recurrent theme in Metcalf's fiction: "It is only the natural world which *makes sense*," which can keep the "soul from care" ("Author's Commentary," p. 202).

"Walking Round the City" is more obviously social in its anger than "The Estuary," but again our state of grace is seen in our relationship with animals ("A dog starv'd at his master's gate / Predicts the ruin of the State"). The inhabitants of the modern city are measured by their reactions to a suffering dog injured in a hit-and-run accident. The owner's quest for help is neatly divided into a series of episodes which reveal some of the factors which have contributed to the numbing of human sensitivity and loss of contact with the natural basis of life. Running through the story and connecting its parts on a symbolic level are images of tackiness and artificiality: glass doors and windows from behind which "faces stared out" impassively (NCW, p. 29) prove to be as impenetrable as barriers of steel; events on television, though distorted in sound and picture, draw attention from and dull reactions to real life; artificial lights daze the senses; formerly important artefacts like eating utensils and religious objects are now stamped out of plastic; people eat from cardboard in the "Pizza Palace[s]." The "Kerb Kings, the Dairy Queens" (NCW, p. 29) have become the sovereigns of our democratic State.

"Robert, Standing" opens with a long, painful description of the severely crippled Robert Hardwick (the name has sexual implications) as he takes a morning bath and prepares for work at his desk amid the "unchanging landscape" (NCW, p. 34) of his room. As Kent Thompson has noted, "The very fact that he is crippled is invoked in the prose, which is at once careful, methodical, and full of close attention to detail."[64] Metcalf uses the limited omniscient point of view to provide a totally objective observation of Robert's difficult manoeuvres; he then moves the centre of focus closer to reveal Robert's heightened sense of his mortality in a jerking vein or muscle and his pounding heart.

With his brother's help, Robert has a degree of self-sufficiency, but the life of a conventional male is impossible. His homemaker's role, his carriage, and the baby powder he dusts on his buttocks and groin indicate some aspects of his life which result from his physical condition. His suffering is Job-like, but there is no hint of complaint; however, he clutches at every opportunity for human contact, and when Mormon missionaries arrive he welcomes them despite his religious scepticism. His lightly ironic humour is wasted on the two women, but his interest is quickened when he notices that one has "absolutely enormous breasts" (NCW, p.38). He politely listens to their presentation despite their insensitivity to the irony intrinsic in their routine arguments and quotations when applied to Robert.

Miss Stevens, one of the missionaries, quotes The Book of Mormon: " 'He who wishes to become a saint must become a child . . . . Submissive, meek, humble, patient, full of love, willing to submit to all things which the Lord seeth fit to inflict upon him . . .' " (NCW, p.38). When the women are finished, Robert agrees to have them back. Out of loneliness, he has allowed himself to be patronized and demeaned by the missionaries, but a moment after they have left, his anger boils to the surface. "Suddenly he pulled the door open again and rammed his chair forward, bucking the wheels over the fibre mat" (NCW, p.40). The illusion of his acquiescence in his state is shattered; Metcalf's use of "rammed," "bucking," and "bellowed" supports Robert's assertion of his maleness and manhood in his defiant shout, "If I was standing up . . . I'd be six foot three" (NCW, p.40). Robert rejects the religious message of meek submission and the smug patronizing of the messengers. The reader is forced by the experience of the story into a recognition that Robert's humanity is undiminished despite his withered limbs.

The Lady Who Sold Furniture was Metcalf's first book; it contained five short stories, including the revised version of "Early Morning Rabbits," and the novella of the title. Structurally the novella is divided into four sections (two long sections bracketing two short), each with a distinct function. The long first section introduces Jeanne, a forty-two-year-old hired housekeeper, and her lover, Peter, who is half her age and just preparing for his first teaching assignment. When the police show up looking for Jeanne at the boardinghouse where she works, she resumes the former pattern of her life. She calls in the Dickensian Mr. Arkle, a dealer in stolen furniture, sells all the movables in the house while the owner is away, and retreats for a holiday to her father's empty cottage near the sea with Peter and her young daughter Anna.

The record of Peter's thoughts and observations as he prepares to embark on his teaching career serves as a counterpoint to Jeanne's vision of ordinary life. His exact, and by implication, affectionate memory of the streets of his university days, with their distinctive humanity, ends with his realization that soon the old brick buildings will be reduced "to an uneven field of rubble" (*LWSF*, p. 17). The future presents itself to him on his first trip to his assigned school, part of a suburban estate whose concrete council houses line streets with picturesque arboreal names, although "there was not a tree in sight" (*LWSF*, p. 17). Human existence and the passage of time under such conditions is conveyed in a short series of bleak consecutive images. In contrast, Metcalf's consistent attachment to the unaggressive beauty of the English countryside and the judgements he implies concerning characters according to their relationship with that nature are expressed in the second section of the novella, with its idyllic pastoral setting. One of the central functions of Jeanne's five-year-old daughter, Anna, is to serve as an inquisitive audience for Peter's demonstration of his knowledge and love of nature. The lists of the popular names of such things as butterflies and sea shells are typical of Metcalf and his belief that "you can only know things when you know their names" (Cameron, p. 422). When Jeanne joins Peter and Anna on one of their jaunts, it is evident that she is relatively uncomfortable, ignorant of nature, and uninterested in their rustic activities; nevertheless, she is gradually drawn into the building of a small dam and soon displaces her daughter in a desperate attempt to divert the waters of a shallow stream. The actions of the adults take on symbolic significance; Peter's forgotten watch is stopped by the water, but time moves on. As they leave, with darkness engulfing the fields, it can be seen that their efforts to stem even this tiny force of nature cannot succeed for long.

The third section of the novella concerns Peter's first day at Gartree Comprehensive School. Despite Jeanne's taunting, Peter had earnestly held to his belief that teaching is "an important job" (*LWSF*, p. 54), but experience quickly proves disillusioning. As he is entering the school set amidst its bleak landscape, he is met by a parody of the nature he has just left: "On the wall facing him was a reproduction of some dim pastoral scene and flanking him two broad-leaved plants in wooden tubs" (*LWSF*, p. 57). Metcalf's picture of school life proceeds to unfold employing many of what have become his stock characters and situations: the authoritarian principal is eccentric to the point of lunacy; the teachers are boring and stupid, and their staff-room talk silly and trivial; the head of the English department is considered "a brilliant chap" for having built a twenty-foot-long papier-mâché model of the Globe Theatre.

The last section finds Peter, after a few weeks on the job, thoroughly bored and dispirited. With Jeanne's assistance, he manages to be released from a few days' teaching through the fabrication of a story concerning his mother catching her arm in a machine (a variation on the folk expression about a lady and a mangle). Metcalf integrated almost all of his early story "Just Two Old Men"[65] into the following transitional scene, in which Peter waits in a pub for a bus he will take to join Jeanne at the house where she has found a new job. The balance of the section is set in the spacious home of the absent Compton-Smythes after a large party Jeanne has given to secretly mark her birthday. At first Peter is as callous as Jeanne in violating the privacy of the owners, whom she has characterized as oppressive snobs, but as he gradually sobers up and sees the careless damage done to the expensive furnishings by Jeanne's guests, his basic respect for property asserts itself, and he tries to clean up the mess.

The novella's last section essentially mirrors the first in incident and character, but Metcalf manages to repeat his earlier comic set piece without diminishing its interest by introducing the overalled and bowler-hatted Henry, a less funny but more reflective extension of Mr. Arkle. Peter is forced into a more open confrontation with the moral questions posed but evaded in the first section. Peter's sensitivity is increased because many of the furnishings in the new house are expensive and tasteful objects of culture and beauty; Henry's memories of his "houseproud" aunt reinforce the human associations of the objects being stolen.

Metcalf's position with respect to modern urban life and its institutions is clear, but while there is sympathy for Jeanne in her anarchistic desire for liberty, she is shown to be inescapably tainted by the world she rejects. Metcalf seems to load the dice against the objectionable ex-RAF bore Jim Rawley, who may be the mean-spirited exploiter Jeanne paints him as, but Metcalf subtly clouds the issue by adding that she had worked for Jim for two and a half years and had intended to stay before the police appeared (*LWSF*, p. 27). Her breezy statement that Jim has insurance (*LWSF*, p. 34) may temporarily assuage Peter, who has already been accused of being stodgy, but it cannot divert the reader.

Jeanne would like to see herself as a "lily of the field," but her carefree pose is belied by her preoccupation with her age and her body's ability to inspire sexual desire. Her determination not to be possessed prevents more than a superficial giving of herself, and that to a lover so young as to preclude the possibility of a permanent relationship. Because she rejects emotional possession, she will not allow emotional or material possession by those around her. A victim, she victimizes, and her actions smack unpleasantly of vindictiveness. The Compton-Smythes may be acquisitive examples of class privilege, and Peter may be too young and idealistic, but Jeanne's actions are morally indefensible as well as futile. However, Metcalf's central concern is with Peter, who is left, clutching his new document case, to work out his own destiny.

"The Tide Line" is an apprenticeship story which presents a child at one of the moments of choice which will gradually determine the direction of his life. At the tideline with its representative mixture of elements — "shrivelled seaweed and driftwood, the flotsam of paper, tar, refuse and sea shells" (*LWSF*, p. 115) — Charles is faced with the choice between the sterile security of his parents' world and the engagingly beautiful but uncertain world of nature. He is unable to overcome his fear and meet the challenging cry of a seabird and so flees back to his parents, clutching the fountain pen which is symbolic of their values.

"Keys and Watercress" (*LWSF*, pp. 118–29) is also one of the eight stories Metcalf specifically listed as being part of an apprenticeship series ("Author's Commentary," p. 199). The fresh physical wound on his knee which David explores in the first paragraph leads directly to the hole in the old man's leg which is described in clearly sexual terms at the story's conclusion (the word "pit" is used in both instances). The bright red of David's blood is repeated in various suggestive associations throughout the story. The references combine with the phallic eels to strengthen the sexual atmosphere surrounding the encounter with the repellent and slightly unhinged old man, who expresses his sexuality through the possessions which are extensions of himself and which he wishes David to handle. When David is confused and frightened by the old man's orgasmic ritual with the keys, he is treated like an unappreciative lover. At the end of the story, David must feel, even if he does not fully understand, the nature of the experience the old man tried to force upon him.

The great strength of both "The Tide Line" and "Keys and Watercress" is in Metcalf's skilled narration, which seems to originate with very young children but which communicates scenes and emotional complexes far beyond the abilities of children to actually state.

Despite a few uncharacteristic technical problems, the delicately lyrical "Dandelions" (*LWSF*, pp. 143–50) is Metcalf's first successful exploration of middle age through a third-person centre of consciousness. George Kenway, bookseller, is uneasily settling into a life physically sustained by his trade in popular paperbacks and books on gardening and the care of budgies; his dream of antiquarian books and scholarly clients is only alive in an occasional fantasy. Metcalf's record of Kenway's thoughts as his mind gently wanders through the details of his day and the associations they call forth has a feeling of exactness which is sustained up to the point of most obvious significance; however, the transition to Kenway's recollection of an instant from his childhood is surprisingly artificial, and the effect of having him see himself as the figure in the "picture" is unconvincing. Metcalf quickly recovers the quality of the experience through the sure capturing of strong sensory impressions — the cool floor through stocking feet, the incandescent dandelions — but in the movement back into the present, he violates his carefully tended point of view. The narrative voice moves too far from Kenway in a single clause: "For a few moments, he stared at the glasses *as though he did not know what they were for*" (emphasis added, *LWSF*, p. 147). The missteps are unfortunate for "Dandelions" contains some of Metcalf's finest writing. The closing paragraphs especially are handled with an almost oriental lightness of touch as the rhythms of the story's measured conclusion reflect the gradual fading of Kenway's visionary gleam.

The decision to write *Going Down Slow*, Metcalf has said,

was largely the result of external pressure on him to further his career by writing a novel. The book's widely praised episodic structure was, in large part, a result of Metcalf's impatience with "having to put connecting bits in and continuing the story. It was the set pieces of the book . . . that [he] really enjoyed because they were the closest to the short story form" (Cameron, p. 403). Metcalf's relative lack of control of the larger form is seen in the sections of the novel which try to fill in character or move the plot forward. These often fail to function organically enough to appear as anything but authorial afterthoughts. However, *Going Down Slow* marks an important juncture in Metcalf's writing career for it integrates a number of strands from his earlier work within a witty and humorous expression of Metcalf's principle that ". . . all writing is political, all great writing subversive."[66]

In many ways, David Appleby is the sum of the many sensitive and intelligent boys and young men glimpsed at isolated moments in the short stories, with Peter Hendricks of "The Lady Who Sold Furniture" being his most immediate ancestor in both time and sensibility. The genesis of the novel's other basic elements is most obvious in the two *Prism* stories about teachers ("The Happiest Days" and "A Process of Time") and the school section of "The Lady Who Sold Furniture." In virtually all its important elements, "A Process of Time" is actually a highly condensed version of the novel, and the name of its central character, Mr. Adams, is used like Appleby's to denote his postlapsarian condition; however, the novel is cast in a new and important context. A few of Metcalf's stories had been specifically or implicitly set in Canada, but *Going Down Slow* is Metcalf's first attempt to deal with his experience as a British expatriate.

Kenneth Gibson identified Kingsley Amis as "the revenant" of *Going Down Slow* and was tempted to see Metcalf, "a ferocious anthologist, as putting together . . . a small anthology of styles to see what dominates and what fades out."[67] But in *Going Down Slow*, Metcalf's overt homages to many of his favourite writers are, aside from that to Amis, mere tippings of the hat, and David Appleby is not simply Lucky Jim in Canada. Although there are many parallels, *Going Down Slow* and *Lucky Jim* are quite different in spirit and intent. Metcalf's first novel appeared a generation after *Lucky Jim*. Part of the loss signified by David

Appleby's name is the disillusionment inherited by educated Englishmen of his generation and class. Amis attributed the title of *Lucky Jim* to an "old song" ("Oh, lucky Jim, / How I envy him."); the title *Going Down Slow* is from a blues of the same name:

> I have had my fun; if I don't get well no more,
> My health is failing me, and I'm going down slow.
>
> Please write my mother; tell her the shape I'm in.
> Tell her to pray for me; forgiveness of my sin.[68]

Even allowing for Amis' irony, the times had clearly changed, and the sin for which David pays is both society's and his own. Jim Dixon spoke for the honesty and decency of the average man; if defeated by the establishment, he could easily retreat to a life with fewer risks of humiliation. David has no such base. When it appears he might be sacked from his teaching position in a Montreal high school, a return to England is not an option he even considers. A provincial in England, David is considered a metropolitan in provincial Canada, where the values of the average man can be added to the sum of all he scorns. In a society of homogenized dullness without class divisions to help channel his anger, David is floating free, and his antagonism becomes generalized misanthropy.

Although *Going Down Slow* is told in the third person, the novel's narrative voice is so close to David's own that they are almost indistinguishable one from the other. The effect is principally achieved by using the cadences and junctures of David's speaking voice throughout the novel for description as well as dialogue. For example, David's habit of searching for the exact word creates the impression of an unmediated, self-conscious narrator addressing the reader:

> David decided that he was probably ill. His head ached. His throat. His throat was definitely dry and sore. Doubtless infected. He pictured the inside of his throat as being like the neck of a guitar strung with red tendons. And now the tendons were studded with white and yellow lumps of infection. Lumps? *Nodules.* Studded with nodules of infection. (p. 12)

Because the voice is felt to be David's, there is a temptation to assess him, rather than the objects of his mockery, and to see Metcalf as having weakened the impact of his argument by trusting it to a frequently obnoxious and unsympathetic character. But although Metcalf clearly supports David's denial of authority and his battle against it, he demonstrates, in David's eventual defeat, the results of foolishness, weakness, or ambivalence in conducting the campaign. As with Jeanne in "The Lady Who Sold Furniture," Metcalf asks that we sympathize with the essential position, not David's methods or personality.

Central to the novel is the problem of David's values. His expressions of nostalgia for England are usually and understandably prompted by Montreal's weather, but he is not interested in returning even for a holiday. He would rather travel to the American South in search of a dream from his youth, "the fabulous, mythic world of the blues, the shining trumpets" (p. 134). His fond memories of his uncle's farm have more to do with Metcalf's usual pastoral associations than with England. At base David is a conservative, but his ambivalence is such that he derides to himself ("*Swooning Swinburne / Tedious Tennyson*" [p. 81]) the English literary tradition he praises to Susan. He doubts the value of his own education while deploring that which Merrymount dispenses. His rebellion is not in favour of the past but of an ideal of elemental individual freedom as symbolized by the crows he calls "rooks":

> He liked their wariness, their wildness. If they nested near houses, unlike swallows or pigeons, they remained independent. They graced inhabited areas with their presence, their gleaming blackness, but remained aloof, suspicious.
> Tough, lordly birds. (pp. 155–56)

The conflict between this ideal and the impulse for reconciliation with social reality is an important one in most of Metcalf's writing.

Metcalf's concept of individual responsibility and his libertarian insistence on a personal and independent attitude to the universe, including human institutions, probably owe as much to his Nonconformist religious upbringing as to his reading of the anarchist philosophers.[69] Through David, he demonstrates what happens when a character with views similar to his own is not up to the challenge. The betrayal of relationships and principles is the novel's central theme.

What does Metcalf hold up as the standard of conduct against which his characters are to be judged? The answer accounts for the novel's weakness in terms of both character and theme. The novel's epigraph, which Metcalf attributes to the blues singer Howling Wolf, states, "The men don't know what the little girls understand" (p. 9). The little girl in question is the unbelievably precocious Susan, who at one point is provided with "a mist of hair like a halo" (p. 61) to identify her as an object of veneration for the purity of her essential and instinctive knowledge. Part of the problem is that when she tries to express what she knows she speaks in vague adolescent platitudes. Metcalf intends David's opposition to her views to reflect his ruinous ambivalence; however, next to Susan, David emerges as a paragon of common sense. But *common* sense and realism are not what is being advocated, for Susan would "*rather* be a romantic" (p. 77).

It is difficult to admire Susan for her hedonism and discriminating sense of culture because Metcalf never dramatizes her in a manner which would sufficiently serve his purpose. We are told that she is beautiful and extremely intelligent. We must accept the former quality, but Susan's ambition to become a writer and her taste for Ingmar Bergman films and African masks smack of authorial projection. When she is physically present in the novel, the evidence argues against accepting David's (and Metcalf's) high estimation of her mental and spiritual capacities. As a repository of the ideals for which the individual should defy the world, Susan is unconvincing.

The collection of stories *The Teeth of My Father* returned Metcalf to his favoured genre but presented him with a problem common to many writers whose primary impulse is autobiographical and whose early work was mainly devoted to an exploration of the process of growing up: the lives of his various fictional personae had caught up to his own experience. In this collection, Metcalf dealt with the problem in a combination of ways. He introduced a new and major thematic concern for art and artists — especially writers; he attempted to deal artistically with his present reality — in one instance, through an overt summation of the past; he imaginatively examined his own future by portraying a writer in old age; he employed narrative points of view not found in his earlier work and expanded his use of the story form in ways which were for him experimental; he recycled earlier work in a way which would delight Mordecai Richler; and he continued to examine experiences of childhood and adolescence, but more often within the expressed context of an adult sensibility. In addition, the humour which he continued to use as an important means of expression was frequently darker and more bitterly ironic.

Five of the stories deal with art and artists. A pessimistic and bitterly funny picture of the artist's social role and his relationship to his audience is presented in "The Strange Aberration of Mr. Ken Smythe." The story is told in the third person through an anonymous traveller, whose experiencing consciousness gradually gives way to a seemingly objective observation of the action. The story's allegorical quality is emphasized by its setting in Edinburgh's Pleasure Gardens, at the entrance of which stands a "massive War Memorial."[70] The Gardens are situated below the statue of Robert Burns, poet of brotherhood and the common man, and the whole scene is brooded over by the national symbol, Edinburgh Castle. As night falls, the traveller symbolically descends into the Gardens to pass a few hours watching a variety show set in "the cave" of a bandshell.

The principal artist figures are a young trumpet player, Heine, and the director of the "Essen International Amity Boys Brass Band," Herr Kunst (whose name literally means "art"). The essence of Kunst's total concern for his music and the effect of his efforts is conveyed in the precision of the following sentences:

> Suddenly onto the stage strode a man in a black suit, halted, faced the silent band. The arm of Herr Kunst rose; the arm of Herr Kunst descended.
> The burst of sound was crisp and perfect, the sections rising and sitting as one man, the soloists flawless. Herr Kunst stood rigid except for the metronome pump of his elbows. (*TMF*, p. 13)

The initial references to "international goodwill" (*TMF*, p. 12) and subsequent allusions to friendship and brotherhood in the announced selection titles become more ironically significant as the story progresses, for Herr Kunst's controlled and austere manner in conducting his disciplined musicians draws attention to characteristics which his onstage "host," Ken Smythe, terms "typically German." The threefold purpose of the German titles announced at intervals throughout the story is to remind Smythe and his audience of the band's nationality, to provoke a response in both, and, frequently, to comment on the action.

RAF veteran Smythe is seen drinking at the rear of the stage, and, as he becomes more inebriated, his increasingly outrageous and racist behaviour draws more attention and approval than the band's performance. His announced memory of bombing Essen during the war stirs shouted support "from the darkness," and when the band in a friendly but unwise gesture plays "Colonel Bogey," there is an intimation of ignorant armies: "On the grass below the stage, a confusion of dark figures marched" (*TMF*, p. 20). The tune ignites the crowd's ugly nationalism and Heine is injured: "A stone, a bottle, something thrown from the darkness" (*TMF*, p. 21).

The story implies that the condition of the artist is one of isolation surrounded by hostility. He must practise his craft among mere entertainers and be presented by buffoons and charlatans to an audience unwilling and unable to appreciate the beauty he offers. Art cannot overcome the barriers of nationalism and race hatred, nor can the artist win over an insensitive audience. For an ignorant audience, when it pays any attention at all, the beauty of the work and the skill of the artist are too often obscured by an irrelevant and destructively morbid concern for the person of the artist himself. Ken Smythe's strange aberration is, of course, nothing of the sort. His name is only a variation on the ordinary, and his moments of unguarded speech are meant to reveal his working-class origins. Pretensions and inhibitions relaxed, the real Smythe emerges as a kind of everyman who is both a member of and a voice for the mob.

"Gentle as Flowers Make the Stones" records a day in the life of poet Jim Haine, whose seedy picaroon existence is the result of his dedication to an art which yields meagre financial returns. The success with which he has freed himself of physical impediments is reflected in the economy of the short paragraph used to describe them:

His possessions, by design, fitted into two large cardboard cartons. Kettle and mug. Sleeping-bag and inflatable

mattress. Clothes. One picture. Writing materials. An
alarm-clock. The few books he had not sold. (*TMF*, p. 25)

Similarly, the seeking of an adequate design for a potentially
sentimental expression of love for a dead child is his attempt to
transmute his personal pain into a manageable objective form —
a form as manageable as are the carved figures of the African
Dogon tribe referred to in a later story, "The Years in Exile."

The effort to adapt Martial's epigram on the death of a pet
slave girl is Haine's attempt to deal with the physical and
emotional loss of his living daughter, thoughts of whom make
her an unburied presence. The complex value he places on the
poem is paralleled in his concern for preserving the single picture
among his possessions. Significantly, it is not a picture of his
daughter, but her portrait of him. Because of the purity of its
expression, the immortality it bestows on its creator as well as its
object is independent of the people or circumstances surrounding
its creation:

> A potato shape in black crayon. A single red eye near the
> top. Seven orange sprouts. He'd typed underneath:
> "Daddy" by Anna Haine (age 2½)
> The newsprint was yellowing, the expensive non-glare
> glass dusty; the top edge of the frame was furred. He wiped
> it clean with his forefinger.
> *Orange arms and legs of course, silly Jim.*
> He tried to recall the name of the girl who'd got it framed
> for him. A painter sort of girl. Black hair, he remembered.
> Frances?
> Sonia?
> But it was gone. (*TMF*, p. 27)

Both the connections and the distancing strategy can be seen in
Haine's expressing his sense of his daughter Anna's loss through a
transposition of Martial's lament for *his* lost child. On one level,
"Gentle as Flowers Make the Stones" deals with the emotional
complex within which it is possible to assert *both* that the artist
uses art to express his life and that his life is subservient to his art.
On a different level, the story is a detailed and graphic description
of one artist's experience of the mysterious forces which work
within him and the psychological and technical manipulation he

employs to translate these impulses into a concrete reality. The story dramatizes a process which Metcalf has described elsewhere as his own ("Author's Commentary," pp. 198–203).

"The Teeth of My Father," the third story written in the art-and-artist series, brings together a number of elements from Metcalf's earlier work and so serves as a partial summary. More importantly, the earlier work is incorporated into a new, or at least more deliberately explicit, thematic context and a more technically complicated formal design. The work is "in a way an attempt to write a short story about the difficulties of writing a short story."[71] Metcalf has also said that the story is "really meant to play with these ideas of truth, nontruth, larger truths than autobiographical truths, lies, who's speaking, who 'I' is, whether you can believe what that person says or can't believe."[72]

"The Teeth of My Father" opens conventionally enough, but Metcalf soon appears to dissolve the distinction between the story's first-person narrator and the implied author. Ostensibly prompted by a new and deeper understanding of his dead father's essential nature, the narrator, in a parenthetic confession, declares that he has "decided to tell the truth" (*TMF*, p. 59) and admits to his past uses of artifice (both in addressing the reader and in spinning tales for his "friend"). This apparent promise of future reliability in fact introduces a more elaborately contrived structure which purports to be autobiography. If fiction is a lie told in the service of truth, Metcalf's story is artistic truth masquerading as deception in the guise of literal truth. Within a framework containing anecdotes, linking passages, and entire stories, "fact" is related in the voice of the now self-conscious first-person narrator; "fiction" is filtered through variously named third-person centres of consciousness.

Metcalf implicitly warns the reader that the whole performance is a conjuring trick by having a voice like that of a variety-show master of ceremonies address the audience over the head of the narrator and give directions as to how one of the segments is to be interpreted:

> *It is instructive, ladies and gentlemen, to examine the psychological implications of this sample of juvenilia if we may assume it to be autobiographical either in fact or impulse.*

Yes, you can assume that. [This is the voice of the narrator.]

What activity is the child essentially engaged in? In nothing more or less than the act of defining his identity. Through which functions does the child perform this act? Through naming, drawing, and most importantly, writing. And with which parent does this suggest identification?

Exactly so. Exactly so. The father!

Who, who I may remind you, is, in the words of the text, "far away." For the perceptive reader, the point requires no further elucidation. (TMF, p. 63)

That the segment in question closed with a plagiarism from James Joyce underlines that the artist often uses highly artificial techniques to express "larger truths"; in addition, it reminds the reader that what is being presented is a miniature portrait of the artist.

What emerges, then, from the sum of the story's segments is not just an affecting picture of an eccentric father but, as the wording of the title implies, the mark he has left on his writer-son. The son's craft is illustrated by the story's final section, in which the father's lessons in the manipulation of language are reflected by the son's highly structured rhetoric. The section, an extended apostrophe, is constructed around four carefully placed declarative sentences, which, despite their surface flatness, pace the story to its emotional climax. Informed by his new and more profound recognition, the narrator expresses both his love for his father and his personal vision of loneliness and human isolation. The section concludes:

Now, ten years later in a life half done, a life distinctly lacking in probity, I use your pen, now twice-repaired, to write my stories, your pencil for corrections.

And I am crying now.

Drunken tears but tears for you. For you. For both of us. Standing on the sidewalk in the cold fall evening of another country, my tears are scalding. (*TMF*, p. 79)

The rhetorical flourish of the repeated phrases beginning with "for" contributes to the heightened feeling of the chantlike lament which unites the son with his priest-father, while the ironic possibilities of the word "probity" serve as a partial counter to the sentimentality inherent in the scene. The return to the discredited narrative voice and to the physical and temporal setting of the opening section is a totally artificial device which is made to seem perfectly natural.

"The Practice of the Craft" (*TMF*, pp. 46–57) is a relative failure because it succumbs to the problem of distance so impressively solved in "Gentle as Flowers Make the Stones" and in the last story in the art-and-artist series, "The Years in Exile" (*TMF*, pp. 80–101), which employs as a first-person narrator a writer who shares many of Metcalf's expressed attitudes and artistic methods and concerns; however, distancing from the implied author is achieved by portraying the narrator as an old man. Like Margaret Laurence's Hagar Shipley, he is "rampant with memory," and the depiction of his rambling thoughts allows Metcalf full use of his elliptical, imagistic, and juxtapositional techniques.

Much of the story's rich and subtle irony results from the interplay between the narrator's thoughts and the total compositional context within which Metcalf places them. The narrator reflects that he will not write again: "I am too old and tire too easily; I no longer have the strength to face the struggle with language, the loneliness, the certainty of failure" (*TMF*, p. 81). But while the narrator seems to be left with only the resources to contemplate his principles concerning the artistic importance of "particular life" (*TMF*, p. 98), Metcalf, in his actual realization of the work, demonstrates the efficacy of those principles. The old man disliked Wordsworth "because he could not do justice to the truth; no philosophical cast of mind can do justice to particularity" (*TMF*, pp. 88–89). Metcalf's deliberate selection and accumulation of details and incidents under the guise of simply recording the old man's random and tenuously connected thoughts demonstrates an artistic alternative to Wordsworth's "abstraction" (*TMF*, p. 89).

The narrator loves objects and their uniquely distinguishing names (". . . such a basket is called a 'trug.' I hug the word to myself" [*TMF*, p. 88]), and the poetry of his lists is typical of those found throughout Metcalf's work:

Scattered above and below the seaweed were the shells,

limpet, mussel, periwinkle, whelk and cockle, painted top
and piddock. Razor shells. The white shields of cuttlefish,
whelks' egg cases like coarse sponge, mermaids' purses.
(*TMF*, p. 84)

Inherent in this stylistic concern for surface detail is a philo-
sophic position which abjures a search for the transcendent in
favour of a sensitive awareness of the material because there is
nothing else in life but life.[73] Because he is dependent on others,
an aspect of the old man's "exile" is his "crotchety" dislike for
the "aluminum and plastic" (*TMF*, p. 80) which typify much of
his physical environment and the modern values it reflects. His
retreat into memory is both an escape from his present and an
expression of what to him is "more real" (*TMF*, p. 82). Barry
Cameron, in his important study of the art-and-artist series, "An
Approximation of Poetry," has stated:

> The story focuses on the inherent psychic split in the
> novelist's mind simply because he is a novelist. Because he
> has "fictionalized" the past, because he has framed "its
> insistence" through the internal fictionalizing process of
> memory, the novelist's visions of his childhood at the age
> of nine or ten are more real to him than his present moment
> in Canada as a famous novelist. The fictionalizing opera-
> tion of memory, as the novelist himself knows, is " 'the
> most basic form of creativity' " (p. 99). Memory, like
> fiction, edits, orders, and preserves experience. Memory
> shapes experience, giving it meaning, and ultimately yields
> through its mythologizing effects a sense of identity. Home
> is a psychic state of oneness, of identity, in which one's
> world is not an external environment but part of one.
> Consequently, the novelist's memories of his childhood past
> in England, because he has mythologized the past, are his
> internal home. (pp. 31–32)

"Because the novelist's real home lies in his visions of the past,"
writes Cameron, "his present moment becomes, as the title of the
story implies, a metaphorical condition of exile and expatria-
tion" (p. 32).
The material of art, then, is not life photographically repro-

duced but life closely observed and recast by the imagination and
the memory. Like Joyce Cary's Wilcher, Metcalf's narrator had
"wished immortal life" for that which had touched him deepest,
and he had "thought [himself] a pilgrim, the books [his]
milestones," but the image which has become "always central in
[the old man's] dream and reverie," taking him back to "the
years when [he] was nine and ten," is that of "the spoiled
mansion, Fortnell House" (*TMF*, pp. 81–83).

Fortnell House is associated not only with the period when the
narrator was physically and emotionally most at one with the
world of nature, but also with the time when he felt most force-
fully his connection with the full range of natural and human
history. During the time of the last Fortnell, Sir Charles, the
mansion had become "the repository of collections of minerals,
fossils, books, weapons, tribal regalia, paintings and carvings.
On his retirement, Sir Charles had devoted his energies to
Christchurch and the county collecting local records, books,
memorabilia and the evidences of the prehistoric past" (*TMF*,
p. 97). The significance of the house and its contents becomes
more complex through the implied association with the primitive
art of the Dogon and the fictionalizing art of the narrator: all are,
to a degree, ritualized and public declarations of the wish to
preserve. Like Sir Charles, the African Dogon (whose carvings
"offer a fixed abode for spirits liberated by death" [*TMF*, p. 83]),
and Cary's Wilcher, the writer too has felt the impulse to bestow
a kind of immortality; however, honesty to his experience will
not allow him to be consoled by ideas of the permanence of art,
for he "has learned how easily things break" (*TMF*, p. 98).

The transience of particular life is seen in the destruction of its
evidence; many of the treasures of Fortnell House are lost
through chance, simple ignorance, public neglect, and wilful
destruction. The evanescence of art itself is seen in the decay of
the Dogon carvings and in the erosion by "time and the weather"
(*TMF*, p. 96) of the carvings on the gate pillars of decrepit
Fortnell House. The old writer does not want his papers to be
"abandoned . . . in the damp to rot" like those in Fortnell
House; however, he knows that they may be "consigned to some
air-conditioned but equal oblivion" (*TMF*, p. 93). The final
significance of Fortnell House is in the narrator's association of
his impending death and its intrinsic mystery with the mansion's

unexplored upper rooms. "Perhaps one night soon," he will not awaken from his dream of childhood but will at last "reach the rooms above" (*TMF*, p. 100).

"The Years in Exile" closes appropriately with the narrator enjoying the pleasure of his imagination. The narrator may have been too old "to frame" the "insistence" of his mental pictures; but Metcalf, in his own working out of the total design of the story, fashioned an "adequate structure" for a work of art which examines the nature of art itself.

In contemplating one of his powerful imaginative "insistence[s]," the aged writer who narrates "The Years in Exile" naturally turned to a consideration of its possible artistic shape: "A short story could not encompass it; it has the weight and feel about it of a novella" (*TMF*, p. 82). Metcalf must have had similar feelings when he turned to the longer form in his next book, *Girl in Gingham*, the title work of which employs with a greater sophistication many of the techniques observed in Metcalf's first novella, "The Lady Who Sold Furniture." Again, as in most of the short stories, the emphasis is on the exploration of a single central character whose consciousness is expressed through a third-person narrator. Metcalf has maintained a tightness of structure in the longer form by closely linking the various parts through an extensive use of foreshadowing and a relatively elaborate use of such recurring and associated images as nautical and marine references. While the texture of the work is as dense as that of the later short stories, the details are often made even more suggestive and resonant through an increased reliance on allusion and symbol. For example, Peter Thornton's first name associates him with a number of Metcalf's earlier characters as does his sensibility. The name also has Christian associations further strengthened by his surname, which implies something of Christ's suffering (a crucifix and the crown of thorns are explicitly mentioned by a minor character); the many references to fish and fishing are clearly a part of this and other complexes which contribute to the story's rich ambiguity.

Robert Lecker and Barry Cameron are the two critics who have most closely examined Metcalf's work, and one must agree with Lecker's observation that Cameron's thorough and "brilliant analysis" of "Girl in Gingham" leaves few new insights to be added by like-minded critics.[74] Cameron first defines Metcalf's general thematic concerns in terms of a series of "dialectics." He goes on to state:

> All these dialectics are implicit in *Girl in Gingham*, but the emphasis falls on art and life, fictional and factual truth, reality and fantasy, comedy and tragedy, and humour and pathos.
>
> *Girl in Gingham* revolves thematically around the motive for — the necessity of and the pain resulting from — "inventing" people, shaping them to fit the contours of our needs and desires, and "inventing" or allowing ourselves to be "invented." ("Invention in *Girl in Gingham*," p. 121)

Lecker states that Peter Thornton's "self-consciousness, the self-reflexive impulse," is "granted to him by a narrator who turns Peter's story into a story about art" (p. 75). Lecker adds:

> Because the search for an ideal girl in gingham is part of Peter's quest for aesthetic fulfillment, he becomes increasingly pre-occupied with Art as the story develops, a pre-occupation frustrated by what Cameron calls "the absurdity of the modern technological world." (pp. 76–77)

Cameron and Lecker provide extremely valuable insights into Metcalf's work, insights which cannot be adequately summarized here. Peter Thornton's idealism and penchant for "invention" do strengthen his impulse to turn life into art; however, it might be useful and not an oversimplification to also view "Girl in Gingham" as expressing one of the most basic and pervasive of Metcalf's themes, the concern for the loneliness and isolation of the individual, both in a cosmic sense and as exacerbated by "the absurdity of the modern technological world," a world Metcalf views with an increasingly dark and sardonic humour.

The novella's opening words establish the cause of Peter Thornton's personal crisis. He is seen after his Fall, his expulsion from the false security of what used to be considered a conventional family life. Divorced by his wife, he is set adrift, deprived of the roles of husband and father on which he founded his identity. Significantly, his deep sense of grief, his feeling of "amputation," results more from his perceived loss of context than from the loss of the particular persons of his wife and son. After the initial trauma of his divorce and his attempts at suicide (to complete the destruction of self), Peter, "with a large weariness and a settled habit of sadness," attempted to start life over, but at thirty-five found himself among life's walking wounded, "active in the world of those whose world was broken."[75] Much of the novella's humour and pathos arises from Peter's encounters with the "sad sisterhood" of unattached women and the eccentricities symptomatic of their dislocation:

He had learned to avoid women who took pottery courses and had come to recognize as danger signs: indoor plants, Alice in Wonderland posters, health food, stuffed toys, parents, menstrual cramps, and more than one cat. (GG, p. 89)

Peter, a man with a rich and perhaps overactive imagination, is unable to visualize himself as a whole personality outside his former context; his quest is for a return to an idealized vision of that context and for the woman who will recreate it. In seeking her, Peter is attempting to reinvent his own sense of identity.

When more conventional means fail, Peter allows himself to be drawn into the world of "CompuMate." Sensitive, intelligent, and well-educated, Peter is a man whose very qualities alienate him from the absurdity of a world where toothpicks are labelled "Inter-Dental Stimulators" and paper plates "Chi-Net." As an appraiser of antiques and *objets d'art*, he is accustomed to discerning the genuine from the fake and ascribing worth to the objects which reflect the human and aesthetic values of a civilization. A sympathetic friend describes Peter himself as "an antique" (GG, p. 95); the essence of Peter's conservatism is expressed in his anachronistic ideal of "a girl in gingham."

It is indicative of Peter's desperation and vulnerability (and a function of his barely controlled imagination) that he is willing to contemplate the possibilities of *"personal growth through deep and meaningful long-term, male-female interaction"* (GG, p. 94) allegedly offered by a computer, the quintessence of the technological age whose values both amuse and repel him. Metcalf frequently conveys the debasement of standards through the abuse of language, and Peter, after presumably having met *"the*

computer's acceptance standards," goes beyond merely acqui-
escing in a system which uses terms such as "CompuMatch,"
"CompuMember," and "Computer Compatible" (*GG*, pp. 94,
95). Metcalf's daring and skill are such that his controlling hand
is unobtrusive in the manipulation of Peter to the point where he
voluntarily participates in the system.

The successful realization of the complex character of Peter
Thornton is one of Metcalf's major artistic accomplishments.
When Peter is most prone to indulging his smug sense of cultural
or emotional superiority, Metcalf reminds him (and us) of his
essential kinship with those he does not admire. This is seen
when Peter's detached and supercilious observation of two
ladies, "a parody of affluent American middle-aged woman-
hood" (*GG*, p. 103), ends in a deflating recognition of *their* pain
and loneliness. It is also seen when he identifies himself with the
equally self-centred Elspeth McCleod ("Sad he; sad she" [*GG*,
p. 115]).

Metcalf has often commented on his lack of interest in plot;
Barry Cameron goes to some lengths to minimize the importance of "meaning" in Metcalf's work and asserts that in "Girl in
Gingham" "Metcalf does not impose meaning on the story; the
story generates meaning in the reader's mind through his experience of it" ("Invention in *Girl in Gingham*," p. 120). However, it
is precisely the areas of plot and meaning and their interrelation-
ship which prevent "Girl in Gingham" from being an unqualified
triumph. To the point in the story when Peter first telephones
Anna Stevens, the tale of his "dismal adventure" has the flawless
illusion of reality, but from that point on it moves gradually into
the area of fantasy. It is as if Peter had finally crossed the line into
a dimension where his imagination created his and the reader's
reality. With Anna's appearance, Metcalf's plot and Peter-
Pygmalion's imagination merge, and the novella's plot becomes
fantasy itself, dominated by its fairy-tale motif. Having allowed
Anna to become flesh, Metcalf must destroy her to serve his
theme, for, contrary to Cameron's assertion, Metcalf *does*
impose his meaning. Despite its fracturing of narrative convention, the deflation of Peter's dreams and the destruction of his
hope for finding a psychic and emotional home must be seen as
the inevitable conclusion for a fairy tale of "these untender
times" (*GG*, p. 129).

"Private Parts: A Memoir" (*GG*, pp. 5–84) purports to be an autobiography in which the author, T. D. Moore, a university professor and fiction writer, lays bare his central anxieties and their cause. Whereas Peter Thornton, who shares Moore's approximate age and his artistic sensibility, used his imagination to escape his present and create his future, Moore attempts to control the functioning of his memory and imagination so that he can accurately capture the past which created his present. Moore's story begins in the literal and symbolic Eden of his uncle's farm, the site of his lost innocence, and moves slowly forward in time through "sequence[s] of anecdote and reflection" (*GG*, p. 17). Also contained within this structure, but moving to its own rhythm, is a sequence of swelling hopes and deflating disappointments. The narrator's war with his Puritan mother, "that battle of wills, a titanic struggle fought against the backdrop of Hell" (*GG*, p. 83), provides most of the story's substance; however, Metcalf makes clear in "Notes on Writing a Story,"[76] an essay on the novella's opening section, that he is more vitally interested in the story as process. It is probably for this reason that his narrator is made to remind the reader from time to time that what is being read is the product of conscious manipulation and that it is impossible for the writer in pursuit of truth to write anything but fiction. Moore interrupts his story for a parenthetical, and more direct, address to the reader: "This will not do. The paragraphs flow too evenly, the sequence of statements rounds off the subject too neatly . . . . To re-read these last paragraphs nauseates me. . . . I have pictured my mother as a joyless puritan. But this is not the whole truth. The fault lies in my writing, feelings hidden behind humour, pain distanced by genteel irony. The truth is ugly and otherwise" (*GG*, p. 17). It should be recalled that the principal narrator of "The Teeth of My Father" began his similarly parenthetical intervention with the words "I have decided to tell the truth" (*TMF*, p. 59), which seemed to introduce a more direct telling of the authentic story. In using the same technique in "Private Parts," Metcalf also added a refinement: instead of using incorporated stories and story fragments which used differing narrative voices and points of view and which the reader was to understand as being at once fictional and autobiographical, Metcalf returned to the uninterrupted narrative voice of T. D. Moore. Having shattered the illusion of Moore as a conventionally reliable first-person narrator, Metcalf paradoxically strengthened it by seeming to move Moore closer to the reader. Moore's complaints about his inability to overcome technique and get to the heart of the truth are designed to create the impression of a more direct and unmediated voice, a voice more capable of intimate confession.

As in "Girl in Gingham," one of the central concerns of "Private Parts" is the question of identity, how it is formed and what sustains it. Structurally, the novella is divided into a long Part I with twelve subsections and a shorter Part II with three subsections. The importance of religion to the story is obvious, and those interested in Christian numerology will recognize the possibilities of Metcalf's divisions. (For example, the significance of the Trinity for the narrator is established early in the story [GG, p. 16]. In the final subsection, the narrator, who names himself for the first time, speaks of his mother and his unknowable father as still being "giant figures on a glaring stage, their lives the myth of my life" [GG, p. 75]. Moore finally unites pictures of his father and mother with those of himself as son, husband, father, and uncertain, isolated individual waiting for his own death.) The novella's structure, then, is organized around the narrator's "self-shaping" (GG, p. 22), his "building for [him]self a new identity" (GG, p. 36) in opposition to his mother and her religious fanaticism in Part I, and, in Part II, the narrator's picture of himself as the adult inheritor of that identity.

The importance of art to the defining and creating of the narrator's identity and the power of his Christian upbringing to affect the way he sees his own experience are revealed in the following:

> At about the age of seven I had my first encounter with Art — an event central to this memoir and as dramatic as Paul's conversion on the Damascus Road.
> Art played no part in the life of my parents or their society. (GG, p. 18)

In the writing of his memoir, Moore is a monologuist whose art depends to a great extent on doing "different voices" convincingly. The sentence which introduces Mr. Montague is both a

comic and meaningful parody of his mother's voice and a statement of fact: "I can remember the monologuist who brought
the certainty of art into my life" (GG, p. 20). It is the narrator's
ultimate substitution of art for religion as a way of dealing with
the world and his perception of it that redeems him. That it
also troubles him is revealed by the increasingly frequent inter-
ventions in which he expresses his dissatisfaction with the
way art, through the functioning of memory, imagination, and
technique, obscures truth. The problem, as it must, remains
unresolved.

The sexually motivated journey towards art recounted in the
novella's first part is often hilariously funny; but the disillusionment and growing awareness of decay and death modulate and
darken the humour of the conclusion. Taken as a whole, "Private
Parts" is a rich and comic *tour de force* which contains the
"echoes, suggestions, allusions, [and] reverberations"[77] Metcalf
sought to achieve. It is not surprising that Robert Lecker states
that "the private parts of the title are sexual, spiritual, emotional,
temporal, spatial, and structural all at once" (p. 90). Clearly
the work's surface naughtiness and scatological method are
employed by the author in the service of a chaste and austere
artistry.

With the writing of his second novel, *General Ludd*, Metcalf
reversed the decision he had made after the publication of *Going
Down Slow* not to return to the form; he also seemed to ignore
his own cautionary dictum: "It is understandable but futile to
take the 20th Century as a personal affront." [78] Metcalf's title is
explained by historian J. L. Granatstein: "The Luddites were a
nineteenth century British group that smashed machinery in
protest both against working conditions and the way the world
was progressing." In Metcalf's novel, he saw "the tale of a new
Luddite." [79] The objects of Metcalf's satire are too numerous to
encompass in a brief summary, but essentially he is concerned
with what he sees as Canada's spiritual malaise and its attendant
lack of taste and cultural values. The "communications media,"
especially television, and the standards they express are both the
cause and the result of our decline. In North America, the old
European traditions of grace and elegance have collided with the
twentieth century, and the most conspicuous casualty has been
language. Metcalf's target in *General Ludd* is so broad and his

attack so ferocious that his satire often eschews the rifle for the large-bore shotgun.

The problem of Jim Wells is a complicated one and, because it is central to the novel, bears close examination. Aside from the obvious reason that he wishes to draw on his own experience, Metcalf uses artists as central figures in his work because they examine life from a perspective which is individual if not eccentric. In this, Jim Wells resembles Metcalf's other artist-heroes (and quasi artist-heroes like Peter Thornton), the closest relative being Jim Haine of "Gentle as Flowers Make the Stones." That Wells is really a stand-in for Haine is implied in the novel itself,[80] but while Haine is seen as an unsavoury character dealing with an ugly world, he is also seen doing what he does best, creating poetry — and in the third person. Wells, who is in a dry spell, is seldom seen doing anything but what he does worst, simply getting through the day — and through the less distancing first-person point of view. The result is a narrator who is used to convey the author's opinions but who, as a human being, has few apparent attractions (his unattractiveness results in major prob-lems for the credibility of Kathy's character). The difficulties of establishing sympathy for the views of an unsympathetic narrator are not insurmountable, especially for a writer of Metcalf's talents, but because Metcalf allowed the insistence of his vision of modern society to take precedence over the satisfac-tory creation of his central character, Wells remains unrealized. Because he is a poet, Wells's despair over illiteracy and the lack of an audience is understandable, but the bitterness of his undiffer-entiated attack on Canadian society and the weakness of the fictional creation from which it flows create an impression of the implied author himself as a snob, one who sees himself as not being a part of the society he disdains. The result is a diverting of the reader's attention from the characters and issues within the fictional construct to the personality of the author, "a blurring between Jim Wells as character and [Metcalf] as writer."[81] The illusion of reality is weakened, and the aesthetic value of the work suffers.

Metcalf's awareness of the problem is made painfully obvious within the novel itself through his often mechanical attempts to breathe life into Wells. Metcalf also uses commentary which seems to come more from the author than the characters. When

Wells rambles boringly and compulsively on, Metcalf, instead of using his skill at compressed or elliptical expression, has Kathy fall asleep or say, "I can't stand much more." The irony is not lost, but one wishes for more editing and less editorializing. Kathy herself plays Sancho Panza to Wells's Quixote. She is Peter Thornton's girl in gingham. Wells tells us, ". . . everything about her enchanted me. She seemed to me to have stepped into the real world of my life from the pages of a fairy tale" (p.91). Unlike Anna Stevens, however, Kathy tragically survives the transition only to remain a figure of fantasy and plot manipulation.

Ironically, both Wells and Kathy become most alive in a brilliantly written section where they are least themselves. In an obvious attempt to give his two central characters, but especially Jim Wells, more depth, Metcalf moved them into the idyllic setting of Wells's decaying farmhouse and an impressively evoked winter landscape. The simple neighbouring farmers are accepted on their own terms, and Jim is seen for once within a context which does not rub him raw. Kathy and Jim begin to take on dimensions as human beings which unfortunately are not sustained by other parts of the novel. Chapter xii demonstrates Metcalf's total control of all the elements of his craft as Wells's brief pastoral idyll modulates almost imperceptibly into images of dissolution and violence.

If Metcalf's handling of his central characters did not adequately serve his purpose, his masterful and often hilariously funny caricatures redeem the work. The thumbnail sketches of university faculty and creative-writing students are accomplished with such a fine sense of precise detail that their living counterparts are pinned wriggling to Metcalf's specimen board. *General Ludd* may be a *roman à clef*, but its secondary characters certainly have counterparts everywhere. They are skewered by Metcalf because they are easily recognizable as personifications of the values and attitudes he is attacking. One of the novel's central concerns is with the abuse of language both as a disease and as a symptom of the larger malaise; it is through the characters' own words that Metcalf most often condemns them.

Among the novel's many memorable creations is Itzic Zemermann, a caricature of the victim who uses his suffering to buy dispensation in areas of life having nothing to do with his afflictions. The scene in which Wells denounces Itzic is superbly paced and loaded with delicately ironic counterpoint. Wells's quotation from Auden's poem as a statement of his credo is central to the novel for it establishes the foundation of Wells's value system and implies the standard on which Metcalf bases much of his satire:

> *Time that is intolerant*
> *Of the brave and innocent*
> *And indifferent in a week*
> *To a beautiful physique*
>
> *Worships language and forgives*
> *Everyone by whom it lives;*
> *Pardons cowardice, conceit,*
> *Lays its honours at their feet.*

(p. 237)

Wells is able to dismiss the questionable quality of his own life on the grounds that he is redeemed by his worship of language. The irony of Auden's infelicitous phrases verging on doggerel is compounded by Wells's insensitivity to the words "beautiful physique" as they apply to Itzic. The scene, which culminates in Itzic's death, manages to combine seriousness and pathos with an underlying black humour.

In *General Ludd*, Metcalf appears to trust his readers less than in his previous works (perhaps because he assumed a wider audience) and is less likely to leave key elements without explanation or significant underlining. An opposing tendency, which stems more from intellectual honesty and artistic integrity, often introduces confusion and ambiguity into elements which at first appeared to be constants. Just when the reader feels that Wells has been comfortably classified, Metcalf shifts the ground. Wells reveals that Auden revised his poem in later life and excised the stanzas quoted, perhaps because the writing was poor, perhaps because ". . . he no longer believed in what he'd written." Wells broods, "Where are we if they're *not* true? . . . If we're *not* pardoned?" (p. 263). Wells's feelings of guilt over Itzic's death, his pain and rage over the life and death of his friend Caverly, his burning and fearful obsession with television, and his conviction that the barbarians are well within the gate all contribute towards making his doubt in his own essential position too much

to bear. He escapes more and more into alcohol and mad anarchistic gestures.

Wells sees himself as guerrilla fighter whose mission it is to
oppose society, but Kathy refuses to take sides. Her betrayal of
Wells is therefore inevitable; Metcalf's scheme allows no
neutrals. In writing *General Ludd*, Metcalf relaxed the tight
control of language, voice, and structure employed in his short
stories for the more diffuse form of the novel. But it is in the
episodes and set pieces that the novel is most impressive, demon-
strating that at present his fundamental impulse as a writer is
correct: his enormous talent is best expressed in the short-story
form. The well-known Canadian critic John Moss has declared
that "*General Ludd* is probably the finest comic novel ever
published in Canada" and that Metcalf "follows comfortably in
the wake of Cervantes, or Fielding, or Trollope, or Waugh at his
very best."[82] If this is accurate, then Metcalf's stature as a short-
story writer must grow enormous in comparison. Metcalf's
importance to the short-story genre in Canada is expressed with
less hyperbole and more authority by the writer-critic Kent
Thompson: "[John Metcalf] is setting a standard; he is an
artistic conscience; he is the preventer of shoddy work. And that
is very important to the development of the short story in this
country, in this language."[83]

NOTES

[1]Quoted by Kent Thompson in "John Metcalf: A Profile," *The
Fiddlehead*, No. 114 (Summer 1977), p. 59. This valuable essay appeared
as part of the "Special John Metcalf Section."

[2]*Prism International*, 4, No. 1 (Summer 1964), 6–30; and 4, No. 2
(Autumn 1964), 28–43. Eight stories published under the general title
"The Geography of Time: A Sequence of Stories by John Metcalf"
included "Early Morning Rabbits," which won the CBC "Young
Writer's Contest Prize" for 1963 and was broadcast on CBC *Anthology*.

[3]Letter received from John Metcalf, n.d. [3 April 1965].

[4]Thompson, "John Metcalf: A Profile," p. 59.

[5]See Douglas Rollins, "The Montreal Storytellers," *Journal of Canadian Fiction*, 1, No. 2 (Spring 1972), 5–6.

[6]John Metcalf, *Going Down Slow* (Toronto: McClelland and

Stewart, 1972). A poorly adapted television version was broadcast in the CBC *Performance* series 11 May 1975. All further references to this work appear in the text.

[7]Barry Cameron, "The Practice of the Craft: A Conversation with John Metcalf," *Queen's Quarterly*, 82 (Autumn 1975), 412–13. All further references to this work (Cameron) appear in the text.

[8]Clark Blaise and John Metcalf, Introd., *Here and Now*, ed. Clark Blaise and John Metcalf (Ottawa: Oberon, 1977), pp. 5–6.

[9]John Metcalf, "Telling Tales," in *Kicking Against the Pricks* (Downsview, Ont.: ECW, 1982), p. 79. All further references to this work (*KAP*) appear in the text.

[10]John Metcalf, rev. of *I Don't Want to Know Anyone Too Well*, by Norman Levine, *The Canadian Forum*, June 1972, p. 39.

[11]Michael Smith, "Interview," *Books in Canada*, Jan. 1979, p. 24.

[12]Anne Montagnes, "A Discovery: John Metcalf, a Newcomer and a Master of the Neat, Pointed Story," rev. of *New Canadian Writing, 1969*, *Saturday Night*, Dec. 1969, pp. 55–56.

[13]Margaret Howard Blom, "The Charm of the Past," rev. of *New Canadian Writing, 1969*, *Canadian Literature*, No. 44 (Spring 1970), pp. 80–81.

[14]Kent Thompson, rev. of *New Canadian Writing, 1969*, *The Fiddlehead*, No. 85 (May–June–July 1970), pp. 102–04.

[15]Peter Sypnowich, "Reverence for Life Is Still Found in English Writing," rev. of *The Lady Who Sold Furniture*, *Toronto Daily Star*, 23 May 1970, p. 59.

[16]Leo Simpson, "Rabbits, Watercress Coming On Excitingly," rev. of *The Lady Who Sold Furniture*, *The Globe Magazine*, 20 June 1970, p. 16.

[17]Eldon Garnet, rev. of *The Lady Who Sold Furniture*, *The Telegram* [Toronto], 6 June 1970, p. 55.

[18]Kent Thompson, rev. of. *The Lady Who Sold Furniture*, *The Fiddlehead*, No. 86 (Aug.–Sept.–Oct. 1970), pp. 167–68.

[19]Simpson, p. 16.

[20]Patricia Morley, rev. of *Going Down Slow*, *Queen's Quarterly*, 80 (Spring 1973), 138–40.

[21]Isaac Bickerstaff [Don Evans], "Physical Education," rev. of *Going Down Slow*, *Books in Canada*, Oct. 1972, pp. 20–21.

[22]David M. Legate, "First but Not a Winner," rev. of *Going Down Slow*, *The Montreal Star*, 16 Sept. 1972, Sec. C, p. 3.

[23]Kenneth Gibson, rev. of *Going Down Slow*, *The Canadian Forum*, Sept. 1973, p. 41.

[24]Robert Weaver, rev. of *Going Down Slow*, by John Metcalf, and *You Cant Get There From Here*, by Hugh Hood, *Saturday Night*, Nov. 1972, p. 51.

[25]William French, "Crisp Satire with a Fine, Surreal Bent," rev. of *Going Down Slow*, *The Globe and Mail*, 26 Aug. 1972, p. 28.

[26]Douglas Barbour, rev. of *Going Down Slow*, *The Canadian Fiction Magazine*, No. 10 (Spring 1973), p. 112.

[27]J. R. Leitold, rev. of *Going Down Slow*, *Dalhousie Review*, 53 (Summer 1973), 367.

[28]David Helwig, "Story Moves Quickly," rev. of *Going Down Slow*, *The Whig-Standard* [Kingston], 4 Nov. 1972, p. 17.

[29]Roy MacSkimming, "Some Outstanding Stories Emerge from Author's Uneven Collection," rev. of *The Teeth of My Father*, *The Toronto Star*, 29 March 1975, Sec. H, p. 7.

[30]Michael Smith, "Victims and Busier Bodies," rev. of *The Teeth of My Father*, by John Metcalf, and *A Private Place*, by Joyce Marshall, *Books in Canada*, Aug. 1975, p. 18.

[31]Kerry McSweeney, "Shoddy on the Outside but Soft Hearts Within," rev. of *The Teeth of My Father*, *The Whig-Standard* [Kingston], 22 May 1975, p. 7.

[32]Brian Vintcent, rev. of *The Teeth of My Father*, *Quill & Quire*, May 1975, p. 40.

[33]Anthony Brennan, rev. of *The Teeth of My Father*, *The Fiddlehead*, No. 105 (Spring 1975), p. 126.

[34]MacSkimming, p. 7.

[35]Barry Cameron, "In Praise of the Craft," rev. of *The Teeth of My Father*, *The Canadian Forum*, Aug. 1975, p. 36.

[36]Barry Cameron, "An Approximation of Poetry: The Short Stories of John Metcalf," *Studies in Canadian Literature*, 2 (Winter 1977), 35. All further references to this work appear in the text.

[37]Wayne Grady, rev. of *Girl in Gingham*, *The Tamarack Review*, Nos. 77–78 (Summer 1979), pp. 99–100.

[38]Roderick W. Harvey, "Private Realities," rev. of *Girl in Gingham*, by John Metcalf, *The Italians*, by Frank Paci, and *Skevington's Daughter*, by John Mills, *Canadian Literature*, No. 84 (Spring 1980), p. 130.

[39]John Mills, rev. of *Girl in Gingham*, *The Fiddlehead*, No. 118 (Summer 1978), p. 175.

[40]Robert Lecker, "Private Art," rev. of *Girl in Gingham*, *The Canadian Forum*, Sept. 1978, p. 28.

[41]William French, "Metcalf Shouldn't Be Classified; Just Enjoyed,"

rev. of *Girl in Gingham*, *The Globe and Mail*, 30 March 1978, p. 15.

[42]Ken Adachi, "Novella Reads like Portnoy's Complaint," rev. of *Girl in Gingham*, *The Toronto Star*, 15 April 1978, Sec. D, p. 7.

[43]Lee Briscoe Thompson, "Guilt in Gingham," rev. of *Girl in Gingham*, *Essays on Canadian Writing*, No. 16 (Fall–Winter 1979–80), pp. 191–97.

[44]Barry Cameron, "Invention in *Girl in Gingham*," *The Fiddlehead*, No. 114 (Summer 1977), p. 120. All further references to this work appear in the text.

[45]John Metcalf, "Notes on Writing a Story," *The Fiddlehead*, No. 114 (Summer 1977), p. 72.

[46]Cary Fagan, "Misguided Accuser," rev. of *General Ludd*, *The Canadian Forum*, Dec. 1980–Jan. 1981, p. 40.

[47]Barbara Campbell, rev. of *General Ludd*, *Quill & Quire*, Oct. 1980, p. 35.

[48]J. L. Granatstein, "Modern Luddite Is Hero of Comic Novel with Bite," rev. of *General Ludd*, *Timmins Press*, 20 Sept. 1980. This review was widely published across Canada in newspapers of the Thomson chain, 20–22 Sept. 1980.

[49]William French, rev. of *General Ludd*, *The Globe and Mail*, 23 Aug. 1980, Sec. E, p. 12.

[50]Rev. of *General Ludd*, *Choice*, 18 (Feb. 1981), 797.

[51]John Metcalf, "Author's Commentary," in *Sixteen by Twelve: Short Stories by Canadian Writers*, ed. John Metcalf (Toronto: Ryerson, 1970), pp. 198–99. All further references to this work appear in the text.

[52]F. S. Flint, "Imagisme," *Poetry* [Chicago], 1 (March 1913), 199.

[53]Ezra Pound, "A Few Don'ts by an Imagiste," *Poetry* [Chicago], 1 (March 1913), 200.

[54]John Metcalf, "Early Morning Rabbits," *Prism International*, 4, No. 1 (Summer 1964), 8.

[55]"Early Morning Rabbits," p. 10.

[56]Marion McCormick, radio interview with John Metcalf, CBC *Anthology*, 19 Dec. 1970.

[57]McCormick, radio interview.

[58]*The Lady Who Sold Furniture* (Toronto: Clarke, Irwin, 1970), p. 110. All further references to this work (*LWSF*) appear in the text.

[59]*Prism International*, 4, No. 1 (Summer 1964), 27.

[60]*Prism International*, 4, No. 2 (Autumn 1964), 33.

[61]*The Canadian Forum*, April 1965, pp. 12–13.

[62]*Edge*, No. 6 (Spring 1967), pp. 19–24.

[63]*New Canadian Writing, 1969: Stories by John Metcalf*, D. O. Spettigue and C. J. Newman (Toronto: Clarke, Irwin, 1969), p. 3. All further references to this work (*NCW*) appear in the text.

[64]Thompson, rev. of *New Canadian Writing, 1969*, p. 104.

[65]*Prism International*, 4, No. 1 (Summer 1964), 21–25.

[66]John Metcalf, "Soaping a Meditative Foot (Notes for a Young Writer)," in *The Narrative Voice: Short Stories and Reflections by Canadian Authors*, ed. John Metcalf (Toronto: McGraw-Hill Ryerson, 1972), p. 154.

[67]Gibson, p. 41.

[68]St. Louis Jimmy [James Oden], "Going Down Slow," *Otis Spann: Walking the Blues*, Candid, KZ31290, 1960.

[69]In England, Metcalf had read George Woodcock and found that many of his own ideas coincided with those of the anarchist philosophers. Letter received from John Metcalf, n.d. [ca. May 1966].

[70]*The Teeth of My Father* (Ottawa: Oberon, 1975), p. 7. All further references to this work (*TMF*) appear in the text.

[71]John Metcalf, Public Reading with Alice Munro, Loyola College, Montreal, 10 Feb. 1975.

[72]John Metcalf, Public Reading, Dawson College, Montreal, 14 April 1975.

[73]See Herbert Gold, quoted by Metcalf in "Soaping a Meditative Foot," p. 154.

[74]Robert Lecker, "John Metcalf: Unburdening the Mystery," in *On the Line: Readings in the Short Fiction of Clark Blaise, John Metcalf and Hugh Hood* (Downsview, Ont.: ECW, 1982), p. 75. All further references to this work appear in the text.

[75]*Girl in Gingham* (Ottawa: Oberon, 1978), p. 89. All further references to this work (*GG*) appear in the text.

[76]See above, note 45.

[77]Metcalf, "Notes on Writing a Story," p. 70.

[78]Metcalf, "Soaping a Meditative Foot," p. 155.

[79]Granatstein, "Modern Luddite Is Hero of Comic Novel with Bite."

[80]*General Ludd* (Downsview, Ont.: ECW, 1980), p. 46. All further references to this work appear in the text.

[81]Geoff Hancock, "An Interview with John Metcalf," *Canadian Fiction Magazine*, No. 39 (1981), p. 122.

[82]John Moss, "Metcalf, John," in *A Reader's Guide to the Canadian Novel* (Toronto: McClelland and Stewart, 1981), p. 197.

[83]Thompson, "John Metcalf: A Profile," p. 63.

SELECTED BIBLIOGRAPHY

Primary Sources

Books

Metcalf, John. *The Lady Who Sold Furniture*. Toronto: Clarke, Irwin, 1970.

――――. *Going Down Slow*. Toronto: McClelland and Stewart, 1972.

――――. *The Teeth of My Father*. Ottawa: Oberon, 1975.

――――, and John Newlove. *Dreams Surround Us: Fiction and Poetry by John Metcalf and John Newlove*. Delta, Ont.: The Bastard Press, 1977.

――――. *Girl in Gingham*. Ottawa: Oberon, 1978.

――――. *General Ludd*. Downsview, Ont.: ECW, 1980.

――――. *Kicking Against the Pricks*. Downsview, Ont.: ECW, 1982.

――――. *Selected Stories*. New Canadian Library, No. 168. Toronto: McClelland and Stewart, 1982.

Contributions to Periodicals and Books

Metcalf, John. "The Geography of Time: A Sequence of Stories by John Metcalf." *Prism International*, 4, No. 1 (Summer 1964), 6–30; and 4, No. 2 (Autumn 1964), 28–43.

――――. "I've Got It Made." *The Canadian Forum*, April 1965, pp. 12–13.

――――. "The Happiest Days" and "A Process of Time." In *Modern Canadian Stories*. Ed. Giose Rimanelli and Roberto Ruberto. Toronto: Ryerson, 1966, pp. 324–31.

――――. "One for Cupid." *Edge*, No. 6 (Spring 1967), pp. 19–24.

――――. "Stories by John Metcalf." In *New Canadian Writing, 1969: Stories by John Metcalf, D. O. Spettigue and C. J. Newman*. Toronto: Clarke, Irwin, 1969, pp. 1–63.

――――. "Author's Commentary." In *Sixteen by Twelve: Short Stories by Canadian Writers*. Ed. John Metcalf. Toronto: Ryerson, 1970, pp. 198–203.

————. "Soaping a Meditative Foot (Notes for a Young Writer)." In *The Narrative Voice: Short Stories and Reflections by Canadian Authors*. Ed. John Metcalf. Toronto: McGraw-Hill Ryerson, 1972, pp. 154–59.

————. Rev. of *I Don't Want to Know Anyone Too Well*, by Norman Levine. *The Canadian Forum*, June 1972, p. 39.

————, and Clark Blaise, introd. *Here and Now*. Ed. Clark Blaise and John Metcalf. Ottawa: Oberon, 1977, pp. 5–6.

————. "Notes on Writing a Story." *The Fiddlehead*, No. 114 (Summer 1977), pp. 68–72.

————. "The Eastmill Reception Centre." *The Fiddlehead*, No. 128 (Winter 1981), pp. 59–76.

Secondary Sources

Adachi, Ken. "Novella Reads like Portnoy's Complaint." Rev. of *Girl in Gingham*. *The Toronto Star*, 15 April 1978, Sec. D, p. 7.

Barbour, Douglas. Rev. of *Going Down Slow*. *The Canadian Fiction Magazine*, No. 10 (Spring 1973), pp. 112–14.

Bickerstaff, Isaac [Don Evans]. "Physical Education." Rev. of *Going Down Slow*. *Books in Canada*, Oct. 1972, pp. 20–21.

Blom, Margaret Howard. "The Charm of the Past." Rev. of *New Canadian Writing, 1969*. *Canadian Literature*, No. 44 (Spring 1970), pp. 80–81.

Brennan, Anthony. Rev. of *The Teeth of My Father*. *The Fiddlehead*, No. 105 (Spring 1975), pp. 123–26.

Cameron, Barry. "In Praise of the Craft." Rev. of *The Teeth of My Father*. *The Canadian Forum*, Aug. 1975, pp. 36–37.

————. "The Practice of the Craft: A Conversation with John Metcalf." *Queen's Quarterly*, 82 (Autumn 1975), 402–24.

————. "Invention in *Girl in Gingham*." *The Fiddlehead*, No. 114 (Summer 1977), pp. 120–29.

————. "An Approximation of Poetry: The Short Stories of John Metcalf." *Studies in Canadian Literature*, 2 (Winter 1977), 17–35.

Campbell, Barbara. Rev. of *General Ludd*. *Quill & Quire*, Oct. 1980, p. 35.

Fagan, Cary. "Misguided Accuser." Rev. of *General Ludd*. *The Canadian Forum*, Dec. 1980–Jan. 1981, pp. 39–40.

Flint, F. S. "Imagisme." *Poetry* [Chicago], 1 (March 1913), 198–200.

French, William. "Crisp Satire with a Fine, Surreal Bent." Rev. of *Going Down Slow*. *The Globe and Mail*, 26 Aug. 1972, p. 28.

——. "Metcalf Shouldn't Be Classified; Just Enjoyed." Rev. of *Girl in Gingham*. *The Globe and Mail*, 30 March 1978, p. 15.

——. Rev. of *General Ludd*. *The Globe and Mail*, 23 Aug. 1980, Sec. E, p. 12.

Garnet, Eldon. Rev. of *The Lady Who Sold Furniture*. *The Telegram* [Toronto], 6 June 1970, p. 55.

Gibson, Kenneth. Rev. of *Going Down Slow*. *The Canadian Forum*, Sept. 1973, p. 41.

Grady, Wayne. Rev. of *Girl in Gingham*. *The Tamarack Review*, Nos. 77–78 (Summer 1979), pp. 99–100.

Granatstein, J. L. "Modern Luddite Is Hero Of Comic Novel with Bite." Rev. of *General Ludd*. *Timmins Press*, 20 Sept. 1980.

Hancock, Geoff. "An Interview with John Metcalf." *Canadian Fiction Magazine*, No. 39 (1981), pp. 97–123.

Harvey, Roderick W. "Private Realities." Rev. of *Girl in Gingham*, by John Metcalf, *The Italians*, by Frank Paci, and *Skevington's Daughter*, by John Mills. *Canadian Literature*, No. 84 (Spring 1980), pp. 129–30.

Helwig, David. "Story Moves Quickly." Rev. of *Going Down Slow*. *The Whig-Standard* [Kingston], 4 Nov. 1972, p. 17.

Lecker, Robert. "Private Art." Rev. of *Girl in Gingham*. *The Canadian Forum*, Sept. 1978, pp. 27–28.

——. "John Metcalf: Unburdening the Mystery." In *On the Line: Readings in the Short Fiction of Clark Blaise, John Metcalf and Hugh Hood*. Downsview, Ont.: ECW, 1982, pp. 59–97.

Legate, David M. "First but Not a Winner." Rev. of *Going Down Slow*. *The Montreal Star*, 16 Sept. 1972, Sec. C, p. 3.

Leitold, J. R. Rev. of *Going Down Slow*. *Dalhousie Review*, 53 (Summer 1973), 367–68.

MacSkimming, Roy. 'Some Outstanding Stories Emerge from Author's Uneven Collection." Rev. of *The Teeth of My Father*. *The Toronto Star*, 29 March 1975, Sec. H, p. 7.

McCormick, Marion. Radio interview with John Metcalf. CBC *Anthology*. 19 Dec. 1970.

McSweeney, Kerry. "Shoddy on the Outside but Soft Hearts Within." Rev. of *The Teeth of My Father*. *The Whig–Standard* [Kingston], 22 May 1975, p. 7.

Mills, John. Rev. of *Girl in Gingham*. *The Fiddlehead*, No. 118 (Summer 1978), pp. 174–78.

Montagnes, Anne. "A Discovery: John Metcalf, a Newcomer and a Master of the Neat, Pointed Story." Rev. of *New Canadian Writing, 1969. Saturday Night*, Dec. 1969, pp. 55–56.

Morley, Patricia. Rev. of *Going Down Slow. Queen's Quarterly*, 80 (Spring 1973), 138–40.

Moss, John. "Metcalf, John." In *A Reader's Guide to the Canadian Novel*. Toronto: McClelland and Stewart, 1981, pp. 196–200.

Pound, Ezra. "A Few Don'ts by an Imagiste." *Poetry* [Chicago], 1 (March 1913), 200–06.

Rev. of *General Ludd. Choice*, 18 (Feb. 1981), 797.

Rollins, Douglas. "The Montreal Storytellers." *Journal of Canadian Fiction*, 1, No. 2 (Spring 1972), 5–6.

St. Louis Jimmy [James Oden]. "Going Down Slow." *Otis Spann: Walking the Blues*. Candid, κz31290, 1960.

Simpson, Leo. "Rabbits, Watercress Coming On Excitingly." Rev. of *The Lady Who Sold Furniture. The Globe Magazine*, 20 June 1970, p. 16.

Smith, Michael. "Victims and Busier Bodies." Rev. of *The Teeth of My Father*, by John Metcalf, and *A Private Place*, by Joyce Marshall. *Books in Canada*, Aug. 1975, p. 18.

——. "Interview." *Books in Canada*, Jan. 1979, pp. 23–24.

Sypnowich, Peter. "Reverence for Life Is Still Found in English Writing." Rev. of *The Lady Who Sold Furniture. Toronto Daily Star*, 23 May 1970, p. 59.

Thompson, Kent. Rev. of *New Canadian Writing, 1969. The Fiddlehead*, No. 85 (May–June–July 1970), pp. 102–04.

——. Rev. of *The Lady Who Sold Furniture. The Fiddlehead*, No. 86 (Aug.–Sept.–Oct. 1970), pp. 167–69.

——. "John Metcalf: A Profile." *The Fiddlehead*, No. 114 (Summer 1977), pp. 57–63.

Thompson, Lee Briscoe. "Guilt in Gingham." Rev. of *Girl in Gingham. Essays on Canadian Writing*, No. 16 (Fall–Winter 1979–80), pp. 191–97.

Vintcent, Brian. Rev. of *The Teeth of My Father. Quill & Quire*, May 1975, p. 40.

Weaver, Robert. Rev. of *Going Down Slow*, by John Metcalf, and *You Cant Get There From Here*, by Hugh Hood. *Saturday Night*, Nov. 1972, pp. 50–51.

Alice Munro (1931–   )

HALLVARD DAHLIE

Alice Munro (1931–   )

HALLVARD DAHLIE

Biography

ALICE ANNE MUNRO was born on 10 July 1931, in Wingham, Ontario, the eldest of three children of Robert Eric and Anne Chamney Laidlaw. Her father was a marginal farmer, raising silver foxes during the depression years, switching to turkey farming during the 1940s, and augmenting the fluctuating family income by working as a night watchman in the local foundry. At a fairly advanced age, he began writing articles and sketches about his own life, and just before his death in 1976 he completed a novel about a pioneer southwestern Ontario family, which was edited and published after his death as *The McGregors: A Novel of an Ontario Pioneer Family* (1979). Alice's mother had been an elementary-school teacher in Alberta and Ontario before her marriage, an occupation she was not permitted to pursue in the unemployment-ridden Ontario of the depression. Like many of the unfulfilled and despairing mothers of Munro's fiction, she expended her energies during the formative years of the three Laidlaw children in the nurturing of a family under conditions of deprivation and hardship. She fought a long and painful battle with Parkinson's disease, to which she succumbed in 1959, a situation poignantly evoked in such stories as "The Peace of Utrecht" and "The Ottawa Valley."

Undoubtedly the Laidlaw family suffered its share of hard times during the depression, but those years seemingly have had no adverse effect on the three children: Alice's sister, Sheila, has become an artist in Toronto, and her brother, William, a professor of chemistry at the University of Calgary. And Alice recalls that though her childhood was at times lonely and isolated, it was on the whole a rich and satisfying one:

> I thought my life was interesting. There was always a great sense of adventure . . . . We lived outside the whole social

structure because we didn't live in the town and we didn't
live in the country. We lived in this kind of little ghetto
where all the bootleggers and prostitutes and hangers-on
lived. Those were the people I knew. It was a community of
outcasts. I had that feeling about myself. . . . I didn't belong
to any nice middle class so I got to know more types of kids.
It didn't seem bleak to me at the time. It seemed full of
interest.[1]

That kind of environment, together with her voracious and
indiscriminate reading, enabled her early in life to develop a
curiosity and excitement about herself and her world that helped
to direct her towards a writing career.

Beginning her schooling in a two-room country school, Alice
completed her elementary and secondary education in the
Wingham public schools, and she recalls that she was an above
average and highly competitive student. She tended towards
being a loner, losing herself in books with romantic and fantastic
plots, and around the age of fourteen or fifteen started turning
her hand to the writing of short stories. She even confesses to the
writing of a somewhat melodramatic novel during this adolescent period, the manuscript of which she is happy to record has
long since ceased to exist. After graduation from the Wingham
and District High School, she attended the University of Western
Ontario from 1949 to 1951, where she majored in English and
began her serious writing, publishing three stories in the university's *Folio*, and selling a story entitled "The Strangers" to Robert
Weaver's CBC program *Canadian Short Stories*.

In December 1951, she married a fellow student at Western,
James Munro, and they shortly moved to Vancouver, where she
continued intermittently with her writing, worked for a couple of
years at the Vancouver Public Library, and began to raise a
family (she has three daughters, born in 1953, 1957, and 1966). In
1963 the Munros moved to Victoria, where they established the
still flourishing Munro's Books, and where she found it possible
to turn to her writing with some semblance of consistency. Her
first marriage ended in 1972, whereupon she returned to Ontario;
today she lives on a farm on the outskirts of Clinton in Huron
County with her second husband, cartographer Gerald Fremlin,
whom she married in 1976.

As indicated above, Alice Munro's writing career began in earnest during her university years, but her first commercial story, "A Basket of Strawberries," appeared in the now defunct Canadian magazine *Mayfair* in November 1953. She continued to publish slick stories intermittently over the next few years in *Chatelaine*, and more recently in such magazines as *Redbook*, *Ms*, and *McCall's*. Simultaneously, however, her serious stories were being picked up by *The Montrealer*, *The Canadian Forum*, and *The Tamarack Review*, and later by such journals as *Queen's Quarterly* and *Ploughshares*. Within the last decade or so, she has joined the long-established Mavis Gallant as one of Canada's regular contributors to *The New Yorker*, and her stories have been included in virtually every anthology of Canadian short stories published in the last twenty years.

Though Alice Munro has now been writing for some thirty years, she is not a prolific writer, and to date has published in book form four collections of short stories and one novel. Her latest short-story collection, *The Moons of Jupiter*, was published in the fall of 1982, too recently, unfortunately, for detailed consideration in this essay. Her first, *Dance of the Happy Shades* (1968), won the Governor General's Award for fiction, as did her third collection, *Who Do You Think You Are?* (1978), published in the United States and England as *The Beggar Maid: Stories of Flo and Rose*. The other collection of stories, *Something I've Been Meaning to Tell You*, appeared in 1974, and her only novel to date, *Lives of Girls and Women* (1971), won the Canadian Booksellers Association International Book Year Award. She has served as a writer-in-residence at the University of Western Ontario and the University of British Columbia, and she recently spent a term at Queensland University in Brisbane as the first Canadian winner of the Canada-Australia Literary Prize.

Tradition and Milieu

Alice Munro occupies a solid position in that group of writers whose careers coincided with the artistic, cultural, and political coming-of-age of Canada after World War II, a period during which the intrinsic value of Canadian experience came to be taken for granted. Unlike those writers who attained their maturity between the two world wars, or who were conditioned by Old World attitudes, sentiments, and values, this younger group felt no obligations or compulsion to see their world in any other terms than those defined by their own vision and experience. Margaret Laurence, Robert Kroetsch, Hugh Hood, Mordecai Richler, Marian Engel, Leonard Cohen, Rudy Wiebe, Margaret Atwood, Clark Blaise — these are some of the major writers, born between the mid-1920s and the early 1940s, who have felt no need either to ignore or to explain the place of Canada in their fiction, and it is to this rich and varied group that Munro belongs.

Their immediate predecessors are clearly recognizable: Frederick Philip Grove, Ethel Wilson, Morley Callaghan, Hugh MacLennan, Sinclair Ross, most of whom—Callaghan and Ross are the exceptions — approached the Canadian fact with a perspective shaped in part by influences from outside Canada. Within the broad scope of Canadian literary development as a whole, this older group of writers can be seen as contributing a fictional extension of the documentary impulse in Canadian literature, a tendency that had its roots in the exploration and settlement literature of the nineteenth century, but which has continued to receive impetus from the utility realizable in its moral and didactic overtones, and from the tangible evidence of nation-building still visible in all parts of the country. To this day, as writers like Pierre Berton and Farley Mowat amply demonstrate, the documentary approach to Canadian experience is very strongly entrenched in our literature.

Aesthetically, of course, this impulse has best been served by realism, and at mid-century Canada was still very much preoccupied with this approach in literature and the other arts. Grove (d. 1948) and Callaghan had been writing realistic novels about Canada's rural and urban worlds for some three decades, and they very much dominated the fictional scene in the period between the wars, just as the Group of Seven dominated the visual arts scene. Middle-class, serious, and practical attitudes remained firmly entrenched, and there was no demand for formal experimentation or any metaphysical reassessment of reality; the imaginative, but recognizable, depiction of man struggling against a vast and harsh country by and large sustained writer and reader alike until well into this century.

But the immediate postwar period also saw the beginnings of a departure from the various forms of realism, a movement that derived from metaphysical as well as social and psychological reassessments of reality. Faint hints of this modulation had sounded occasionally in some of the fiction of the traditional realists, as in Ross's *As For Me and My House* (1941) and Grove's *The Master of the Mill* (1944), but essentially it was a manifestation of the cosmic reverberations produced by the holocaust of the war and lingering uncertainties of its aftermath. In fiction, a major aesthetic formulation of this development appeared in the work of Malcolm Lowry, an exile who exploited the simultaneous existence of wonder and terror in the coastal landscape he so quickly adopted as his private paradise, as it were. Over the next couple of decades, such indigenous writers as Sheila Watson and Robert Kroetsch contributed their metaphorical versions of Canadian landscapes and mythologies, and it may well be that their works represent the vanguard of a fictional movement that will accelerate if the intellectual and artistic climate of the nation is appropriately modified.

For the moment, however, there is seemingly no profound or pervasive break with the basic tenets of realism, and perhaps the most that one can detect is a tension between the traditional and experimental aesthetic patterns and their accompanying metaphysical rationales. And, in a very real sense, Munro occupies both these fictional worlds: her fiction is tangibly rooted in the social realism of the rural and small-town world of her own experience, but it insistently explores what lies beyond the bounds of empirical reality. She has said that she is "very excited by what you might call the surface of life,"[2] but her fiction clearly reflects that it is what the surface conceals rather than what it reveals that is central to her vision. If she does not subscribe to the formal experimentation of such writers as Audrey Thomas and Robert Kroetsch, she does evoke their metaphysical disturbances and uncertainties, a situation which in her fiction takes on an added intensity simply because the world she normally depicts is such an empirically recognizable one. In this respect, she has much in common with one of our most traditional novelists, Ethel Wilson, who, in novels such as *The Equations of Love* and *Love and Salt Water*, frequently juxtaposes simple social reality against sudden dimensions of the irrational or terrifying.

Munro is clearly a central figure in the short-story tradition in Canada, a tradition that goes well back into the nineteenth century, and one that, at least until fairly recently, has earned Canada more international recognition than the novel. And many of the writers whom she acknowledges as having influenced her are internationally recognized practitioners of the short story: Katherine Mansfield, Mary Lavin, Edna O'Brien, Eudora Welty, Flannery O'Connor, Shirley Faessler, Mavis Gallant. Regardless of their diverse origins, these writers have in common an ability to transform a mundane, ordinary world into something that is unsettling and mysterious, and most of them are rooted strongly in a particular region. Munro acknowledges novelists as well — James Agee, Wright Morris, Ethel Wilson, Brian Moore — for their compassion, I would think, for their subtleties and delicacies of style, as well as for the tangible worlds out of which they write.

The most pervasive influence, as she has frequently explained, has been that of the American writers of the South, and it is both the regional and the Gothic impulses in their fiction that she has been very much in tune with and has adapted to her own particular world. ". . . I felt there a country being depicted that was like my own," she has said. ". . . the part of the country I come from is absolutely Gothic. You can't get it all down."[3] As in the American South, the traditions and sense of propriety in Munro's Huron County are both strongly entrenched and threatened by the very distortions they produce, a situation which is further intensified by the desperate lives led by so many of the inhabitants.

It is this qualitative texture of the regional South, rather than any formal influence, that Munro acknowledges, though, as she concedes, her *Lives of Girls and Women* has structural similarities to Welty's *The Golden Apples*. It is difficult, however, to trace her techniques to any particular development in the short story, for hers is a uniquely private fictional manifestation, born simply of precise observation and what seems to be a perpetual sense of astonishment about her world. On the whole, regional writers in Canada have not been formal experimenters, for their concern has been with the verification of human experience and intuition deriving from the peculiarities of the region, rather than the creation of fictional worlds whose integrity resides in the conjunction of words. Like Margaret Laurence, Ethel Wilson, or Ernest Buckler, Munro has been strongly influenced by place, and like them, too, she has learned to distil its peculiarities in characters and intense moral confrontations rather than in abstractions.

Critical Overview and Context

Though Alice Munro has been writing for some three decades, critical attention of any extended sort did not appear until the beginning of the 1970s, when serious response to her 1968 collection of stories began to formulate. She had received, it is true, some attention during the 1950s and 1960s, particularly from *Tamarack Review* editor Robert Weaver, who was consistent and perceptive in his praise of her work, but she earned only a line or two of objective mention in the 1965 edition of the *Literary History of Canada: Canadian Literature in English* (compared to more than a page of strong praise in the revised 1976 edition). It was, however, the awarding of the Governor General's Award for *Dance of the Happy Shades* that signalled to the country as a whole the arrival of a new force in Canadian literature, even though the initial response to that event focused more on who Alice Munro was than on the substance of her fiction.

To date, serious critical attention has been limited to interviews, articles, and reviews published in scholarly and academic journals; no monograph or full-length study as yet exists, though I know of one that is under way as I write this. The first graduate thesis on Munro's work came out of Queen's University in 1972, and in the ensuing decade her fiction has received increasing attention from graduate students across the country as well as abroad. A half dozen or so interviews with Munro have been conducted since Mari Stainsby published the first one in 1971,[4] and though some of these are livelier than others, all elicit much the same information about her life and career, about the various influences on her work, and about her opinions on being simultaneously a writer and a woman in Canada.

Scholarly articles on Munro show a steady but not spectacular growth, with the majority of them thematic in nature, though a few also address structural and stylistic matters. The titles of the articles are revealing, suggesting not only the richness of Munro's fiction but also the versatility of her critics. Where one speaks of isolation and rejection, another counters with confinement and escape, a third with resolution and independence, and yet another with transience; one discusses her vision, and not to be outdone, another her double vision; we have private landscapes and wonderlands, both with and without the looking glass; child-women and primitives vie with the masculine image and the growth of a young artist in her fiction; two critics link her with James Joyce, one with the American South, and a third with myth and fairy tale. In short, scholarly criticism of Munro to date seems to be following the standard exegetical route that all writers routinely undergo, perhaps particularly those whose fiction is relatively uncomplicated and accessible to a wide range of readers.

The articles which examine *Dance of the Happy Shades* — and only one is concerned exclusively with this book — have in common a tendency to set up either opposing or complementary tensions within the stories and thus to formulate keys to specific interpretations. In some cases, it is Munro's own phrases that provide the opening the critic requires, particularly when the situation evoked by that phrase seems to constitute a repeating pattern in her fiction. Thus, for example, in my 1972 article on *Dance*,[5] I picked up on Helen's parenthetical observation in "The Peace of Utrecht" about the depressive effect of "unconsummated relationships" and saw this as a recurring dilemma for those many Munro characters caught up in situations of isolation and rejection. Similarly, Rae McCarthy Macdonald in her 1976 article[6] takes the observation that the scissors-man in "The Time of Death" is in some respects like "a madman loose in the world" to buttress her convincing argument that a central pattern in Munro is the tension between the normal world and the irrational "other" world which so many characters appear to be partially occupying. In an earlier article that same year, Beverly Rasporich saw much the same pattern operating throughout Munro's three books, but with a persuasive narrowing of focus: what she sees as Munro's central concern, the exploration of the feminine psyche, receives a vivid reflection through what she calls "the grotesque and hysterical reality of Munro's 'other' world."[7]

Extended criticism of *Lives of Girls and Women* began

appearing about the mid-1970s, and to date it is this book that has attracted the greatest amount of attention. In a 1975 article,[8] Tim Struthers analyses this novel within the perspective of its being a *Künstlerroman*, drawing a number of parallels between it and Joyce's *Portrait*, as well as making an interesting observation on the closing words of *Lives* and *Ulysses*. Del's final word, "Yes," Struthers suggests, moves this novel, as did Molly Bloom's in *Ulysses*, from irony to affirmation, a position, I think, that the "Epilogue" itself supports. W. R. Martin in a 1979 article[9] pursues the Joycean parallels in Munro, observing, as Struthers does, the "artist" similarities that link *Lives* and the *Portrait*. But he concentrates his analysis on the tonal and structural similarities between *Dance* and *Dubliners*, particularly the correspondences between two of Munro's stories, "Dance of the Happy Shades" and "The Time of Death," and Joyce's "The Dead." Struthers' other article on Munro (1974, rev. 1978)[10] constitutes an interesting analysis of her frequently asserted debt to writers of the American South, arguing that it is manifested both thematically and formally. His demonstration of Munro's debt to Eudora Welty is more convincing, I think, than the case he makes for her formal affinities with the journalism / photography combination of James Agee and Walker Evans in their *Let Us Now Praise Famous Men*, though one can certainly find in many of Munro's stories tonal echoes of Agee's novel *A Death in the Family*.

The three articles on Munro published in 1977 reflect the eclectic nature of current criticism of her work: David Monoghan concentrates on the twin relationships of vision and form that the opening "Flats Road" section of *Lives* has with the rest of the novel;[11] Marcia Allentuck argues that *Lives*, along with the stories "The Office" and "Material," provide evidence that the emotional dependence women experience with men is difficult, if not impossible, to overcome;[12] and John Moss shapes his analysis of *Lives* to the overall theme of his *Sex and Violence in the Canadian Novel*.[13] Del's progress from childhood to maturity, he argues, that is, her evolution as an artist, is reflected among other ways by her progression from the vicarious sexuality adumbrated in Uncle Benny's world to her total sexual fulfilment in the "Baptizing" section, where in effect the artist merges with the person she has created.

In the last four years or so, criticism of Munro has begun

moving away from its thematic slant towards a concern with structure and style, though there is as yet no study exclusively devoted to these formal aspects. In a detailed study of *Lives*,[14] Rae McCarthy Macdonald picks up on her earlier article and demonstrates how Del is compelled to make continuous commitments to one world or the other — to the ordinary world or to the "other country," as it were. The process, she suggests, is rendered credible and dramatic through the episodic structure of the novel, a structure which paradoxically reveals by the time of Del's maturity that the two worlds were not that separate after all, that, indeed, this dual vision of the world was in fact an illusion. This notion, the doubleness of reality, is central to a fine study by Helen Hoy,[15] who argues convincingly that Munro consistently employs the stylistic devices of paradox, juxtaposition, and oxymoron to reflect the coalescing of the seemingly prosaic and the seemingly marvellous in life. Hoy's is the only article to date to deal to any extent with *Who Do You Think You Are?*, and with respect to that book she tentatively explores the idea that it introduces a new layer of ambiguity to this concept of reality, wherein the commonplace achieves its own intrinsic mystery.

If there is the beginning of a consistent ideological stance in Munro criticism, it lies, not surprisingly, in the feminist approach. Both Rasporich and Allentuck, in the articles referred to above, edge into this area, but the strongest position taken to date is that by Bronwen Wallace in an article published in 1978.[16] Wallace pursues, with reference mainly to the collections of stories, Munro's own implication made in an interview that women, as members of a subject race, have visions and perceptions that are qualitatively different from those of men; indeed, she concludes her perceptive study by arguing that the presence of so many selves in a woman constitutes her unique strength rather than a weakness. In an article published the following year, Nancy Bailey combines a feminist approach with a Jungian analysis of the androgynous nature of the female-artist figure. It is an intriguing study, though for me it was more instructive at times about Jung than about Munro, as, for example, when she interprets Bobby Sherriff as "the Wise Man or the fourth stage of animus development."[17] Nevertheless, Bailey's article may well mark the advent of the kind of sophisticated and intellectual

approach that will be required if Munro's subsequent fiction
assumes more complexity.

In general, however, there is as yet no sustained body of
Munro criticism which adopts any consistent dialectic or ideological stance, even though some of the titles of the articles
discussed here bear family resemblances to one another. What we
have at the moment is a growing collection of discrete articles,
eclectic in nature, all of which shed interesting and useful light on
the meanings and structures of Munro's fiction.

Munro's Works

As suggested above in "Tradition and Milieu," Alice Munro
belongs in two fictional worlds, that of literary realism and that
in which empirical reality is transformed into something qualitatively quite different. The materials of her fiction are the ordinary
everyday components of the recognizable worlds of southwestern Ontario and the Pacific coast, and up to a point her
artistic exploitation of this material constitutes, as she confirmed
in a 1981 interview, "the perfect literary equivalent to a documentary movie."[18] But in many respects her fiction represents the
very antithesis of literal documentation: the tones and nuances of
her art bespeak a sensitive and profound explorer of empirical
reality, one who is not at all comfortable with untested moral and
philosophical precepts. The statement of the narrator in "The
Peace of Utrecht" that ". . . there is no easy way to get to Jubilee
from anywhere on earth"[19] clearly has its documentary cartogra-
phic relevance, but it can stand as a caution to the reader, too,
that entry into Munro's fictional world is not as easy or direct as
it seems. Yet a statement from a later story reminds us that this
world *is* accessible, given our willingness to transcend the literal:
"The world that we accept — you know, external reality . . . is
nothing like so fixed as we have been led to believe. It responds to
more methods of control than we are conditioned to accept."[20]

Formally, Munro's concern with this conjunction of appearance and reality has to date been more frequently manifested in
the short story than in the novel, though two of her first four
books, *Lives of Girls and Women* and *Who Do You Think You
Are?*, suggest the interchangeability of these two genres. It seems

that the more concentrated form of the short story allows her to attach added intensity to the dilemmas her protagonists face, or, perhaps more accurately, to leave them with those tensions suspended that a novel would more typically resolve. For what Munro characteristically explores are those areas of reality and experience which are *not* resolvable: the imprecise boundaries between the rational and the irrational, the juxtaposition of familiar and comfortable worlds and sudden intrusions of terror, and the relationships among the many facets of certainty, uncertainty, and illusion. In this respect, her two collections of disparate short stories, *Dance of the Happy Shades*, and *Something I've Been Meaning to Tell You*, can be seen as tentative explorations of these junctures, while *Lives of Girls and Women* and the interrelated stories of Flo and Rose in *Who Do You Think You Are?* reflect these dilemmas being brought to some degree of resolution.

Munro's moral and metaphysical concerns are reflected in the formal structures of her fiction. Characteristically, a kind of illusory balance operates between the conventional fictional elements of plot, setting, and character, on the one hand, and, on the other, complex psychological and even psychic verifications of the experiences in question. On the surface, much seems straightforward — family relationships, ordinary friendships, love affairs — but Munro's vision often invests these situations with a degree of moral chaos and a destructive force rather than with the positive tendencies we customarily associate them with. The discoveries the characters make in these relationships, both about themselves and about the larger world, threaten not only their day-to-day ideas and values, but seemingly at times the cosmic order itself. The reader who struggles with the paradoxes and ambiguities of these fictional situations is constantly compelled to reassess character and motive, and ultimately realizes that "normal" characters in the conventional meaning of that word rarely exist in Munro's world. In effect, what frequently happens in her fiction is that the reader comes to the kind of realization that Rose does in "Simon's Luck": he is disturbed by "those shifts of emphasis that throw the story line open to question, the disarrangements which demand new judgments and solutions, and throw the windows open on inappropriate unforgettable scenery."[21]

Munro's dramatization of what we might see as this conjunction of existential possibility and existential terror operates inconsistently throughout her fiction: that is, there is no obvious progress towards one or the other of these states of existence. Del Jordan in *Lives of Girls and Women* expresses the former option when she articulates her belief that girls like herself can "go out and take on all kinds of experiences and shuck off what they didn't want and come back proud,"[22] whereas the narrator of "Dance of the Happy Shades" fears that ". . . things are getting out of hand, anything may happen" (*Dance*, p. 212). An awareness of this existential contradiction makes control of one's life and the act of survival both challenging and despairing, and while Eugene's statement about external reality in "Walking on Water," referred to above, suggests the flexibility of Munro's vision, her fiction also supports the narrator in "The Ottawa Valley," who recalls that in her mother's universe, "luck was not without its shadow . . ." (*Something*, p. 228). In sum, Munro's total vision is predicated more on faith of some kind than on despair, though like other dualities in her fiction, faith and despair also vie inconsistently with each other.

It is this kind of flexible vision that informs the fifteen stories of *Dance of the Happy Shades*, the title of which ironically suggests the interplay of these various contradictions. Munro's use of a first-person narrator in eleven of these stories suggests her concern with the subjective dimensions of reality, and the fact that the narrator or reflector of the action is in most cases a youthful, sensitive girl underscores the tentative nature of this reality. In most of the stories, the narrator stands uneasily between two positions: on the one hand, she is an active participant in, or even the instigator of, the action, and on the other hand she stands apart from it as a kind of intuitive moral critic. What she gains — or perhaps more accurately, what she seems frequently to be on the point of gaining — is the kind of compromised moral stance that Del and Rose achieve in Munro's longer works: the realization that a more or less permanent state of moral tension is both inevitable and acceptable.

A basic pattern in many of these stories reveals the sensitive narrator figure emerging from her experiences to a position where she senses that morality itself is an elusive aspect of reality, and that human relationships create by their very interaction a perpetually shifting dimension of this morality. Appropriately, the narrator in coming to these realizations is frequently in positions of isolation and rejection, where genuine human relationships seem at best tentative; what Munro labels "unconsummated relationships" in "The Peace of Utrecht" (*Dance*, p. 194) defines the situations in many other of the stories as well, notably "Walker Brothers Cowboy," "Postcard," and "Thanks for the Ride," even though in these last two stories there is an actual sexual consummation.

"Walker Brothers Cowboy," one of the four stories Munro wrote specifically for *Dance of the Happy Shades*, can in one sense stand as an appropriate prologue to her entire chronicle of various feminine lives. It is not only that the youthful Del Jordan is to reappear in a literal sense in "Images" (*Dance*, pp. 30–43) and as the central figure in *Lives*; more to the point, it is that her dimly unfolding realizations in this first story emerge as a theme upon which many variations are played throughout Munro's first four books. The realism of this story is conveyed through the physical and domestic details of Del's circumscribed life, details which reinforce the theme of isolation: the momentary glimpses Del has of the children of Tuppertown who "separate into islands of two or one . . . occupying themselves in . . . solitary ways" (*Dance*, p. 2) are paralleled by the divisions within the Jordan family, particularly in the isolation of the mother from her husband and children. Within the realistic framework of adolescence, Del rejects her mother's obsession with propriety, her lack of imagination, her inward-turning nature, and her preference to remain in the seclusion of her home, "always darkened by the wall of the house next door" (*Dance*, p. 5). Just as realistically, she is drawn to her father, who knows "the quick way out of town" (*Dance*, p. 6) and whose adventures both within and outside his "territory" fill her with anticipation.

In this situation, Ben Jordan is a partner in an "unconsummated relationship" not only with his wife but also with an earlier love, Nora Cronin, who now lives "outside his territory," and it is this situation that constitutes the beginning of Del's moral confusion. She senses that something is wrong from the moment they arrive at Nora's place — she notices her "abrupt and somewhat angry" laughter and hears her speak "cheerfully and aggressively" — but it is not until Nora dances in a frenzied

manner with her and then is turned down by Ben that the full
extent of her isolation is made manifest. "I can drink alone," she
informs Ben, "but I can't dance alone" (*Dance*, p. 17), an expression of human rejection that ranks with Prufrock's poignant
lament "I have heard the mermaids singing, each to each. / I do
not think that they will sing to me." Del intuitively comprehends
her father's dilemma, and their mutual collusion further reinforces her mother's isolation:

> My father does not say anything to me about not mention-
> ing things at home, but I know . . . that there are things not
> to be mentioned. . . . So my father drives . . . and I feel my
> father's life flowing back from our car in the last of the
> afternoon, darkening and turning strange, like a landscape
> that has an enchantment on it, making it kindly, ordinary
> and familiar while you are looking at it, but changing it,
> once your back is turned, into something you will never
> know, with all kinds of weathers, and distances you cannot
> imagine. (*Dance*, pp. 17–18)

This realization is not unlike that experienced by the narrator
of "Dance of the Happy Shades," who speculates that in her
world, too, "things are falling apart." Her world is not the ordinary one of a normal family relationship, but a unique and somewhat trivial one, the annual music recital conducted by the aged
Miss Marsalles. The ostensible formal order of that event —
"Everything was always as expected . . ." (*Dance*, p. 214) —
becomes gradually more tenuous as the community's mothers
and daughters subject themselves to this recurring routine:

> Here they found themselves year after year — a group of
> busy, youngish women . . . who were drawn together by a
> rather implausible allegiance — not so much to Miss
> Marsalles as to the ceremonies of their childhood, to a more
> exacting pattern of life which had been breaking apart even
> then but which survived, and unaccountably still survived,
> in Miss Marsalles' living room. (*Dance*, p. 215)

But chaos — or at least a perversion of normality — follows upon
this order as a group of retarded children straggle in to take their

turn in the recital. "Something has happened, something unfore-
seen, perhaps something disastrous . . ." muses the narrator,
who senses that "there is an atmosphere in the room of some
freakish inescapable dream" (*Dance*, pp. 221, 222).

Munro employs two agents or forces here to effect a conjunction between the "normal" and the "abnormal" worlds — the
music and Miss Marsalles herself. Music and madness have
traditionally been common juxtapositions throughout literature,
and in this story the music played by Dolores Boyle emanates
from the world of madness, though paradoxically it renders that
label meaningless, for "it is something fragile, courtly and gay,
that carries with it the freedom of a great unemotional happiness" (*Dance*, p. 222). The other operative force is Miss Marsalles herself, who, near the end of one long life, appears to be
partially occupying another, from which vantage point she can
impose a harmony over the two disparate worlds. She manifests
no surprise at Dolores' playing — ". . . people who believe in
miracles do not make much fuss when they actually encounter
one" (*Dance*, p. 223) — but when the music stops, the gap
between the two worlds is reestablished. As the mothers and
daughters depart, they know they have lost their former superiority over Miss Marsalles because they recognize that the music
which is "that one communiqué from the other country where
she lives" (*Dance*, p. 224) cannot be comprehended by "other
people, people who live in the world" (*Dance*, p. 223).

A different kind of tension separates the protagonists of "The
Peace of Utrecht," not only from each other, but from all the
forces that normally tend to bring people together — the past,
family ties, the very home itself. In this story, these elements are
presented as disturbing forces; the narrator significantly defines
"home" as a "dim world of continuing disaster" (*Dance*, p. 191),
and the mother as merely a force she and her sister Maddy have
to "*deal with*" (*Dance*, p. 198), evoking in them mainly the
memories of "the complex strain of living with her, the feelings of
hysteria . . . [and] a great deal of brutal laughter" (*Dance*,
p. 201). Even after the funeral, when in a sense this disturbing
element has been vanquished, there is no possibility of a
reconciliation between the two sisters: ". . . we will have to look
straight into the desert that is between us and acknowledge that
we are not merely indifferent; at heart we reject each other . . ."
(*Dance*, p. 190).

In a number of these stories, isolation is a product of the process of mutual exclusion practised by protagonist and antagonist alike, a confrontation produced not only by age or by sex, but occasionally by deliberate assumptions of superiority or detachment. There is frequently a degree of dissimulation practised by these characters: the narrator of "Images," for example, "pretended not to remember her [Mary McQuade]" (Dance, p. 30), and Mary in "The Shining Houses," in "pretending to know less than she did," articulates the advantages attainable in assuming such a stance: ". . . this way, remembered episodes emerged each time with slight differences of content, meaning, colour, yet with a pure reality that usually attaches to things which are at least part legend" (Dance, p. 19). Del Jordan of "Images" unconsciously strives towards this realization as well, and she is able at the end to overcome her earlier fears of Mary, as well as that of the grotesque "other world" of Joe Phippen; in her resolution, she combines both experiential verification and an inchoate recognition of something beyond that, "like the children in fairy stories who have seen their parents make pacts with terrifying strangers, who have discovered that our fears are based on nothing but the truth" (Dance, p. 43).

"Images," like "Walker Brothers Cowboy," dramatizes the bridging of youthful innocence and adult experience, a pattern that is duplicated, not infrequently with ironic modulations, in a number of other stories as well. It is whimsically traced out in "An Ounce of Cure," wherein the conventional relevance of the proverb is undercut by reversing the situation, that is, by making the disease (Martin Collingwood) less deadly than the prevention (straight whisky), and more seriously in "Boys and Girls," where the narrator's isolation and insecurity have cosmic as well as psychological and sociological derivations. First of all, as a child in her upstairs bedroom, separated from "the warm, safe, brightly lit downstairs world," she reflects that she and her brother "were not afraid of outside" but they "were afraid of inside" (Dance, p. 112). It is not the tangible world of snowdrifts and biting winds that poses the terror, but rather the dark and shifting shadows of the unfinished upstairs. The more complex source is the paradoxical nature of her own self as defined by the adult world: she is rejected by her father and brother because she is a girl, and by her mother and grandmother because she is not enough of a girl. "I no longer felt safe," she reflects. "The word *girl* had formerly seemed to me innocent and unburdened, like the word *child*; now it appeared that it was no such thing. A girl was not, as I had supposed, simply what I was; it was what I had to become" (*Dance*, p. 119). Isolation here is more deliberately accompanied by the impulse to freedom than it is, for example, in "Images" or "Walker Brothers Cowboy," though Munro suggests, through the catching and slaughtering of the mare the girl had earlier set free, the illusory nature of freedom in a world of experience and obligations.

Hostility derived from sexual exploitation or from sexual deprivation constitutes another isolating force in Munro's world, a theme which is more subtly developed in her later stories in *Something I've Been Meaning to Tell You* than in this first collection. But it operates here, too, especially in "Thanks for the Ride" and "Postcard," and, in less threatening ways, in "Red Dress — 1946" and "Sunday Afternoon." In the first two, sexual consummation constitutes part of the experience, but the dominant note in both is that of desperation and hysteria. In "Thanks for the Ride," Lois cloaks her hysteria in the trappings of formality: she introduces the innocent narrator to her mother and grandmother, she dresses up before they embark on their sexual escapade, and at evening's end she expresses the formal title words, modified by events into something of a vulgar joke. Her voice is "the loud, crude, female voice, abusive and forlorn" (*Dance*, p. 58), as though it expresses all the pent-up desperation of a life circumscribed by the conventional hypocrisy and expediency of her family and town, a situation against which she, her mother, and her grandmother seem united in a kind of desperate league.

The narrator — one of the few male narrators in Munro — is caught between the vulgar crudity of his cousin George and a kind of residual impulse towards innocence, and is thus in a no-win situation, even though he gains admittance to the adult world of sexual experience. Like Salinger's Holden Caulfield, he wants initially to preserve the ideal of innocence:

This girl lay against my arm, scornful, acquiescent, angry, inarticulate and out-of-reach. I wanted to talk to her then more than to touch her, and that was out of the question; talk was not so little a thing to her as touching. (*Dance*, p. 53)

This hostility, for the moment, keeps them apart, and after it erupts into overt action, a kind of metamorphosis overcomes them both: the narrator "did not want to talk any more, having discovered another force in her that lay side by side with her hostility, that was, in fact, just as enveloping and impersonal" (*Dance*, p.56). The force of love almost surfaces to transform the mechanical act of intercourse into something resurrectional for Lois as well as for the narrator, but it ultimately cannot transcend her conditioned cynicism.

In "Postcard" Helen sees her ongoing sexual relationship with Clare as a kind of holding action in preparation for what she (and the town generally) sees as their inevitable marriage. There is something perverse and almost grotesque in her attachment to him, as though intuitively knowing he is going to betray her, she therefore wishes to reinforce her illusion so much that it becomes a reality. Thus, when the tangible fact of his marriage to the Florida woman is brought home to her, her reactions alternate from disbelief, to resignation, to hysteria, and finally to a kind of mystical incomprehensibility. Her realization that Clare "was a man who didn't give out explanations, maybe didn't have any" (*Dance*, p.145) seems to transform him in her mind into something unreachable, and she "felt for the first time that [she] wanted to reach out [her] hands and *touch* him" (*Dance*, p.146), as though reducing their earlier sexual relationship to something subordinate—not unlike Gatsby's dismissal of Daisy's and Tom's physical love as something that was "only personal."

In "Red Dress—1946" and "Sunday Afternoon," the theme of isolation is played out against barely suggested worlds of sexual possibilities, and both stories end on a note of positive anticipation. Nothing much happens here — in one the young girl is asked to dance, and in the other she is gently kissed in a prolonged and slightly erotic fashion — but both protagonists move into a position where they realize that ". . . there were things [they] had not taken into account . . . and ways of living . . . that were not so unreal" (*Dance*, p.170). The adolescent girl in "Red Dress" momentarily is in danger of rejecting the conventional world of boys and dances for the mysterious, somewhat exhilarating Mary Fortune and her hostility towards boys. The tensions here between the "other world" and the "ordinary world" are not as disturbing as in "Dance of the Happy Shades" or in *Lives*, but for the narrator they seem real enough, as she realizes she will no longer "be safe behind the boundaries of childhood" (*Dance*, p. 151).

Most of the dilemmas in Munro's stories are psychological and moral rather than purely social or sociological, but in two or three the social world emerges as a major component. "The Time of Death" allows us to witness the sudden catastrophe that overcomes a poverty-stricken family living in filth and despair; it is a tale that more than any other in Munro evokes the grim Gothic tales of Flannery O'Connor or William Faulkner. The events in it are related obliquely to us through the consciousness of the sympathetic yet severe Allie McGee, who in a sense serves as the town's chorus. The townspeople are aware of the desperate state of the Parry family — of their hopelessness as well as of their pitiful pretensions — because in a very real way they have helped to shape it. The boy who was killed by scalding water had even by the age of eighteen months achieved a state akin to adult lifelessness: "Benny was long and thin and bony and his face was like his father's — pale, mute, unexpectant; all it needed was a soiled peaked cap" (*Dance*, p. 93). His death, in the literal sense, is a wrenching experience; in a symbolic sense, it represents the externalization of the qualities within the Parry family and the community which signify the inevitability of death: dirt, sickness, muteness, hysteria, fantasy. The world they live in contributes to this hopeless state in its readiness to exploit them, and in its failure to understand their dilemmas; its more grotesque dimensions are represented by the scissors-man — the "madman loose in the world," as the omniscient narrator describes him.

This story, in part because of the sociological slice of life that is revealed, is unrelievedly despairing; there is no character and no impulse to promise relief. This is not so in the other story with a strong social basis, "The Shining Houses," where the central observer and participant reflects a philosophy and vision of life that are intrinsically superior to the self-righteous efficiency of her suburban neighbours. While the story receives its genesis from the sociological phenomenon of urbanism, its ramifications are played out in moral and psychological terms. Mary is physically a part of the suburban world, but as the defender of the isolated and threatened Mrs. Fullerton, she stands apart spiritually from the values of that world. Mary is not an uncritical or sentimental champion of Mrs. Fullerton; indeed, at times she finds her somewhat disagreeable, and when she tries to justify her position rationally, she finds nothing tangible about the old lady to sustain her:

> She was trying desperately to think of other words, words more sound and reasonable than these; she could not expose to this positive tide any notion that they might think flimsy and romantic, or she would destroy her argument. But she had no argument. She could try all night and never find any words to stand up to their words, which came at her now invincibly from all sides: *shack, eyesore, filthy, property, value.* (*Dance*, p. 27)

In a tangible and literal way, Mrs. Fullerton stands in complete isolation from the suburban world encroaching upon her, not unlike Lowry's Sigbjørn Wilderness, who faced a constant eviction threat from his West-Coast shack as well. But the major difference lies not so much in her geographical or social separation from her neighbours; rather, it lies in the sense of internal order and self-sufficiency her house reflects through its harmony with the world around it: "Here was no open or straightforward plan, no order that an outsider could understand; yet what was haphazard time had made final" (*Dance*, p. 22). The outsiders live in what Munro obviously sees as a qualitatively inferior world, in "new, white and shining houses, set side by side in long rows in the wound of the earth" — "those ingenuously similar houses that looked calmly out at each other, all the way down the street" (*Dance*, p. 23). Munro presents a devastating description of the interiors of these houses, and thus we are not at all surprised when we meet their inhabitants.

Mary realizes she has no chance against the real-estate logic of her world, and that in spite of her refusal to sign the petition, the eviction order will in all likelihood go through. In her most explicit note of social protest in this collection, Munro offers a blistering portrait of the self-important upholders of progress:

> . . . it did not matter much what they said as long as they were full of self-assertion and anger. That was their strength, proof of their adulthood, of themselves and their

seriousness. The spirit of anger rose among them, bearing
up their young voices, sweeping them together as on a flood
of intoxication, and they admired each other in this new
behaviour as property-owners as people admire each other
for being drunk. (*Dance*, pp. 27–28)

Isolation in this story clearly spells out a strong moral victory,
though the reader experiences a sense of depression or anger,
too, in the realization that Mary's voice is feeble indeed against
the logic of real estate and progress.

Taken together, most of the stories in *Dance of the Happy
Shades* reflect a recognizably realistic world whose components
never leave one entirely comfortable, a situation rendered both
ambivalent and complex by Munro's sensitive use of irony,
paradox, and understatement. The collection's title, of course,
prepares us for the ambivalent and unpredictable world that
unfolds, and virtually all of the stories — "The Shining Houses"
is the exception — constitute formally satisfying modulations on
the theme struck by the title. In an oversimplified sense, the
progression has been from the terrestrial reality of Del's world in
"Walker Brothers Cowboy" to the supraterrestrial implications
of "Dance of the Happy Shades," and Del's initial curiosity
about the boundaries of her father's "territory" receives in the
process many answers.

In this respect, "A Trip to the Coast" emerges perhaps as one
of the most appropriate stories, for the ordinary, realizable possibility contained in its title is suddenly rendered immeasurably
complex and elusive by the grandmother's death. The grand-
daughter's day had begun with a "delicate premonition of
freedom and danger" (*Dance*, p. 174), and throughout the day
her tentative sparring with her grandmother prepares us for some
manifestation of what this impulse will mean; her death both
releases and immobilizes May:

> She sat with her legs folded under her looking out at the
> road where she might walk now in any direction she liked,
> and the world which lay flat and accessible and full of
> silence in front of her. (*Dance*, p. 189)

It is appropriate, I think, that this passage evokes the final lines
of Milton's *Paradise Lost*, for like their Edenic counterparts

Munro's characters are compelled to embrace the unknown possibilities of an experiential world in exchange for what lies within "the boundaries of childhood." The essential difference, of course, is that in Munro there is really no prelapsarian world to start with, but only a few dim, vestigial echoes of it sounding from time to time.

Like *Dance of the Happy Shades*, *Something I've Been Meaning to Tell You* is also a collection of disparate stories, yet here, too, there is a curious unity, attributable more to metaphysical than to formal elements. The title of the collection in this respect applies to more than the opening story, for in many of the others we become witness to the impossibility of communication, a situation engendered not only by fear or selfishness or love, but also by the nature of what is to be communicated.

Throughout *Dance*, we might recall, the characters frequently respond to various situations and experiences by loud and involuntary laughter: there is the "great deal of brutal laughter" in "The Peace of Utrecht," Nora Cronin's "abrupt and somewhat angry" laughter in "Walker Brothers Cowboy," Lois' "loud, crude, female voice" in "Thanks for the Ride," and the "hungry laughter" of the class in "Red Dress — 1946." The laughter at times constitutes a defensive stance, and at other times aggression, and it is only when the character senses the import of the moment, as in "A Trip to the Coast," that laughter is held off. "She wanted to laugh . . ." we are told as May watches the hypnotist working his spell on her grandmother. "But she did not laugh because she had to wait to see what her grandmother would do" (*Dance*, p. 188).

In *Something I've Been Meaning to Tell You*, on the other hand, the response is as frequently silence, though Munro with one of her more memorable characters in "The Ottawa Valley" deftly exploits Aunt Dodie's tendency to nervous laughter: "She was small and sharp-faced and laughed at the end of every sentence" (*Something*, p. 228). Only occasionally in this collection is laughter dramatized as a response to a particular experience; in "The Found Boat," which deals with the tentative surges of adolescent sexuality, Carol's and Eva's paroxysm of giggling at the end seems an appropriate response to the temporary, mutual hostility engendered by their sexual horsing around with the three boys: innocence has been maintained, but it is precarious.

Throughout these stories in general, however, it is the inability
to communicate, the reduction to silences, the futility of words,
that qualify any resolution arrived at, and that render these
stories on the whole more disturbing than those in *Dance of the
Happy Shades*. Variations of the title words recur frequently
enough throughout the collection to suggest a consistent vision
here: "What is here that is not being told?" ("Marrakesh");
"This is a message . . . but I don't see how I can deliver it" ("The
Spanish Lady"); ". . . and so I must believe that we get messages
another way, that we have connections that cannot be investi-
gated . . ." ("Winter Wind"); the title words of "Tell Me Yes or
No"; and, most powerfully, the concluding passage of "The
Ottawa Valley," where the narrator articulates her ultimate
frustration:

> If I had been making a proper story out of this, I would have
> ended it, I think, with my mother not answering and going
> ahead of me across the pasture. . . . I didn't stop there . . .
> because I wanted to find out more, remember more. I
> wanted to bring back all I could. Now I look at what I have
> done and it is like a series of snapshots . . . . The problem,
> the only problem, is my mother. And she is the one of
> course that I am trying to get; it is to reach her that this
> whole journey has been undertaken. With what purpose?
> To mark her off, to describe, to illumine, to celebrate, to *get
> rid*, of her; and it did not work, for she looms too close, just
> as she always did. . . . I could go on, and on, applying what
> skills I have, using what tricks I know, and it would always
> be the same. (*Something*, p. 246)

There is a nice irony in these, the last lines of this book: we as
readers accept the narrator's poignant lament about her own
mother, but at the same time we reject these lines in their function
as the disclaimer of Alice Munro the artificer, for throughout
these stories she has admirably succeeded in communicating the
"something" she has wanted to tell us.

As in *Dance*, most of these stories are told from a first-person
point of view, but there is a shift of perspective here as far as the
narrator is concerned. In both *Dance* and *Lives*, the emphasis
is on the youthful, female protagonist trying to come to terms
with the adult world, but here it is frequently the other way

around: grandmothers trying to understand granddaughters ("Marrakesh"); an elderly man trying to resolve his bewilderment with youth ("Walking on Water"); or, as in the title story, elderly sisters being compelled to face a reality transformed by their distortions of the past. As in the earlier stories, certain themes recur from story to story: unconsummated relationships, sexual awakenings, infidelities, death for old and young alike, and human misunderstandings. There are sharp and unflattering comments on the academic world ("Material"), delightful ironies of life ("How I Met My Husband"), explorations of cruelty, persuasion, and revenge ("Executioners"), and portraits of parasitic and amoral youth ("Forgiveness in Families" and "Marrakesh").

In "Walking on Water," the elderly Mr. Lougheed is in a sense bewildered by two forces or attitudes emanating from the world of the younger generation, neither of which satisfactorily explains his world to him. There is first of all the intellectual irrationality of Eugene, whose vision so far transcends the empirical aspects of his world that he elects suicide when he realizes he cannot "walk on water" — that is, control external reality. Lougheed's reaction to him is bewilderment, sorrow, and eventually a capitulation to a kind of weariness that suddenly overtakes him after Eugene's disappearance. His response to the other form of irrationality that besets him — the selfish, solipsistic self-indulgence of the hippies who inhabit his boarding-house — is one of bitterness and anger. He inadvertently catches two of them in the act of copulation in the hallway, but it is he, by their laughter and derision, who is made to feel guilty. Like Saul Bellow's Mr. Sammler, Mr. Lougheed is undoubtedly threatened by the sexuality of the young, but "what he objected to in this generation . . . was that they could not do a thing without showing off. Why all this yawping about everything, he asked. They could not grow a carrot without congratulating themselves on it" (*Something*, p. 71).

This is not the same kind of protest we heard earlier in "The Shining Houses"; it is psychological in its derivation rather than sociological, and is in part a product of rejection, as we also see in Munro's fine West-Coast-based story, "Material." The attack here at the outset is directed against the falsities and sycophancy associated with the academic-literary world, and it is manifested

in what is ostensibly a lingering sense of resentment felt by the
narrator against her ex-husband Hugo:

> Sometimes I see his name . . . on the cover of some literary
> journal that I don't open — I haven't opened a literary
> journal in a dozen years, praise God. Or I read . . . an
> announcement of a panel discussion at the University, with
> Hugo flown in to discuss the state of the novel today . . . .
> Then I think, will people really go, will people who could
> be swimming or drinking or going for a walk . . . [go] . . .
> and sit in rows listening to those vain quarrelsome men?
> Bloated, opinionated, untidy men, that is how I see them,
> cosseted by the academic life, the literary life, by women.
> (*Something*, p. 24)

Munro saves this story from becoming merely an anti-
academia tirade by shifting the focus from the narrator's bitterness to her moving response to a story by Hugo she discovered a
dozen or so years after their separation, and her rationalizing
that she should write him a letter and "apologize . . . for not
having believed he would be a writer" (*Something*, p. 43). A
major point of this story is that she does not send such a letter—it
was, indeed, "something" she *meant* to tell him — for as she
attempts to write it, her words are transformed into sharp, bitter
outbursts against Hugo. She is ultimately unable to forgive him
for his double betrayal: in life, and in art, for in his story he had
immortalized their former landlady's daughter, whom they had
privately nicknamed "the harlot-in-residence." "She has passed
into Art," the narrator ironically reflects. "It doesn't happen to
everybody" (*Something*, p. 43). There may be other reasons why
spouses of writers become bitter, but this kind of betrayal,
Munro seems to suggest, must surely be a major one. The
implications of the title word become clear, and one is reminded
of Brendan Tierney's similar fictional exploitation of human
"material" in Brian Moore's *An Answer from Limbo*.

"We were strong on irony," Hugo's ex-wife ruefully recalls,
and this recollection has, of course, its specific aptness within the
context of that story. But it also points to an underlying element
in Munro's fiction in general: hers is an irony which both enlarges
the possibilities of experience and helps define her characters'

attributes that operate within a given situation. In some cases, the irony is delightful and benign, as in "How I Met My Husband," which is not without its touches of an O. Henry or Somerset Maugham ending—inevitability combined with moral relief — and sometimes, as in "The Office" from her first collection, the irony turns the story into a cryptic *tour de force*. What we have here is the simultaneous creation of two imaginative worlds, that created by the narrator in her arrangement of words, and that created by Mr. Malley, who arranges facts and implications to create a world that fits his views on women writers. ". . . I arrange words, and think it is my right to be rid of him" (*Dance*, p.74), muses the narrator, but she implicitly acknowledges that Mr. Malley's outrageous distortion of the facts creates its own kind of credible truth as well. Furthermore, of course, there is the irony residing in the contradictions posed by the narrator's proclaimed need for an office in which to write: Mr. Malley becomes at once both its justification and the force which renders it unworkable.

In other stories, Munro's irony operates to fuse fact and fancy into a nexus where it becomes both impossible and unnecessary to sort them out. In *Dance of the Happy Shades*, this situation is in a sense presexual, though the sexual dimension is occasionally implied in the world that is emerging for the youthful protagonist. In *Something I've Been Meaning to Tell You* and in *Who Do You Think You Are?*, these situations become increasingly sexual, for Munro seems to suggest that it is in such relationships that identities and roles become most frequently confused and interchangeable. Thus, "Tell Me Yes or No" turns on an ambiguity at the end which can spell out either complete control or a bitter desperation, and in the title story of this collection Munro balances the elements of event and fantasy so delicately that one is never sure exactly what the "something" is that Et has it in mind to tell the husband of her dead sister.

One clue to the meanings of these ambiguous stories lies in their formal structure, which reveals the nature of the reality that the narrator or protagonist is attempting to resolve. "Something I've Been Meaning to Tell You" consists of fifteen sections in which past and present events alternate inconsistently (though the second-to-last section leaps into the future and thus relegates all the others into the past). Indeed, there is a sense in which past and present are clearly interchangeable: Blaikie Noble returns to Mock Hill to drive a tour bus, and he again becomes a disturbing element in the lives of Char and Et, a situation identical to that of thirty years earlier. And, of course, Et's deliberate fabrication of Blaikie's elopement on this later occasion constitutes the event to render the cycle complete, though the harmony is broken, Char's suicide attempt this time being successful. In a sense, therefore, though Et is permanently on the brink of telling Arthur "something," just as all her life she has had to tell on somebody in order to achieve a recognition to match her sister's, the proliferation of events as reflected by these fifteen sections continually modifies just what it is that she is going to tell. Char remains in death, as in life, a perpetually beautiful and statuelike force, who in a very real way has denied Et even her final triumph.

"Tell Me Yes or No," on the other hand, is much more tightly structured, though its first-person point of view clearly reinforces the ambiguities of the relationship which is described. The brief prologue prepares us for the priority of the narrator's imagination, but the concluding passage of the fourth and last section (which constitutes both continuing action and epilogue) brings into question the distinction between invention and reality. In between are two roughly equal sections of summary and recollection, which obtain their authority from the sheer credibility of the events recalled: here is a realistic world of campuses and strollers and lunches and sexual assignations, and the narrator makes clear that she recognizes the moral issue involved. "Love is not in the least unavoidable, there is a choice made," she realizes. "It is just that it is hard to know when the choice was made, or when, in spite of seeming frivolous, it became irreversible" (*Something*, p. 111).

The realistic world created in these middle sections carries over into the final part, where both it and the narrator are transformed into something else. The real world becomes "this city of my imagination," while the narrator assumes the dual role of herself and the other betrayed mistress; what is not clear is just how much the narrator has in fact invented, and how much she is desperately rationalizing:

> Never mind. I invented her. I invented you, as far as my purposes go. I invented loving you and I invented your

death. I have my tricks and my trap doors, too. I don't understand their workings at the present moment, but I have to be careful, I won't speak against them. (*Something*, p. 124)

Not unlike Hugo's ex-wife in "Material," the narrator here assumes a position characterized by bitterness and the sense of rejection, a stance directed in part against the selfishness of men, but in part also against their own insufficiency. In a statement explaining her artistic credo, which is of particular relevance to this story, Munro has remarked upon the interchangeability of the words "remember" and "invent": ". . . the kind of remembering I mean is what fictional invention is; but I wanted to show, too, that it is not quite deliberate."[23]

These words, with very little distortion, could be spoken by Del Jordan at the conclusion of *Lives of Girls and Women*, for that book is on one level the chronicle of remembered events given a kind of fictional transformation. Throughout its separate but related episodes, Del never emerges as anyone who is consciously or willingly trying to save herself — that is, what she does is in a very real sense "not quite deliberate." It is true that from the outset she is in a state of incipient rebellion against the prevailing values of Jubilee, but she is also susceptible to — and indeed desirous of — some of the sordid experiences that befall her companions who, as Del later recalls, "faded into jobs and motherhood" (*Lives*, p. 196). It is, for example, curiosity as much as it is any streak of prurience that causes her to participate in Mr. Chamberlain's blunt and clumsy sexual overtures or to submit herself to the mechanical pawings of a local dance-hall creep.

Her progression from this stage of sexual perversion through the clinical sexual experimentation of Jerry Storey to consummation with Garnet French illustrates the confusions, contradictions, mysteries, and delights that beset an ordinary adolescent, and Del does achieve a genuine measure of satisfaction in recognizing that she is both "endangered and desired." But it is also a manifestation of the philosophy of life she takes unto herself in an intuitive way, in response to her mother's earnest stricture that it was up to women themselves to bring about changes in the lives of girls and women:

... I felt that it was not so different from all the other advice
handed out to women, to girls, advice that assumed being
female made you damageable, that a certain amount of
carefulness and solemn fuss and self-protection were called
for, whereas men were supposed to be able to go out and
take on all kinds of experiences and shuck off what they
didn't want and come back proud. Without even thinking
about it, I had decided to do the same. (*Lives*, p. 177)

In retrospect, it can be seen clearly that Del's experiences all
along contribute to this code, from her reading of Uncle Benny's
blazing tabloids, which make her "bloated and giddy with
revelations of evil, of its versatility and grand invention and
horrific playfulness" (*Lives*, p. 5), to her rejection of the potential
destruction she sees in her relationship with Garnet French.
Paradoxically, this final affirmation of her own authority and of
her own self derives not so much from any accumulation of
wisdom that all these experiences might have generated — a
kind of experiential counterpart to her mother's encyclopaedic
mission to bestow wisdom — but rather through an epiphany
which proclaims the residual import of innocence: "We had seen
in each other what we could not bear, and we had no idea that
people do see that, and go on, and hate and fight and try to kill
each other, various ways, then love some more" (*Lives*, p. 240).
There is always a strong sense of amazement at the human condition in Munro, a quality that seems to be born of her recognition
that ordinary people have an intangible talent or gift: not necessarily for wisdom or goodness or truth or beauty, though that
happens, too, but more frequently for lucking it out, for intuiting
a move or an action that will get them out of a present
predicament.

Keeping in mind Munro's artistic disclaimer that "this novel is
autobiographical in form but not in fact" (*Lives*, copyright
page), we can interpret Del's progression through the seven
sections (excluding the "Epilogue") in a number of ways. First,
in the narrow sense of the title's implication, these segments
depict in recognizable stages Del's life as she literally changes
from a girl to a woman, but of course the fact that all three title
nouns are plural warns us that it is not quite that simple. At first,
it is other lives which touch Del's life, but as her life converges

with, and passes by, that of her mother, it takes on its own significance, and she becomes unwittingly an agent of the transformation of others. In the "Flats Road" section, it is Uncle Benny's world, with its perversities and illogicalities, a "world like a troubling distorted reflection" (*Lives*, p.25), that overpowers Del to a point of immobility. But though his world, in a sense, has nothing more substantial about it than remembered tabloid headlines and the brief appearance of a frightful mail-order wife, "like something he might have made up" (*Lives*, p.27), the effect his life has on Del's acceptance of her parents' world is tangible indeed:

> But [my parents] were connected, and this connection was plain as a fence, it was between us and Uncle Benny, us and the Flats Road, it would stay between us and anything. . . . And upstairs seemed miles above them, dark and full of the noise of the wind. Up there you discovered what you never remembered down in the kitchen — that we were in a house as small and shut-up as any boat is on the sea, in the middle of a tide of howling weather. They seemed to be talking, playing cards, a long way away in a tiny spot of light, irrelevantly; yet this thought of them, prosaic as a hiccough, familiar as breath, was what held me, what winked at me from the bottom of the well as I fell into sleep. (*Lives*, p.26)

It is only in this opening section that Del's life is detached from her conscious control, and she is "held" here, in the absolute sense, by her parents for the last time. From this point on, her intuitive recognition of the plurality of experience enables her to begin the other growth process that parallels her sexual transition from girl to woman, her growth as a creative artist, which allows her to realize the relationship between factual remembering and "fictional invention." The two processes are not entirely separable, of course, and formally, the episodic structure of the novel is appropriate for this exercise since it allows Del to overlap her recounting of experience, so that the same event can have more than one significance. Process, too, or preparation, becomes more important than completion or event: it is, for example, Del's state of mind before Uncle Craig's funeral, rather than the funeral itself, that achieves significance, and later, in "Changes and Ceremonies," it is the rehearsals and preparation for the operetta that occupy Del's recollections. "What happened, after the operetta?" Del muses. "In one week it had sunk from sight" (*Lives*, p. 139), and she is quickly reassured again by the preparation for the next event — the final examinations.

Del ultimately comes to the realization, as the narrator did in "Material," that artistic growth is more than feeling or spontaneity, that it involves a conscious decision to order experience and to detect significances. The moment in *Lives* when Del's two growth processes — her sexual and her artistic — completely converge is dramatized by achievement of her first orgasm, and it is then that she intuitively senses a fundamental change in her relationship with Garnet and with reality:

> But I was amazed to undergo it in company, so to speak; it did seem almost too private, even lonely a thing, to find at the heart of love. . . . We had come out on another level — more solid, less miraculous, where cause and effect must be acknowledged, and love begins to flow in a deliberate pattern. (*Lives*, p. 229)

In a real sense, this is as far as sexual consummation can go, and thus Del's life has literally completed its transition from girl to woman. And again, as with the funeral, the operetta, the final examinations, the completed event quickly assumes a reduced reality, and other preparations and ceremonies take over. Thus, Garnet's attempt to baptize Del would not only ritualize their sexual relationship, but it would formalize her psychological and creative surrender to something that she is not ready to accept, reflected in the ironic truth in Garnet's accusal "You think you're too good for it" (*Lives*, p. 238). It is not an easy decision for her, and she is saved from Garnet — as Rose is not to be saved from Patrick — more by his unavailability than by her willpower. Her final thoughts, "*Garnet French, Garnet French, Garnet French. Real Life*" (*Lives*, p. 242), reflect her ongoing struggle with the doubleness of reality, adumbrated for her long before in the "Flat's Road" section, where the "marvellous" of Uncle Benny's world clashed with the "ordinary" of her parents' world. Just as the latter tenuously won out there, so for the moment "real life" wins out over the "dark side, the strange side" of life represented by Garnet.

This choice *seems* to be vindicated in the "Epilogue" to *Lives*, but Del is left troubled and unsure. On the one hand, she recognizes that "people's lives, in Jubilee as elsewhere, were dull, simple, amazing and unfathomable . . ." (*Lives*, p. 253), and like her Uncle Craig, she too is "greedy" and "voracious" for all details of Jubilee. But on the other hand, she suddenly realizes that Bobby Sherriff, whom she had thought she had "doomed to fiction," in fact inhabits a world she does not comprehend. Like the ladies at Miss Marsalles' recital who fail to understand "that one communiqué from the other country where she lives" (*Dance*, p. 224), so Del receives a stylized message from Bobby Sherriff, "a letter, or a whole word, in an alphabet I did not know" (*Lives*, p. 254). In her greed for Jubilee, Del the artist ironically inherits all the worlds that Del the girl and woman experienced, and she begins to grasp the nature of her dilemma. "It is a shock," she muses, "when you have dealt so cunningly, powerfully, with reality, to come back and find it still there" (*Lives*, p. 251). This realization, we will see, is not unlike that which Rose ponders over numerous times in *Who Do You Think You Are?*.

The ten interrelated stories that comprise this book (for which "Simon's Luck" and the title story were specifically written) together constitute a much more ambiguous world than that presented in *Lives*, though the two books have much in common. Both depict the growth of a young girl to maturity, and both conclude this growth with the juxtaposition of the protagonist against a character who simultaneously inhabits the normal world and the irrational world. Bobby Sherriff's counterpart in *Who*, Ralph Gillespie, has acquired his status by doing imitations of one of West Hanratty's most grotesque characters, Milton Homer, and so adept has he become at this imitative role that people gradually find it increasingly difficult to keep the two identities separate. Rose, briefly attracted to Ralph during her high-school days, discovers as an actress years later that she can imitate *his* imitation of Milton, and thus the title question of this book assumes an ongoing irony.

This book is, on the whole, more despairing than *Lives*; the humour is bleaker, the contradictions more threatening, and the resolutions more tentative. The third-person point of view allows Munro more distancing and detachment from the particular dilemmas Rose faces, and it allows her to divide her sympathy fairly evenly between Rose and Flo. In this process, Flo emerges with a much greater stature than did Del's mother in *Lives*, for we see her operating very clearly within a tangible moral and survival code that consistently reveals her strength as the stories proceed. Her death, foreshadowed in "Spelling," like that of May's grandmother in "A Trip to the Coast," contributes a kind of triumph over all those who have tried to manipulate her life. Another modification over *Lives* lies in the book's overlap structure; whereas in the earlier book it was somewhat incidental, here it is integral to the organization of Rose's experiences, and we are therefore able to observe her from a number of angles simultaneously.

Rose has much in common with Del and with other youthful protagonists in Munro's fiction, for she too feels a need "to pursue absurdities" (*Who*, p. 1) in her incipient rebellion against her parents. In the "Royal Beatings" section, there is, however, no clear-cut moral issue on which to act; both Flo, as the instigator of the beating, and Rose's father, as its administrator, are uncertain about the legitimacy of their cause; as its victim, Rose protests more pain than she actually experiences. All three are therefore undergoing a ritual which in that particular family is only a vestigial remnant of what Flo had herself gone through. And a grim parallel to it is reflected in the beating administered to Becky Tyde's father by three stalwart citizens of the town, a beating which leads to his death. Compared to Uncle Benny's blazing headlines, the reality of horror in West Hanratty is grim indeed.

Throughout the separate episodes of this book, Munro's constant use of retrospection and anticipation not only allows us to see an experience in a larger context, but compels us to make some moral judgement on it. For example, the "royal beating" episode just referred to allows Rose immediately to speculate on what will be the uneasy compromise effected between herself, her father, and Flo:

> Rose will understand that life has started up again, that
> they will all sit around the table eating again, listening to

the radio news. Tomorrow morning, maybe even tonight. Unseemly and unlikely as that may be. They will be embarrassed, but rather less than you might expect considering how they have behaved. They will feel a queer lassitude, a convalescent indolence, not far off satisfaction. (*Who*, p. 19)

But the full moral ramifications of this experience are delayed until years later, when Rose as an actress living in Toronto again hears on the radio news an interview with an oldtimer who turns out to be Hat Nettleton, one of the three men who had beaten up Tyde. "Horsewhipper into centenarian," Rose muses. "Oldest resident. Oldest horsewhipper. Living link with our past" (*Who*, p. 22). Another irony resides in the fact that Nettleton (incidentally, a character resurrected from "Executioners") is in the same nursing home as Flo, herself a victim of another beating, but who at the time of the interview, "had stopped talking," "had removed herself, and spent most of her time sitting in a corner of her crib, looking crafty and disagreeable, not answering anybody, though she occasionally showed her feelings by biting a nurse" (*Who*, p. 22). Whose was the victory? In light of Nettleton's public recognition and Flo's Bartlebyian triumph of silence, Rose from this delayed vantage point must wonder about her far-off minor and temporary victory over her parents.

Between adolescence and marriage, Rose in effect plays many variations on this survival game, and she early learns that trying to be neutral is more dangerous than taking sides. "Learning to survive, no matter with what cravenness and caution, what shocks and forebodings, is not the same as being miserable," she recognizes. "It is too interesting" (*Who*, p. 27). Among the "interesting" routes to survival is that which takes the protagonist through to an understanding and experiencing of the sexual drive, and, as was the case with Del Jordan, it is curiosity, "more constant, more imperious, than any lust" (*Who*, p. 62), that impels Rose along that route. Her routine adolescent experiences are both voyeuristic and vicarious; and, given the grimmer vision that informs this book, are blunter and more ambiguous than their counterparts in *Lives*. She watches, "interested but not alarmed" (*Who*, p. 27), as Shortie McGill *performs* (Flo's expression) upon his sister Franny in the boys' toilet; she cravenly

nurses her schoolgirl crush on the beautiful Cora, imitating her
every word and gesture, and we detect here the incipient manifes-
tations of what Rose eventually will come to understand:

> The opening, the increase, the flow, of love. Sexual love,
> not sure yet exactly what it needed to concentrate on. It
> must be there from the start, like the hard white honey in
> the pail, waiting to melt and flow. There was some sharp-
> ness lacking, some urgency missing; there was the inci-
> dental difference in the sex of the person chosen; otherwise
> it was the same thing, the same thing that has overtaken
> Rose since. The high tide; the indelible folly; the flash flood.
> (*Who*, p. 33)

The vicarious and the voyeuristic are partially resolved in the
"Wild Swans" section of the book, one of the most subtle narratives anywhere in Munro, but Rose's experience here remains in
that ambiguous area that lies between fantasy and reality: Rose
must clearly know, but the reader is never sure, whether she has
been violated in fact or only in fancy. "Her imagination seemed
to have created this reality," she muses, "a reality she was not
prepared for at all" (*Who*, p. 61), and yet the reality of the man is
tangible enough, with "something crude and pushy and childish
about him" (*Who*, p. 64). What the book's dustcover calls "a
bizarre sexual initiation" takes on all kinds of ambiguities as
Munro's verb-tense modulations confuse present possibilities
with future actualities and as we are made aware of the relationships between the progress of the man's hand and the unfolding
landscape Rose watches through the train window.

Just as Del Jordan's landscape had changed from profuse to
erotic to postcoital during her vicarious escapade with Mr.
Chamberlain, so we witness a change here, represented by the
difference between landscape and cityscape. Either in fancy or in
fact, Rose knows she will soon surrender, a decision made as the
train crosses the Niagara Escarpment:

> . . . as they looked down at the preglacial valley, the silver-
> wooded rubble of little hills, as they came sliding down to
> the shores of Lake Ontario, she would make this slow, and
> silent, and definite, declaration, perhaps disappointing as

much as satisfying the hand's owner. He would not lift his eyelids, his face would not alter, his fingers would not hesitate, but would go powerfully and discreetly to work. Invasion, and welcome, and sunlight flashing far and wide on the lake water; miles of bare orchards stirring round Burlington. (*Who*, p.63)

But after the experience is over, the landscape changes to urban blight, as, "victim and accomplice," she is "borne past Glassco's Jams and Marmalades, past the big pulsating pipes of oil refineries" (*Who*, p.63). And in a kind of surrealistic vision, she imagines the inhabitants of the city united in some obscene league reenacting her fallen state, "where even the children seemed to be frolicking lewdly in the schoolyards, and the very truckdrivers stopped at the railway crossings must be thrusting their thumbs gleefully into curled hands" (*Who*, p.63). Though she emerges from this escapade manipulated but chaste, she nevertheless remains suspended between the dualities which are responsible for her confusion over the reality / fantasy nature of this moment. ". . . that she had come as close as she had, to what could happen, was an unwelcome thing," she rationalizes, yet she is still eager for a kind of metamorphosis or transformation to a stage where she could "enter on preposterous adventures in [her] own, but newly named, skin" (*Who*, p.64).

In her subsequent sexual experiences — with Patrick, both as lover and husband, with Simon and other casual lovers, in her strangely voyeuristic *ménage à trois* with Clifford and Jocelyn — this stranger on the train "remained on call, so to speak . . . ready to slip into place at a critical moment" (*Who*, pp.63–64). It is as though Rose is forever condemned to inhabit a world whose reality she is unsure of, an uncertainty that derives in part from her own chameleonlike nature, and in part from the unpredictability of the physical details of the real world — weather, train and bus schedules, cancelled meetings, and so on. Imitation, duplicity, deceit, dissimulation — strategems she casually utilizes to resolve momentary crises — have become by the end of the book indistinguishable from other aspects of her operative reality.

Within this perspective, the title words of this book have a precise relevance to Rose's situation, and though the literal words are hurled at her only twice, once by Flo, and once by her teacher, Miss Hattie, Rose is aware of their lingering presence, and of their import:

> This was not the first time in her life Rose had been asked who she thought she was; in fact the question had often struck her like a monotonous gong and she paid no attention to it. But she understood, afterwards, that . . . [t]he lesson she was trying to teach here was more important to her than any poem, and one she truly believed Rose needed. It seemed that many other people believed she needed it, too. (*Who*, p. 196)

The question, too, where it is not directly articulated, is dramatized in a number of situations throughout the book: in Rose's transformation when she enters high school across the bridge in Hanratty, in the sorority girls' amazement that Patrick Blatchford should be attracted to her, in her ongoing rivalry with her half brother Brian, and, indeed, in her very choice to become a radio and television actress. And, of course, in terms of the structure of this book, it is appropriate that the question be articulated only in the opening and closing sections: in between we are witness to the many experiential searchings that Rose undertakes to find answers to that elusive question. It is appropriate, too, that the book ends on another question, one that not only evokes the dilemma Del had found herself in with Bobby Sherriff, but also signifies that in a world where chance rules as much as design (Ralph's life was "one slot over from her own"), there is in effect no answer Rose can give, except that she is a changeling of sorts shaped and altered by her tenuous and shifting human relationships.

The realization that Rose the seasoned actress arrives at here derives ultimately from the same kinds of experiences that the youthful Del Jordan was only beginning to anticipate in "Walker Brothers Cowboy," the opening story of Munro's fictional chronicle. In between we have been witness to the many variations that it is possible to play on a single theme, a theme that in its simplest form reflects the tensions generated between the Hanratty / Jubilee derivations of the Munro protagonists and their impulse for a larger and richer experience. We are moved by her achievements here much the same as the people in "Royal Beatings" were moved by the skills that Rose's father displayed in his furniture-repair shop, and we wholeheartedly transfer Rose's compliment about her father to Munro herself: "That was his pride: to startle people with such fine work . . ." (*Who*, p.2). In our astonishment at what Munro has accomplished, and in our attempt to recognize the underlying components of her talents, we can perhaps do no better than consider a statement by one of her acknowledged influences, Eudora Welty:

Art . . . is never the voice of a country; it is an even more precious thing, the voice of the individual, doing its best to speak, not comfort of any sort, indeed, but truth.[24]

NOTES

[1]Alan Twigg, "What Is: Alice Munro," in *For Openers: Conversations with Twenty-Four Canadian Writers* (Madeira Park, B.C.: Harbour, 1981), p.18.

[2]Graeme Gibson, "Alice Munro," in *Eleven Canadian Novelists Interviewed by Graeme Gibson* (Toronto: House of Anansi, 1973), p.241.

[3]Gibson, p.248.

[4]Mari Stainsby, "Alice Munro Talks with Mari Stainsby," *British Columbia Library Quarterly*, 35, No. 1 (July 1971), 27–30.

[5]Hallvard Dahlie, "Unconsummated Relationships: Isolation and Rejection in Alice Munro's Stories," *World Literature Written in English*, 11, No. 1 (April 1972), 43–48.

[6]Rae McCarthy Macdonald, "A Madman Loose in the World: The Vision of Alice Munro," *Modern Fiction Studies*, 22 (Autumn 1976), 365–74.

[7]Beverly Rasporich, "Child-Women and Primitives in the Fiction of Alice Munro," *Atlantis*, 1, No. 2 (Spring 1976), 5.

[8]J. R. (Tim) Struthers, "Reality and Ordering: The Growth of a Young Artist in *Lives of Girls and Women*," *Essays on Canadian Writing*, No. 3 (Fall 1975), pp.32–46.

[9]W. R. Martin, "Alice Munro and James Joyce," *Journal of Canadian Fiction*, No. 24 [1979], pp.120–26.

[10]J. R. (Tim) Struthers, "Alice Munro and the American South," in

Here and Now, Vol. 1 of *The Canadian Novel*, ed. John Moss (Toronto: NC, 1978), pp. 121–33.

[11]David Monoghan, "Confinement and Escape in Alice Munro's 'The Flats Road,' " *Studies in Short Fiction*, 14 (Spring 1977), 165–68.

[12]Marcia Allentuck, "Resolution and Independence in the Work of Alice Munro," *World Literature Written in English*, 16 (Nov. 1977), 340–43.

[13]John Moss, "Alice in the Looking Glass: Munro's *Lives of Girls and Women*," in *Sex and Violence in the Canadian Novel: The Ancestral Present* (Toronto: McClelland and Stewart, 1977), pp. 54–68.

[14]Rae McCarthy Macdonald, "Structure and Detail in *Lives of Girls and Women*," *Studies in Canadian Literature*, 3 (Summer 1978), 199–210.

[15]Helen Hoy, " 'Dull, Simple, Amazing and Unfathomable': Paradox and Double Vision in Alice Munro's Fiction," *Studies in Canadian Literature*, 5 (Spring 1980), 100–15.

[16]Bronwen Wallace, "Women's Lives: Alice Munro," in *The Human Elements: Critical Essays*, ed. David Helwig (Ottawa: Oberon, 1978), pp. 52–67.

[17]Nancy Bailey, "The Masculine Image in *Lives of Girls and Women*," *Canadian Literature*, No. 80 (Spring 1979), p. 117.

[18]Twigg, p. 15.

[19]Alice Munro, *Dance of the Happy Shades* (Toronto: Ryerson, 1968), p. 196. All further references to this work appear in the text.

[20]"Walking on Water," in *Something I've Been Meaning to Tell You: Thirteen Stories* (Toronto: McGraw-Hill Ryerson, 1974), p. 75. All further references to this work appear in the text.

[21]*Who Do You Think You Are?* (Toronto: Macmillan, 1978), pp. 172–73. All further references to this work appear in the text.

[22]*Lives of Girls and Women* (Toronto: McGraw-Hill Ryerson, 1971), pp. 177. All further references to this work appear in the text.

[23]Alice Munro, "The Colonel's Hash Resettled," in *The Narrative Voice: Short Stories and Reflections by Canadian Authors*, ed. John Metcalf (Toronto: McGraw-Hill Ryerson, 1972), p. 183.

[24]Eudora Welty, "Place in Fiction," in *The Eye of the Story: Selected Essays and Reviews* (New York: Random House, 1978), p. 117.

SELECTED BIBLIOGRAPHY

Primary Sources

Munro, Alice. *Dance of the Happy Shades*. Toronto: Ryerson, 1968.
———. *Lives of Girls and Women*. Toronto: McGraw-Hill Ryerson, 1971.
———. *Something I've Been Meaning to Tell You: Thirteen Stories*. Toronto: McGraw-Hill Ryerson, 1974.
———. *Who Do You Think You Are?* Toronto: Macmillan, 1978.
———. *The Moons of Jupiter*. Toronto: Macmillan, 1982.

Secondary Sources

Allentuck, Marcia. "Resolution and Independence in the Work of Alice Munro." *World Literature Written in English*, 16 (Nov. 1977), 340–43.
Bailey, Nancy. "The Masculine Image in *Lives of Girls and Women*." *Canadian Literature*, No. 80 (Spring 1979), pp. 113–20.
Conron, Brandon. "Munro's Wonderland." *Canadian Literature*, No. 78 (Autumn 1978), pp. 109–12, 114–18, 120–23.
Cook, D.E. "Alice Munro: A Checklist (to December 31, 1974)." *Journal of Canadian Fiction*, No. 16 [1976], pp. 131–36.
Dahlie, Hallvard. "Unconsummated Relationships: Isolation and Rejection in Alice Munro's Stories." *World Literature Written in English*, 11, No. 1 (April 1972), 43–48.
———. "The Fiction of Alice Munro." *Ploughshares*, 4, No. 3 ([Summer] 1978), 56–71.
Dombrowski, Eileen. "'Down to Death': Alice Munro and Transience." *The University of Windsor Review*, 14, No. 1 (Fall–Winter 1978), 21–29.
Gibson, Graeme. "Alice Munro." In *Eleven Canadian Novelists Interviewed by Graeme Gibson*. Toronto: House of Anansi, 1973, pp. 237–64.
Hoy, Helen. "'Dull, Simple, Amazing and Unfathomable': Paradox and Double Vision in Alice Munro's Fiction." *Studies in Canadian Literature*, 5 (Spring 1980), 100–15.

Macdonald, Rae McCarthy. "A Madman Loose in the World: The Vision of Alice Munro." *Modern Fiction Studies*, 22 (Autumn 1976), 365–74.

———. "Structure and Detail in *Lives of Girls and Women*." *Studies in Canadian Literature*, 3 (Summer 1978), 199–210.

MacKendrick, Louis K., ed. *Probable Fictions: Alice Munro's Narrative Acts*. Downsview, Ont.: ECW, 1983.

Martin, W. R. "Alice Munro and James Joyce." *Journal of Canadian Fiction*, No. 24 [1979], pp. 120–26.

Metcalf, John. "A Conversation with Alice Munro." *Journal of Canadian Fiction*, 1, No. 4 (Fall 1972), 54–62.

Monoghan, David. "Confinement and Escape in Alice Munro's 'The Flats Road.' " *Studies in Short Fiction*, 14 (Spring 1977), 165–68.

Moss, John. "Alice in the Looking Glass: Munro's *Lives of Girls and Women*." In *Sex and Violence in the Canadian Novel: The Ancestral Present*. Toronto: McClelland and Stewart, 1977, pp. 54–68.

New, W. H. "Pronouns and Propositions: Alice Munro's Stories." *Open Letter*, 3rd ser., No. 5 (Summer 1976), pp. 40–49.

Packer, Miriam. "*Lives of Girls and Women*: A Creative Search for Completion." In *Here and Now*. Vol. 1 of *The Canadian Novel*. Ed. John Moss. Toronto: NC, 1978, pp. 134–44.

Rasporich, Beverly. "Child-Women and Primitives in the Fiction of Alice Munro." *Atlantis*, 1, No. 2 (Spring 1976), 4–14.

Stainsby, Mari. "Alice Munro Talks with Mari Stainsby." *British Columbia Library Quarterly*, 35, No. 1 (July 1971), 27–30.

Struthers, J. R. (Tim). "Reality and Ordering: The Growth of a Young Artist in *Lives of Girls and Women*." *Essays on Canadian Writing*, No. 3 (Fall 1975), pp. 32–46.

———. "Alice Munro and the American South." In *Here and Now*. Vol. 1 of *The Canadian Novel*. Ed. John Moss. Toronto: NC, 1978, pp. 121–33.

Thacker, Robert. "Alice Munro: An Annotated Bibliography." In *The Annotated Bibliography of Canada's Major Authors*. Ed. Robert Lecker and Jack David. Vol. V. Downsview, Ont.: ECW, 1984, 354–414.

Twigg, Alan. "What Is: Alice Munro." In *For Openers: Conversations with Twenty-Four Canadian Writers*. Madeira Park, B.C.: Harbour, 1981, pp. 13–20.

Wallace, Bronwen. "Women's Lives: Alice Munro." In *The Human Elements: Critical Essays*. Ed. David Helwig. Ottawa: Oberon, 1978, pp. 52–67.

Sheila Watson (1909–)

STEPHEN SCOBIE

Sheila Watson (1909–   )

STEPHEN SCOBIE

Biography

THE MAJOR FACT about Sheila Watson's biography is that she does not have one; or, rather, that she would regard it as irrelevant. She would doubtless prefer that this section not be included in the study of her work. Like T. S. Eliot, the "invisible poet,"[1] she has cultivated a style of impersonality, and, though biographical elements do enter into her writing, she would hold to the principle that only the text itself is of legitimate interest to the critic.

Her life has been fascinating, not in terms of any major dramatic events, but in terms of the people she has known, and the periods of Canadian intellectual history she has been a part of. But it is a story which she can only tell herself — as, indeed, all her friends have been urging her to do for years. Once, over an excellent meal of Pacific salmon cooked by her husband, Wilfred, I heard her embark on a series of personal anecdotes, until Wilfred remarked, "Now, now, Sheila, you're getting biographical." It was a joke, but the caution and reticence which the joke implies have been fundamentally characteristic of Sheila Watson's attitude towards any biographical criticism of her writing.

The facts of her life may be briefly stated — and in this account I am deeply indebted to the short biography prepared by Diane Bessai and David Jackel for their tributary volume *Figures in a Ground: Canadian Essays on Modern Literature Collected in Honor of Sheila Watson* (1978).[2] Sheila Watson was born on 24 October 1909 in New Westminster, B.C., where her father, Dr. Charles Edward Doherty, was Superintendent of the Provincial Mental Hospital. Her childhood on the grounds of the hospital is reflected (and, of course, changed, mythologized) in some of her short stories, notably "Antigone." Her upbringing was strictly Roman Catholic, her primary and secondary schooling being with the Sisters of Saint Anne in New Westminster, and her first two years of university being at the Convent of the Sacred Heart in Vancouver. She studied English at the University of British Columbia, graduating with Honours in 1931; in 1932 she obtained an Academic Teaching Certificate; and in 1933 she completed an M.A., with a thesis on Addison and Steele.

Over the next ten years, Sheila Watson taught school in New Westminster, Langley Prairie, Duncan, Mission City, and—most significantly, from the point of view of her writing — in Dog Creek, a tiny community on the Fraser River between Ashcroft and Williams Lake. "I didn't choose," she recalled later, "it chose me. It was the only place in 1934 that said, 'Come, and teach our children.' "[3] Years later, it was to become the model for the setting of The Double Hook.

In 1941 Sheila Doherty married Wilfred Watson, "playwright, poet, teacher and literary theorist,"[4] a marriage which has lasted to this day. "To be with Sheila and Wilfred Watson," Henry Kreisel has written, "is to be in the presence of two of the most original, the most stimulating minds in the country."[5] After the war, the Watsons lived in Toronto, Powell River, and Calgary before settling in Edmonton, where they both held positions in the Department of English at the University of Alberta.

In Toronto, Sheila Watson pursued her academic interest in the works of Wyndham Lewis, the English painter, novelist, and polemicist, under the direction of Marshall McLuhan, "who had known Lewis while he lived in Toronto and Windsor during the war years, and was the only professor of English in Canada who had any extensive knowledge of Lewis's work at that time" ("Sheila Watson: A Biography," p.3). Her doctoral study, "Wyndham Lewis and Expressionism," supervised by McLuhan, was completed in 1965.

During the 1950s, Sheila Watson began publishing a small number of short stories, and was also working on her novel, The Double Hook. According to Bessai and Jackel, the novel was completed during her residence in Calgary between 1951 and 1953, but it was not published until 1959 ("Sheila Watson: A Biography," p.2). A Swedish translation appeared in 1963, and a French one in 1976.[6]

From 1961 until 1975, Sheila Watson taught at the University of Alberta. "In the winter, on very cold days, you can see her small figure, wrapped up in a huge, yellowish fur coat of indeterminate ancestry, walking across the snow-covered campus," Henry Kreisel recalls. "She seems vulnerable, fragile almost. A strong gust of wind might blow her away. But that's an illusion. The small figure creates a space of its own, asserts itself, and yet seems an integral part of the landscape."[7] For generations of staff and students in Edmonton, Sheila Watson was indeed "an integral part of the landscape." She and Wilfred formed the unquestioned centre around which the literary life of the city revolved. Wilfred was writing prolifically — plays, poems — but even Sheila's silence commanded attention and respect. Endlessly generous in devoting time to her students, she illuminated the lives and the studies of all those privileged to work with her.

In 1971 she was instrumental in founding *White Pelican: A Quarterly Review of the Arts*, whose initial editorial board consisted of Sheila Watson, Stephen Scobie, Douglas Barbour, John Orrell, Norman Yates, and Dorothy Livesay.[8] The magazine ran for eighteen issues, 4½ years, during which time it published some of the most advanced work in writing and graphics being done in Canada. *White Pelican* also published two books of poetry, Wilfred Watson's *The Sorrowful Canadians*, and Miriam Mandel's *Lions at Her Face*, which won the Governor General's Award in 1973.

In 1974 a special issue of *Open Letter*[9] collected all of Sheila Watson's published writing outside of *The Double Hook*. (See below, "The Short Stories," for a fuller account of the contents of this issue.) Apart from two translations of stories by Madeleine Ferron in Philip Stratford's *Stories from Québec*,[10] this collection represented the total of her new publications until the appearance of the startling short story *And the four animals* in May 1980.[11] *Figures in a Ground*, a collection of essays in her honour, was published by Western Producer Prairie Books in 1978; after her retirement from the University of Alberta, a special prize in Canadian literature was inaugurated in her name by the Department of English.

Sheila Watson retired from the University of Alberta, at the rank of full professor, in 1975, and Wilfred Watson retired two years later. In 1980 they left Edmonton and returned to

Vancouver Island, just north of Nanaimo, on the coastline where Wilfred had spent much of his childhood. Retirement has dulled nothing of the sharpness of Sheila Watson's mind, or of the energy of her contribution and commitment to the continuing cause of contemporary Canadian literature.

Tradition and Milieu

In the absence of any detailed biographical or autobiographical account of the development of Sheila Watson's cultural theories and ideals, it is dangerous to speculate on the influences upon her writing of the biographical facts sketched in the previous section. The biography does, however, hint at the range of ideas and influences to which she was exposed: something of the characteristic duality of her thinking, the pattern of the double hook, may be seen in the various juxtapositions of convent schooling and avant-garde literature, of the need for order and the need for disorder, of the local and the cosmopolitan, of conservative tradition and endlessly youthful intellectual inquiry.

"If men live at all," says the doctor/father in "Antigone," "it is because discipline saves their life for them."[12] Insofar as the short stories can be taken as reliable guides, we may suppose that the experience of growing up among people with disordered minds produced a sense of the need for order: an order reinforced by the conservative tendencies of a religious upbringing and a convent schooling. At the same time, however, the hospital environment must also have encouraged a sense of tolerance for the sheer range and oddity of the human psyche. Antigone, after all, is engaged in an act of rebellion, which authority accepts.

The religious element is seldom obtrusive in Watson's writing — certainly, *The Double Hook* is in no way a narrowly dogmatic novel — but it is always, undeniably, present. Watson does not preach in her works, but neither does she avoid the implications of her beliefs. She responded, of course, to the intellectual Christianity of Eliot; but it was the much more secular Wyndham Lewis who became the focus of her academic interest.

To speak of Watson's "tradition and milieu" is, in effect, to speak of the whole culture of modernism, which was obsessed equally by the impulse to order and by the desire, in Ezra Pound's

phrase, to "make it new." It was in some ways a very conservative culture, looking back to all-encompassing world views,
steeped in the literature and mythology of previous ages; yet, for
its contemporaries, it was also revolutionary, an avant-garde, the
latest thing. While Watson was a student at the University of
British Columbia, Bessai and Jackel record, ". . . no unnecessary
and artificial distinctions were made between modern British and
American writing; the students read contemporary authors as
their works became available: Eliot, Pound, Virginia Woolf,
Dorothy Richardson, Lawrence, Hemingway, Faulkner, Dos
Passos" ("Sheila Watson: A Biography," p. 1). Watson still
recalls the excitement of reading Eliot's *Four Quartets* one by
one, as they were published. (And yet, at the same time as she
was absorbing the most advanced of international literature, she
was teaching grades four, five, and six in Duncan, Mission City,
and Dog Creek.)

The Double Hook displays, in its individual way, many of the
characteristics of modernism. Its theme is essentially conservative — the need for social traditions and religious rituals as the
means by which moral value may be given to community life —
while its form is experimental. It is tightly controlled, Imagistic
in its conciseness; like Eliot and Joyce, it uses mythology as a
medium for correlating multiple layers of allusion and meaning.
The modernist influence on Watson would have found strong
reinforcement in the literary atmosphere of Toronto in the
middle to late 1950s, at the time of the so-called "mythopoeic"
school of Canadian writing, under the tutelage of Northrop Frye.
In 1957, when Watson was studying in Toronto, the Governor
General's Award for poetry was won by Jay Macpherson's *The
Boatman* — and in 1955, of course, the award went to Wilfred
Watson's *Friday's Child*. (Sheila Watson has always been an
ardent supporter and advocate of her husband's writing.)

Again, however, one must caution against ascribing too great
an importance to these influences. During the 1950s, Watson
spent more time in Calgary than she did in Toronto, and her
major contact in Toronto was not Frye but McLuhan — who, as
has frequently been stressed, was himself of a conservative cast of
mind, deploring the very trends which he was so acutely
describing. By her own account (which will be discussed in more
detail in "The Double Hook," below), she began writing *The*

264   SHEILA WATSON

Double Hook as a reaction *against* the prevailing literary climate
and received opinions on the validity of the "regional" novel.

While there may have been some influence, then, from the
"mythopoeic" poetry of the 1950s, it is harder to see any
significant relation between Watson's work and earlier prose
fiction in Canada. The passionate but clumsy intensities of Frederick Philip Grove; the dreary and derivative banalities of Morley
Callaghan; the urbane and academic essay-writing of Hugh
MacLennan: none of these prepares us for the grace and intellectual daring of *The Double Hook*. Watson does not stand as the
culmination of any movement in Canadian fiction: she stands at
the start. It is she who made modern Canadian writing possible.
There is no point in listing names of those who have been
influenced by her; such a list would have to include every serious
writer in Canada for the last twenty years.

After 1961, when she was appointed to the University of
Alberta, Edmonton became the focus for Watson's literary life.
Here her influence was most directly felt by the students, especially the graduate students in early twentieth-century British
literature, whose work she stimulated and nurtured, but the
clearest record of her contribution during these years is to be
found in the pages of *White Pelican*. The magazine was run by an
editorial board, each of whose members was responsible for individual issues, but the overall guidance and inspiration of the
editorial policy may still be identified as Watson's. A partial list
of contributors to *White Pelican* will give some notion of its
range and importance: Douglas Barbour, Ted Blodgett, Wayne
Clifford, Frank Davey, Samuel R. Delany, Gail Fox, Gary
Geddes, Aritha van Herk, Roy Kiyooka, Henry Kreisel, Karen
Lawrence, Dennis Lee, Douglas Lochhead, Pat Lowther, Miriam
Mandel, Steve McCaffery, Barry McKinnon, George Melnyk,
Shirley Neuman, bpNichol, Michael Ondaatje, P. K. Page,
Monty Reid, Harry Savage, Stephen Scobie, Sid Stephen, Sharon
Stevenson, Wilfred Watson, Tom Wayman, Jon Whyte, Rudy
Wiebe, Norman Yates. The title was chosen, characteristically,
for its regional associations as much as for its mythological
image. The white pelican nests and breeds in Western Canada
but also moves freely across international borders; an editorial
in the first issue discoursed eruditely on the Greek origins
of the name, offered quotations from Sir Thomas Browne and

William Wordsworth, and concluded with a remark by Frank Michler Chapman, curator of the American Museum of National History, on the possibility of ". . . European and American Pelicans, following in the wake of an advancing favorable isotherm . . . meet[ing] again on the shores of the Polar Sea."[13]

In terms of the literary traditions and milieu within which Sheila Watson has lived, and to which she has made such major contributions, it might well be said that her whole career has constituted just such an "advancing favorable isotherm."

Critical Overview and Context

The first criticism of *The Double Hook* came before the novel was even published. Nervous at the then unheard-of venture of giving a "serious" novel its first publication in paperback form, McClelland and Stewart included an advance comment from Professor F. M. Salter, who described it as "a book of amazing beauty, artistry and power," and predicted that the author "will find her audience among those whose reading muscles are capable of exercise and development; and of these the number will grow, since the most infectious thing in the world is enthusiasm."[14]

The growth, however, was to be slow, at least in terms of informed critical response; it was not until ten years after its publication that *The Double Hook* began to accumulate a serious critical literature. Perhaps it was inevitable that time had to pass before the full impact of the novel could be felt. For example, in the 1961 edition of *Creative Writing in Canada*, Desmond Pacey says only that *The Double Hook* is "technically the most adventurous" of a group of recent novels: ". . . obliquely and allusively, by a technique which resembles that of gathering what goes on in a closed room by listening at the keyhole, she gradually reveals to us a disturbing story of lust and jealousy in a small British Columbian settlement." Pacey then goes on to devote twice as much space to Charles E. Israel, whom he believes "will eventually rank as an important novelist."[15]

Much more perceptive was the commentary by Hugo McPherson in the 1965 edition of the *Literary History of Canada: Cana-*

dian Literature in English: "This story, as simple as a medieval folk ballad, is told with a poetic compression and allusiveness, and a vividness of imagery that make its regional setting both a sharply realized *here* and 'an everywhere.' Repeatedly the style kindles echoes from Eliot and Faulkner, Job and the *New Testament*, and Anglo-Saxon poetry, but Mrs. Watson is so fully in control that idiom and action never gape apart. . . . *The Double Hook*, indeed, is the most literary, and probably the most sophisticated novel of the period."[16]

In its time, *The Double Hook* has received more than its fair share of bad criticism. The entry on Sheila Watson in Clara Thomas' *Our Nature — Our Voices* (1972) is adequate if unexciting, apart from the following astonishing statement: "On its simplest level, [*The Double Hook*] can be read as a mystery story. The mother, Mrs. Palter, is killed. Who is her murderer?"[17] Since there is no such character as "Mrs. Palter," and since we are told on the first page who killed the mother, this is indeed a mystery.

No better is an essay by Jan Marta on "Poetic Structures in the Prose Fiction of Sheila Watson." Marta has an interesting, indeed a vital, topic, but the essay is vitiated by incredibly sloppy scholarship. More than half the essay is given over to an analysis of the "prose" and "poetry" settings of the novel's "epigraph": "The epigraph to *The Double Hook*," Marta writes, "provides . . . a verse original for the main text which elaborates its message. It heads the text graphically, yet as 'epigraph' would have been composed after or 'in addition' to the text. . . . In that sense, the prose poetry of the novel is pre-poetic. The fact that the epigraph constitutes a poetic form of Kip's prose thoughts in the text strengthens the bond between text and epigraph, between prose and poetry."[18] All this is sheer nonsense, and only demonstrates that Marta has neither read Douglas Barbour's bibliographical note "Editors and Typesetters,"[19] which explains the origin of the "epigraph," nor even consulted the first edition of *The Double Hook*, where the "poetic form" is set as prose!

Returning to respectable criticism, we find that the first major essays did not begin to appear until 1966, seven years after the novel's publication. Between 1966 and 1974, there is what we might call the "first wave"of criticism, essays which performed the basic tasks of elucidation and interpretation. This phase was begun by John Grube in his introduction to the New Canadian Library edition of 1966.[20] Grube provides a straightforward exposition of the themes of the novel, and a brief discussion of the "regional" question. Although his ideas are unexceptionable, he gives little sense of the importance or excitement of the novel; he attains effortlessly that level of mediocrity which seems endemic to NCL introductions.

Three major essays explored the background of the novel's allusions and imagery. First was Margaret Morriss' "The Elements Transcended" (1969), which established and expounded the idea that ". . . the initial symbolic structure of the novel is elemental, incorporating earth, air, fire and water." Tracing this pattern of imagery enabled Morriss to articulate some of the basic ideas for the orthodox thematic reading of *The Double Hook*: "The mythic structure . . . is the archetypal pattern of redemption through death and rebirth, the religious ritual celebrating the re-entry of love into the wasteland."[21] Then, in 1972, the mythological background in the Indian legends of Coyote was clearly laid out by Leslie Monkman in "Coyote as Trickster in *The Double Hook*." Referring to Paul Radin's book *The Trickster: A Study in American Indian Mythology* (London, 1956), Monkman characterizes Coyote as a malign presence who has "driven the community into silence and submission," who is associated with "fear and death," and who "functions . . . in satanic opposition to Old Testament Jehovah."[22] The other major pattern of reference in the novel, to the Bible, was the subject of Beverley Mitchell's "Association and Allusion in *The Double Hook*" in 1974.[23] Mitchell's conclusions were somewhat different than Monkman's (for a more detailed discussion of her interpretation, see below, "The Double Hook"), but her essay is valuable in its identification of biblical quotations in the novel.

This "first wave" of criticism was rounded out in 1974 by Nancy J. Corbett's "Closed Circle,"[24] which, though not contributing anything very original, provided a convenient summary of the received interpretations, and also, more importantly, by the appearance of the special Sheila Watson issue of *Open Letter*. In addition to printing all of Watson's published and unpublished writings outside *The Double Hook*, this issue provided two indispensable critical tools: the bibliographical notes on the text of the first edition of *The Double Hook*, and Watson's own introduction to a public reading from the novel, which is the only public statement she has ever made about her work.

After 1974 the criticism of *The Double Hook* moved into its second stage, the exploration of more detailed aspects of the book, and the search for new insights, new ways to approach its central concerns. Two notable essays pioneered this phase. The first was Barbara Godard's " 'Between One Cliché and Another': Language in *The Double Hook*," which dealt with "the radical exploration of the limits of language undertaken in *The Double Hook*," and argued that ". . . it is above all a story of 'the coming of the Word,' a dramatization of the beginnings of language and cultural order in a primitive people."[25] Godard's essay seems to me the most intelligent and the most stimulating yet to appear; my only complaint would be that she does not go far enough. We still need a much more detailed linguistic analysis of Watson's style, of the precise ways in which it operates at these "limits of language." This criticism is also made, partly, by the only critic who has so far responded to Godard, Dawn Rae Downton, in "Messages and Messengers in *The Double Hook*."[26] Downton's article concentrates on characters who have up until now been seen as "secondary," namely, William, Kip, and Heinrich, all of whom she sees as messengers. While her final claims for Heinrich's importance are somewhat overstated, Downton's essay nevertheless constitutes, along with Godard's, an important step forward in Watson criticism.

In this discussion, I have been talking exclusively about the criticism of *The Double Hook*. Other areas of Watson's writing have scarcely been explored at all. The republication of *Four Stories* garnered a few reviews, but as yet we have no major critical studies of the short fiction. Nor has anyone attempted the (admittedly daunting) task of responding to the critical essays by Watson collected in *Open Letter*. The richness and complexity of thought and language in both these areas would surely demand the most careful and exhaustive study. And while many writers (including myself) have made general assertions about the pervasiveness of Watson's influence on subsequent Canadian writing, no one has attempted a detailed study of any writers or works in which this influence could be significantly demonstrated. The state of Sheila Watson criticism is, therefore, endlessly challenging: the greatest part of the work remains to be done.

Watson's Works

A. The Short Stories

A 1981 issue of *Quill & Quire* proclaimed that the last twenty years of Canadian literature can be characterized as "the Atwood generation."[27] While not wishing to deny either the inherent quality of Margaret Atwood's work, or the dominance of her role in the public perception of Canadian writing, I feel impelled to put forward an alternative candidate. If a "generation" can indeed be defined in terms of a single writer — which is itself a debatable proposition — then it can be argued that the credit should go, not necessarily to the author or authors whose works form the culmination of the movement, but to the writer who made it all possible, who opened the doors, who got the whole thing started. And in Canadian literature, I would submit, that writer is Sheila Watson.

The crucial date in the development of contemporary Canadian literature is 1959. The Governor General's Award-winning novel from that year was Hugh MacLennan's *The Watch That Ends the Night*, which is a romantic, pseudophilosophical soap opera. Despite some shuffling of the time-scheme, its narrative style is entirely conventional, straightforward, and dull; like most of MacLennan's novels, it displays his great virtues as an essayist. It marks, perhaps inadvertently, the end of the first stage of the development of fiction in Canada; it looks backward, to a tradition of the novel that was already moribund.

By contrast, look at another novel published in the same year, 1959: Watson's *The Double Hook*. The literary context in which Watson operates, and with which she assumes her readers will be familiar, is far more sophisticated, subtle, and complex than MacLennan's. She made it possible for Canadian writers to assume that their readers were not naïve colonials; she placed the Canadian novel firmly within the modernist tradition, at the same time as she anticipated much of what we are forced to call, for want of a better word, post-modernism. *The Double Hook* arises out of the Canadian literary milieu of the 1950s — the influence of Northrop Frye, the fascination with mythology, the agonizing over "regional" versus "universal" novels — but it also looks forward, adumbrating most of the major features of the vital Canadian literature of the next twenty years.

Barbara Godard places Watson within that modern tradition
of writers for whom language itself has become problematical, so
that "... the only subject left for writers was that of their difficult
relationships with their medium . . ." (" 'Between One Cliché
and Another,' " p. 152). She points to Watson's connections both
with Gertrude Stein, the "mother of us all" in our struggles with
language, and with bpNichol, who has often acknowledged *The
Double Hook* as one of the seminal works in his own "apprenticeship to language." Godard admits that Watson's experiments
with language are less radical than those of younger writers like
Nichol or, in Quebec, Nicole Brossard, but she nevertheless
concludes that "... in the very act of making the medium of her
art her subject, by exploring the coming of the word, Watson
belongs in this company of revolutionaries" (p. 165).

To see Watson in such a "revolutionary" or "post-modernist"
context, however, is not to deny that she is also, in many ways,
"traditional" and "modernist." Indeed, any study of Watson
must continually return to the paradoxical nature of her vision,
her insistence on combining opposites, on seeing opposites
always as existing in necessary correlation. Even this habit of
mind itself may be described either in modernist terms, as
duality, or in post-modernist terms, as duplicity: it is what is
summed up, ultimately, in the image of the double hook itself.
Thus, the "traditional" elements in Watson's vision, such as her
Roman Catholicism, or her scholarly devotion to Wyndham
Lewis, T. S. Eliot, and the writings of "high modernism," have
to be balanced on the one hook, against, on the other hook, the
"revolutionary" concern with self-reflexive language poised on
the knife-edge of silence. To maintain such a balance requires,
not only considerable breadth of knowledge and reference, but
also extreme mental agility: a kind of intellectual highwire act,
which delights the audience by its daring, and by its grace. It is
precisely because Watson is able to perform this act, apparently
effortlessly, that I believe her writing is more important, and her
influence more pervasive, than those of Margaret Atwood.
Speaking for myself, both as a writer and as a critic, it is the
Sheila Watson generation that I belong to.

I am aware that such a claim may seem outrageous in view of
the fact that, after twenty years, *The Double Hook* remains
Watson's only novel, and that her other writing is, to say the
least, not extensive. As mentioned earlier, the 1974 issue of *Open*

Letter gathered all the extant writings outside *The Double Hook* into a single, 190-page issue.[28] It included one previously unpublished story, "The Rumble Seat," and three which had appeared prior to the novel: "Brother Oedipus" (1954), "The Black Farm" (1956), and "Antigone" (1959). (These are dates of publication, not of composition.) There were six essays on Wyndham Lewis, mostly dating from the 1960s, and four essays on other topics, two of which—on Michael Ondaatje and Gertrude Stein—were first published in *White Pelican*. The *Open Letter* issue also contained an edited transcript of the talk Watson gave in 1973, introducing a reading from *The Double Hook*. There was a note on the textual problems of the first edition, but the rest of a long interview with her, prepared by Douglas Barbour and myself, was, at her own request, not included. This issue represents the total of her publications from 1959 to 1979.

These years were not, however, devoid of activity or influence. Her work with graduate students at the University of Alberta, her editorship of *White Pelican*, her advocacy of the truly revolutionary work of Wilfred Watson in both drama and poetry: all these constitute a continuing and important influence during the years when *The Double Hook* itself became a classic, claiming generations of new readers in a way which no other Canadian novel of the 1950s has been able to do.

In 1979 The Coach House Press republished the four stories from the *Open Letter* issue, under the noncommittal title *Four Stories*. *Four Stories* are distinguished, above all, by their high level of intellectual wit. Although only "The Rumble Seat" is avowedly comic in the main line of its action (such as it is — "plot" is not a prominent feature in any of the stories), all four are comic in the immediate, line-by-line texture of their language. Allusions and aphorisms abound; the play of ideas and concepts is as dazzling as it is, on another level, serious:

> Must we, roared our uncle slanting forward, live by the clock after the clock-maker has been sacked? Are we a mechanical sequence, an organized seriality? Has not Bergson proved beyond a doubt that we are snakey and submarine? The soul of man Berdyaev observed no longer rests on secure foundations. We float, we flood, we flounder. Finally we are redundant.
>
> Our uncle himself had arrived at the perils and anguish.

He clasped his hands. Are we, he mourned, flotsam
or jetsam? Have we survived or are we being thrown
overboard?

His voice rose on a hectoring note. According to modern
theory he should have been cool. He was behaving in an
unaccountable way. ("The Rumble Seat," in *FS*, p. 55)

This passage is typical of many in *Four Stories*. In a few
concise, witty sentences, it traces the main features of the history
of ideas on God and Time from the deist "clock-maker" of the
eighteenth century through to his "sacking" by the God-is-dead
theology of the 1960s. The caricature of Bergson introduces the
image of the "submarine," which is then extended into the
uncle's anguished speculation about the true position of man in
the universe: "flotsam or jetsam." The final paragraph provides
an ironic distancing, as well as slipping in a sly comment on
McLuhan, whose "modern theory" had it that television (to
which the uncle is reacting) is a "cool" medium. The irony of the
closing sentence is compounded by the question of the narrator's
identity, to which we shall return shortly. A great part of the
value of *Four Stories* lies simply in the enjoyment of this intellectual play, in an appreciation of Watson's sly, and too often
overlooked, sense of humour.

Wit plays a great part in establishing the setting of these
stories, a setting which is simultaneously local and universal,
realist and mythological. I will argue later that, in *The Double
Hook*, these two realms are synthesized into a single landscape —
a landscape which in fact makes its first appearance in the
"other" short story, *And the four animals*. In *Four Stories*, it is
less a synthesis than a juxtaposition. The two levels never merge
as fully or as convincingly as they do in the novel. The effect of
inserting classically named characters into a recognizable B.C.
setting is rather arbitrary. It is most successful in "Antigone,"
where the setting of the mental hospital provides a context
slightly removed from the realist world, and in "The Rumble
Seat," where the idea of Oedipus being interviewed by Pierre
Berton is exploited for the satirical potential implicit in the very
split between the two.

At the beginning of "Brother Oedipus," Watson introduces
the juxtaposition with her customary wit. "Our brother's name

was Oedipus," it opens (*FS*, p. 7), casually conflating the mythological, from Sophocles to Freud, with the autobiographical. The cover of the book shows the mental hospital outside New Westminster, B.C., where Watson's father was superintendent and where she was born. "Perhaps our father, who was a doctor, chose the name in some moment of illumination as he snipped and sewed together fragments of human life" (*FS*, p. 7). There is in this sentence the familiar detached irony of Watson's wit, and yet also an affectionate memory; the evocation of character is vivid and realistic, and yet the resonances of the words expand to whatever level of universality the reader is prepared to accept. In its rhythm and balance, the sentence gives to the reader; in its reticence, it gives no more than it should. And then a paragraph later, with a perfectly straight face: "Of all of us Oedipus was most attached to our mother" (*FS*, p. 7).

Classical mythology does not, of course, record that Oedipus had any brothers or sisters. The narrator of *Four Stories* is in fact male, although this does not become apparent until page 17, when Oedipus refers to him as "my sensible brother here." So strong is the reader's assumption of an autobiographical link that this revelation of gender comes as something of a shock. The narrator remains, throughout, a very shadowy character, more an observer than a participant in the action; like Tiresias, he hovers between male (the character, unnamed) and female (the author, Sheila Watson) and between past (the classical names) and present (the B.C. setting). At times he is clearly the voice for the author's irony, distancing Watson's sardonic commentary through the minimal means of an insubstantial persona; at other times, he is little more than a narrative convenience.

So, in these stories, Watson, like the father in the first paragraph, seeks for "some moment of illumination" — the radiance of light indwelling, or merely the decorations on the margins of manuscripts — as she also snips and sews amid the "fragments of human life." Within the peculiar temporal setting of her stories, simultaneously contemporary and timeless, Oedipus stumbles again towards the truth set plainly before him; Daedalus, the maker of wings, is destroyed by his mechanistic vision's inability to accommodate paradox; Antigone, at home with the dead, conducts a burial in defiance of authority and proudly declares, "It's my funeral" (*FS*, p. 46).

"There are three R's," Oedipus declares in the first story, "which our masters never bothered their heads about — recognition, rejection, and redemption" (*FS*, p. 15). The naming of the characters is itself a kind of recognition, sometimes a self-recognition, of which they are uneasily aware:

> Oedipus himself turned full into the screen.
> Dwellers in our native Thebes, he said, I am Oedipus who knew the famed riddle.
> He seemed to be trying out a role.
> This is Toronto, Pierre said. Riddles are beside the point. Here we have obstruction, obscurantism, and worse.
> We must, he said turning to Oedipus, demythologize.
> For me it is too late, Oedipus answered . . . . (*FS*, p. 53)

Yet, though the characters pursue paths similar to those by which we "recognize" them, they do not always reach the familiar destination. For this Oedipus, mother and wife are safely separate, even if they can still combine to give him problems; it is Daedalus, not Icarus, who flies too close to a black sun, and goes up, not down, in flames; Antigone's defiance this time does not bring her the expected (desired?) punishment.

The characters also experience rejection: the figure of the father, so memorably evoked in the first paragraph, remains always a distant and shadowy absence, never truly a part of his children's experience except as an exemplar of rejection, and of discipline. Rejection is also implicit in the quest of Daedalus, who attempts to reject all colours, all impurities, all paradoxes, all complexities, reducing his world to a perfect black, the absence of colour, only to find in the end that at the level of the absolute there is only impurity, paradox, complexity, and white — the presence of all the colours. *"All black is white"* he concludes. *"There are no eternal verities"* (*FS*, p. 36). The later novelist would say that Daedalus had fallen victim to Coyote.

Redemption is little more than hinted at in *Four Stories*, although it is to become the major theme of *The Double Hook*. Daedalus dies (like Greta) in a fire which is still the "consuming fire" of a jealous God rather than the "refining fire" of a Redeemer. Antigone gains a moment of mercy, when the Jehovah-like figure of the father "simply turned away" (*FS*, p. 48), but this is scarcely redemption, merely a suspended sentence. In "The Rumble Seat," Watson burlesques Pierre Berton's study of organized religion in Canada, *The Comfortable Pew*, but the action of the story is inconclusive. If the two children do attain a moment of perfect happiness in their cushioned seat poised above the central heating, it is modified by several layers of context: the florid style of Oedipus' own narrative, the acerbic commentary of the watching uncle, and the fatuous presence of the interviewer, the television God, who has "lost control" of his creation:

> Pierre was shifting uneasily. He had lost control. In a moment he would have to end the interview. He would have to make some significant gesture before tired, drained, and quiet, as the public press assured us, he would decompress under a spot-light in some darkly elegant bar. (*FS*, pp. 61–62)

It is in language, above all, that the processes of recognition, rejection, and redemption take place. The precision of Watson's verbal wit — in that last sentence, the elegance of "darkly elegant," the deadly deflation of "decompress" — continually forces the reader to *recognize* the rightness of what she is saying. At the same time, she herself practises the life-saving discipline of rejection: one novel and five stories, in over twenty years. And however ambiguous the notion of redemption may be in her stories — all the way from her father "sew[ing] together fragments of human life" to the birth of Felix at the end of *The Double Hook*—it is clear enough in her language. Watson, truly, "purified the dialect of the tribe": her writing focused attention on itself, in the self-reflexive style of modernism, and with the open-ended explorativeness of post-modernism, and thus set the example which all the most important writers of the last twenty years in Canada have had to follow. From Leonard Cohen to bp Nichol, from Phyllis Webb to Jack Hodgins, they have seen that it is the language itself which must first be redeemed: if the truth does not happen at that level, then it cannot happen anywhere else; if the language is dead, then the message is unredeemed. Again, it is in this sense above all that I would argue that Sheila Watson made this generation of Canadian writing possible; she made it new.

Four Stories occupies a unique place in Watson's literary work.

In a sense, with their range of reference and their quiet comedy, the stories resemble her conversation more closely than do *The Double Hook* and the other story. This "other" story, *And the four animals*, is much more closely linked to the novel than it is to *Four Stories*; it may serve, indeed, as a useful introduction to the issues of *The Double Hook*. For this reason, and because it is far less widely known, I have decided to devote to it the major part of this section on the short stories.

It was in May 1980 that a "new" Sheila Watson short story appeared — an occurrence which should have been a major event on the Canadian literary scene, but which, in fact, has passed almost unnoticed. The story was published as one of The Coach House Press's MS Editions, which is a series of "computer line-printer copies of works-in-progress, run off and bound up 'on demand' as orders are received at the Press" (*And the four animals*, colophon). The series allows for ongoing revisions to be entered into the computer, and it already includes drafts of works by George Bowering, Frank Davey, Eli Mandel, bpNichol, Michael Ondaatje, Fred Wah, and others.

Watson's story is somewhat different from the other publications in the series. Although described on its title page as a "First Draft, May 1980," it is, strictly speaking, neither a first draft nor a work-in-progress. The actual first draft was written in the early 1950s, around the same time as the other stories, several years before the publication of *The Double Hook*. This earlier version, which was never published, was then revised and rewritten very recently, and given directly to Coach House. As I have said, *And the four animals* is more closely linked with *The Double Hook* than the other four stories are, but it is impossible to say which elements predate the novel, and which elements come from the recent revision. However, it seems reasonable to assume that the basic outline of the story, and the quality of the landscape, were present in the earlier version, and, with these provisos, it is possible to use it as an approach to the thematic and stylistic concerns of the novel.

Whereas the setting of *Four Stories* is derived, as I have said, from a juxtaposition of classical myth with the autobiographical details of the mental hospital where Watson's father was superintendent, the setting of *And the four animals* derives from the B.C. interior, from the area around Dog Creek, where she went as a schoolteacher in 1934. And whereas the mythological background of *Four Stories* is primarily Greek, with a bizarre admixture of Pierre Berton, *And the four animals* takes us into *The Double Hook* territory, "under Coyote's eye." *And the four animals* is little more than a sketch — less than a thousand words — but like all Watson's writing it is extraordinarily *packed*. Into its 3½ pages, it compresses the basic ideas of mythology, narration, perception, and duplicity which will be the informing principles of *The Double Hook*.

The first consideration which links the story with the novel is the creation of a *landscape*. That bare, minimal landscape in which the "yellow limbs" of the foothills combine with the "blue sky" to create "only a fugitive green" (*And the four animals*, n. pag.) is recognizably the landscape of *The Double Hook* — that is, it is *simultaneously* a specific, localized setting (the B.C. interior in the drought years of the 1930s) *and* a symbolic, mythological country, whether the myth is that of Eliot's "Waste Land" or that of the Indian tales in which Coyote "walked early on the first day" (*And the four animals*) of creation. This paradoxical effect — the "double hook" of realism and symbolism — is achieved through the minimalism of the writing. We are given not so much a landscape as the *signs* of a landscape, not so much description as the semiotic conventions of description reduced to their most basic forms. In an almost Cubist manner, Watson puts her landscape through analytical and synthetic phases, and, like a Braque collage, the result is both recognizably a landscape and unmistakably an artifice. Description is rendered in its essential terms, its "bare bones" — and, indeed, Ezekiel's vision of the Valley of Dry Bones has been evoked as a source for passages in *The Double Hook*.[29] Similarly, one of the most important image-patterns in the novel has been identified as deriving from the classical four elements.[30]

Part of the effect on the reader is to combine the specific with the universal. The reader of *The Double Hook* has a strong sense of a particular location — *this* place, in *this* time — but there is really very little in the text to support such a feeling. We may know from Watson's biography that the model for the setting is Dog Creek, British Columbia, 1934, but in the novel itself the community is never named or localized. We know that there is a valley in some foothills, but there is nothing in the text to indicate *which* foothills, or even which country. Apart from a few stray references to cars and trucks, nothing prevents us from postulating any date in the last two hundred years. *And the four animals* is even more minimal in setting, and its time-scale is frankly mythological: "In the place of the hills before and after have no more meaning than the land gives" (*And the four animals*, n. pag.).

This style of writing arose, in part, as Watson's response to the problem of the "regional" as against the "international" novel. In her 1973 statement, reproduced in *Open Letter*, she said of *The Double Hook* that it was conceived

> in answer to a challenge that you could not write about particular places in Canada: that what you'd end up with was a regional novel of some kind. It was at the time, I suppose, when people were thinking that if you wrote a novel it had to be in some mysterious way, international. It had to be about what I would call something *else*. And so I thought, I don't see why: how do you . . . how are you international if you're not international? if you're very provincial, very local, and very much a part of your own milieu. ("What I'm Going to Do," p. 182)

The argument against "regional" writing was a late vestige of Canadian colonial insecurity. It was not so much that a novel could not be regional as that the region could not be Canadian. Hugh MacLennan used to tell the story of a film producer, discussing the possible adaptation of one of his novels, who insisted on shifting the locale to the United States; when MacLennan protested, the producer argued, "Listen, boy meets girl in New York City, you got a story. Boy meets girl in Winnipeg, who cares?"[31] One thinks also of Morley Callaghan's *The Loved and the Lost*, published in 1951, which is about racial prejudice and tension in Montreal, but the two races involved are black and white!

More respectably, the argument in favour of "international" writing arose out of Northrop Frye's emphasis on mythological and archetypal images and themes. One had to strike straight through to the universal, avoiding the limitations of local references, which only a minority of readers would understand. Watson was never as much influenced by Frye as she was by

Marshall McLuhan, but even so, McLuhan also insisted that regional differences and particularities were being rendered irrelevant as the world became the "global village." Clearly, however, Watson resisted the pressures of these arguments; as the above quotation shows, she felt that these demands were for a literature about "something *else.*" At the same time, paradoxically as always, she recognized the need to go beyond the limitations of the *merely* "regional" novel.

As a student of modernist writing, she had two great examples before her of novelists who had combined universal significance with highly localized settings: James Joyce and William Faulkner. (They bear, incidentally, the same first names as the first two characters mentioned in *The Double Hook.*) Eliot's interpretation of Joyce's use of myth as a structural principle in *Ulysses* had, by the 1950s, taken on the status of dogma, but in *Ulysses* one can always feel the *distance* between Dublin and the Aegean. Odysseus is an extended analogy for Leopold Bloom, rather than an integral part of his phenomenological experience. In Watson, myth is not kept at arm's length, but is much more radically fused with the local landscape. *And the four animals*, especially, takes place — literally — entirely in the place and in the time of myth, yet it never loses a sense of locality, a place which it takes in our world as well as "some[where] *else.*"

As for Faulkner, he is clearly relevant to the use of dialogue in *The Double Hook*: a stylized form of rural speech, with short, clipped sentences, repeated phrases, and sudden flashes of profundity and poetry. The brief chapters with their constantly shifting viewpoints may recall, for example, *As I Lay Dying*, which also, of course, features the dominating presence of a dead mother. But again, Watson cannot be defined by the sum of her influences: her world view is different from Faulkner's since it allows for the Christian possibilities of grace and endurance. In Faulkner, the jump from the particular to the universal is most often achieved within the characters' minds, in their thoughts, insights, and visions, while the landscape remains localized, and secular. In Watson, it happens in both the characters' minds *and* the external landscape; the foothills also are mythologized. Her landscape is more abstract than Faulkner's, more symbolic, shifting its status between reality and dream, between the time of myth and the time of man.

And the four animals, then, represents a first sketch for the

landscape of *The Double Hook*, the major difference being that
it is farther back in mythological time, it is not yet peopled —
except by the dogs, by Coyote, and by the observing eye. For this
is a landscape which both exists, autonomously, and also is being
brought into existence: it is a landscape created, a landscape
perceived. Throughout the story, one is aware of "the watching
eye," which is both a passive spectator of the action and,
increasingly, an active participant in it. The eye creates its world;
the speaking voice brings into the being of language only what
the eye has already seen.

At first sight of the dogs, "the watching eye could not record
with precision anything but the fact of their presence. . . . The
watcher could not have said whether they had come or whether
the eye had focused them into being" (*And the four animals*,
n. pag.). The dogs maintain an independent existence, as
phenomena in an objective, exterior world; but there is already a
tension between that view and the eye's subjective claim, that
perception equals creation. In its negative form, that claim is
quickly seen to have its validity: "The eye closed and the dogs
sank back into their proper darkness." What the eye does not
see, does not exist.

Next, both views are seen in equal balance: ". . . the sky was
in the eye yet severed from it," and "The dogs were against the
eye and in the eye." Objective and subjective worlds coexist, held
in the tension of the moment. But as the story moves more deci-
sively into the arena of myth, the subjective view becomes
dominant. "The eye closed. It opened and closed again. Each
time the eye opened the dogs circled the hill to the top . . ." —
as if they are obeying the eye's commands. The perceiving
consciousness is now controlling the action, determining its
direction.

At last, the eye becomes unambiguously creative: "Now when
the eye opened there were four dogs . . ," and whereas the eye
had not been able, earlier, to be sure of the origin of the first
three, the fourth is certainly "whistled up from his own depths."
But the eye has done more than just create: it has also entered
into its own creation; as a participant in the action, it both
perceives and controls. "Now when the eye opened there were
four dogs and a man and the eye belonged to the man . . . ." The
idea that perception creates reality is ultimately solipsistic. The

eye has become a man, and the man in turn has become the landscape: "Now when the eye opened there were four dogs and a man and the eye belonged to the man and stared from the hill of his head along the slope of his arm on which the four dogs lay." Reality, and the narration of reality, thus become closed systems, subject to the law of entropy. The "watching eye" becomes the agent through which its own creations consume each other, and themselves. The final mention of eyes in the story relates, not to the observer's eye, but to the dogs' eyes: ". . . the man stood rolling the amber eyes in his hands and these he tossed impartially to the waiting jaws."

There is no direct equivalent in *The Double Hook* to this pervasive presence of a watching eye, though the importance of sight, and the moral responsibility which goes along with the gift of seeing, are crucial to all characters. For instance, Kip is also a watcher who attempts to enter the action, to catch the glory that he sees, and he is rewarded with blindness. James has a vision of "Eyes everywhere. In the cottonwoods the eyes of foolhens. Rats' eyes on the barn rafters. . . . Eyes multiplied. Eyes. Eyes and padded feet" (*DH*, p. 37). Each of the characters creates his or her own reality in terms of what he or she *sees* — most clearly in Part I, where the figure of the old lady continues to be *seen* by each member of the community long after her death. At the end of the novel, James's return to the community is marked by Lenchen's vision — "I see James" — and by Ara's movement of withdrawal — "Ara didn't want to look at James" (*DH*, p. 128). Above all, the whole novel takes place, in the words of its opening, "under Coyote's eye" (*DH*, p. 13). Coyote lays claim to the role of the perceiver/creator/destroyer: if everything takes place under his eye, then it is he who performs that ultimate and ambivalent role ascribed to the watcher in *And the four animals*.

But Coyote, of course, is a liar. Coyote always tries to take credit for more than is his due. Coyote is the Trickster God, the apotheosis of malign destiny and capricious chance. If anything can go wrong, it will: Coyote is the divine agent of Murphy's Law. I will have much more to say, later, about Coyote's role in *The Double Hook*, but here it is worth noting that nowhere in the novel are Coyote's character and attributes more concisely or poetically summed up than they are in these two lines from the story: "Coyote, the primitive one, the god-baiter and trouble-maker, the thirster after power, the vainglorious" (*And the four animals*, n. pag.).

The hills are "Coyote's house" (*And the four animals*), or at least he lays claim to them, in the arrogant, untrustworthy way in which he has attributed power and glory to himself ever since he walked, early, on the first day of creation. But Coyote is not the only religious presence in the story: there are also the dogs. The dogs arrive in the story ambiguously, either naturally, coming "around the curve of the hill," or mythologically, "out of the hill itself," or as creatures of fiction, summoned by the observing eye. They are defined at first in opposition to the land, between which and them the eye recognizes no "congruence." Rather, they are "aristocrats" whose appearance is "elegant and lithe," who move "with rhythmic dignity." They are the products of breeding, that is, of human manipulation and control of the animal world. As the story proceeds, they can be more particu-larly classified as "Labrador retrievers, gentle, courteous, and playful with the sedate bearing of dogs well schooled to know their worth, to know their place, and to bend willingly to their master's will." They have become eminently *civilized*, and have lost, in the process, most of their native independence, their dignity, even their capacity to survive outside human protection.

Originally, the dogs (or their ancestors) had belonged to the land, to "Coyote's house." "They, too, were gods . . . ." But now they are alienated, cut off from this level of their being. Now they are "*in* the land but not *of* it" (my emphasis); no longer savage gods, they are "civil gods made tractable by use and useless by custom." Some force — identified in the story only as "time" — has now "yielded them up to the timeless hills," where their uselessness means that ". . . they would starve or loose [sic] themselves in wandering." They have become "aliens," or "exiles returned as if they had never been."

The central fact about the dogs, then, is that the ostensible benefits of "civilization" have caused a moral and physical degeneration which renders them incapable of surviving in their native landscapes. Their coats may shine ebony, their bones may be accurately adjusted, but they can no longer even climb a hill. "Each time they reached the height of land with more difficulty. At last all three lay pressing thin bellies and jaws against the unyielding earth." They have been reduced to a state of "insensibility."

I use that word because it is Watson's word; it comes from her 1973 comments on *The Double Hook*, in a passage which is crucial to any interpretation of the novel, but which is also, I believe, relevant to this story: ". . . there was something I wanted to say: about how people are driven, how if they have no art, how if they have no tradition, how if they have no ritual, they are driven in one of two ways, either towards violence or towards insensibility . . ." ("What I'm Going to Do," p. 183). Watson is talking here about the human characters in her book, especially the Indians, and the traditions and rituals she has in mind are religious, specifically Christian. But the state of insensibility of the novel's characters certainly resembles the "lackluster" condition of the dogs, and the same imagery continues to be used. In *The Double Hook*, Theophil — for whom this insensibility is terminal—is described on his mattress: "He lay loose there like a dog on a rumpled sack" (*DH*, p. 71). And William says of Felix— unfairly, as it turns out—that "he spends all his days lying round like a dog in a strip of sunlight taking warmth where he finds it" (*DH*, p. 123).

If, then, one is looking for symbolic interpretations of the dogs in this story, they could be seen as representing the degeneration of Indian culture under the impact of white civilization, or, more generally, as representing man in his fallen state, alien and exile in the world which was created for him, existentialist man in the wasteland of the twentieth century. Moreover, the scope of such symbolic interpretations is vastly increased when one considers the context provided by the *title*, a context which reinforces the mythological, Christian, and indeed apocalyptic tone of the narrative.

The title comes from the Revelation of Saint John the Divine: "Then I heard all the living things in creation — everything that lives in the air, and on the ground, and under the ground, and in the sea, crying, 'To the One who is sitting on the throne and to the Lamb, be all praise, honour, glory and power, for ever and ever.' And the four animals said, 'Amen'; and the elders prostrated themselves to worship" (v. 13–14). The four animals have been described in the preceding chapter: "In the centre, grouped round the throne itself, were four animals with many eyes, in front and behind. The first animal was like a lion, the second like a bull, the third animal had a human face, and the fourth animal was like a flying eagle. Each of the four animals had six wings and had eyes all the way round as well as inside; and day and night they never stopped singing" (iv.6–8).[32]

Like all the symbols in Revelation, the four animals are subject to a plethora of interpretation. Since the time of the second-century church father Irenaeus, they have been identified with the four evangelists, the most familiar association being the Lion with Saint Mark. In rabbinical tradition, ". . . there are four supreme orders in the world: among all created beings, mankind; among birds, the eagle; among domestic animals, the ox; and among wild animals, the lion."[33] Sources for the descriptions have been traced in Ezekiel, in Isaiah, in 1 and 2 Samuel, and in the Psalms. They have been seen as constellations, as signs of the zodiac, as "the four quarters of heaven," "the four corners of the earth," the four winds, the four elements — "Four," says the Jerusalem Bible succinctly, "symbolises the universe."[34] G.B. Caird describes them as "the supporters of the firmament . . . the bearers of God's throne," and concludes: "It is safe to assume that in John's vision they represent the whole created cosmos of heaven and earth."[35]

This is, obviously, far too great a weight of symbolism to bring to bear on one story, and it would be foolhardy to attempt interpretive readings which would accord consistently with the theological commentaries. But there are several points of contact, which offer intriguing and provocative suggestions about ways to read the story. One could argue that the identification of the four animals with the four elements, "the whole created cosmos," is an ultimate step in the universalizing of a local landscape. The traditional reading of the four animals as the four evangelists would accord with the idea that the degeneration of the dogs represents the decline of religion in a people without ritual. Intriguingly, this symbolic reading is attributed to Irenaeus, whose major contribution to early Christian theology was to insist on the importance of the previously neglected Gospel of Saint John: for Irenaeus, there had to be four dogs, not three. Irenaeus used Greek philosophy to stress the fourth gospel's view of Christ as the Logos, the Word. (Barbara Godard interprets the whole of The Double Hook as a novel of "the coming

of the word" ["'Between One Cliché and Another,'" p.149].)
Finally, one could associate the insistence on *eyes* in Saint John's
description with the pervasiveness of the watching eye in the
story.

However, it would probably be unwise to push any one of
these interpretations too far. More important is the simple fact
that the title sets the whole story in the context of Apocalypse.
The ideas of Revelation and eschatology operate in the background of the story rather than in the foreground; they set tone
and atmosphere rather than provide clues for schematic interpretations. This view of the function of the title may be supported by
noting that it belongs to the recent revision of the story, not to the
original draft. All my quotations from Saint John have been
taken from the Jerusalem Bible, the official modern Roman Catholic translation with first appeared in 1966, well *after* the first
draft of the story was written. The Greek original is Καὶ τὰ
τέσσαρα ζῶα ἔλεγον, Ἀμήν. In the King James translation ζῶα is
rendered, slightly inaccurately, as "beasts"; in the Douay Catholic version, which preceded the Jerusalem, they are, accurately
if not poetically, "the four living creatures." The earliest use of
"animals" that I have been able to trace is in a 1962 translation by
Richmond Lattimore.[36] So the title *And the four animals* is, in
fact, post-1966 — and Wilfred Watson has told me, in conversation, that it was a discussion of this phrase which prompted the
reworking of the older version.

The overtones of apocalypse certainly carry over into the
climactic action of the story, where the account of the four
animals being fed to each other and consuming themselves until
only one tooth remains has the primal quality of myth or legend,
although it is not based on any *particular* Indian myth or legend.
Rather, it stands in relation to traditional myths in much the
same way as I suggested earlier that Watson's landscapes stand in
relation to conventional descriptions. Again, we are given not so
much a myth as the *signs* of myth, the semiotic gestures of mythical narrative reduced to their most basic forms, an analysis or
deconstruction of the process of mythical storytelling. But at the
same time, even here, we should allow for the possible presence
of Watson's dry and quiet sense of humour — so quiet that it is all
too often ignored, or simply not noticed. This story may be
myth, but it is also a grimly humorous literalization of the cliché

"dog eat dog." The narrator, the observing eye, is also evidently unwilling to "let sleeping dogs lie."

But if the story is a myth, what kind of myth is it? Creation or destruction, redemption or apocalypse? In keeping with the insistent duality of Watson's work, I have to argue that it is, ultimately, both. On the negative side, one can see the dogs' terminal insensibility turning to self-destructive violence. On whatever symbolic level you care to read the dogs — from decultured Indians to alienated man to demythologized evangelists — there is a gloomy logic to this self-consumption. The agent of this holocaust may be a man, but the dogs cooperate all too willingly in their own fate, fawning graciously, begging decorously, bowing and slavering. In this negative view, the man could be seen as an incarnation of the "vainglorious" Coyote, or even the Devil, the true "beast" of the Revelation. Disturbingly, the man is also, as previously noted, the narrator of the story, the observing eye which creates what it sees. Do all authors destroy their characters at the same time as they create them? The eye can close, and the word can lapse into silence; "bringing a character into being" involves also a vast nonbeing, the space of silence surrounding the few precarious words. This is then a myth of the end of the world, a negation, an apocalypse.

It is, admittedly, harder to argue for a positive view of the ending, even if most end-of-the-world myths do allow for a cyclical beginning, Balder's return, the Second Coming, the New Jerusalem. But Watson recognizes that the process of redemption must sometimes start with a cleansing violence. *The Double Hook*, which I will argue is a novel of *re*generation, begins with matricide and proceeds through a blinding and a suicide by fire before it arrives at its final birth. The dogs, we are told, would in any case have starved or lost themselves in wandering; instead, they are given a death with the mythological overtones of sacrifice and re-creation. The single tooth which the man takes and hides in his belly is surely reminiscent of many teeth or bones, in mythological stories, which spring back into life. Admittedly the story ends before this cycle can be completed; but I see at least the possibility of reading it, not only as apocalypse, but also as a perverse creation myth. And from this positive side, the man is also transformed. If he is Coyote, attempting destruction, he is as usual fooled: the trickster is tricked into doing good in spite of himself. The observing, creative eye also has a redemptive vision. The word—whether it is the theological Word of Irenaeus, or the creative word of a literary tradition—is still spoken against the silence.

The strength of the image, I submit, is that it maintains and balances both possibilities, holding them upon the double hook, which is the most basic pattern of Watson's work. Her writing cannot be reduced to the oversimplifications of schematic interpretation; the images have too great a density, too assertive an insistence on the autonomy of their own being. But in this brief sketch of a story, she sets out the essentials of her narrative vision: its landscape, its mythology, its perception of insensibility and violence, its project of ambiguous redemption. All that is missing is the scale of human beings living in society; for that, she has to go beyond the short story into the more extended form of the novel. Within the totality of Sheila Watson's work, *And the four animals* stands as an introduction, or a prologue, to the greater achievement of *The Double Hook*.

B. The Double Hook

"I began the writing of *The Double Hook*," Watson recalled in 1973, "as an answer to a challenge. When it was written—I can't remember when it started: I can remember when I first thought about it, it was right in the middle of Bloor Street — it was in answer to a challenge that you could not write about particular places in Canada: that what you'd end up with was a regional novel of some kind" ("What I'm Going to Do," p. 182).

I have already commented, in relation to the creation of a landscape in *And the four animals*, on Watson's approach to the problem of the regional novel as it was perceived in Canada in the 1950s. On the larger scale of the novel, both sides of the paradox — the sense of a *particular* locality, the sense of a *universal* setting — are extended and intensified. It is possible to read *The Double Hook* in terms of a realist novel, to trace the psychological development of the characters, to define them in the contexts of their race, their upbringing, their milieu. They are, Watson has said, "figures in a ground, from which they could not be separated" ("What I'm Going to Do," p. 183). At the same time, it is also possible, and indeed necessary, to see the action as symbolic, the characters as representative, the place as universal, and the time as timeless.

Many aspects of the novel form, as opposed to the short story, favour the "realist" impulse. The minimalist technique of *And the four animals* cannot be stretched even to the limited extent of a fairly short novel (128 pages, including titles). The very fact of having to present characters speaking dialogue, and doing everyday things like eating food and mending fenceposts, shifts the narrative away from the mythological mode of four dogs consuming each other. *The Double Hook* has moved from the time of myth to the time of man; human society is now the foreground, and the symbolic background must emerge in indirect ways, such as "association and allusion."[37]

The movement towards the general takes place even at the level of the characters' own habits of speech. Everyone seems to talk naturally in aphorisms, transforming every particular incident into an occasion for universal truth. For example, at the key moment when James has decided to return to the community and remembers that he has no money left to pay the stabling costs for his horse, he says, "Write it down . . . . I'll pay when I'm next in town." This is a particular comment on his own present situation, but immediately he generalizes it, giving it an impersonal, universal application. "There are times when a man spends more than he has and must go on credit." Even then he feels further compelled to offer a generalizing comment on his own generalizing comment: "Unless a man defaults, he said, a debt is a sort of bond" (*DH*, p. 115).

William, whom Watson devastatingly sums up in the comment "He only felt, but he always felt he knew" (*DH*, p. 14), is especially fond of this generalizing habit of speech and is ready with an aphorism for every occasion, but to a greater or lesser extent all the characters share the same fondness. It is so prevalent that Watson is able to make fun of it, as in an exchange between Kip and Theophil which pushes it to the extremes of parody. "These eyes seen plenty," Kip begins, again at the particular level. Voicing his disapproval, Theophil shifts naturally to the general mode: "It's not always right for the mouth to say what the eyes see . . . . Sometimes, too, it's better for the eyes to close." Kip is quite ready to play the game, and replies in kind: "Sure, Kip said. Sure. But sometimes, he said, when the eye's open a thing walks right in and sets down." Theophil immediately picks up on the figure of speech of "walks right in" and extends it: "The best thing to do, Theophil said, is to shoo it out. If you had a back door now, you could just keep it moving on." Having introduced the image of the back door, however, Theophil cannot resist an aphorism on back doors as well, and the whole hilarious exchange topples over the edge of exaggeration into absurdity: "Back doors do have their points, he said, though they're powerful mean for letting in the draughts" (*DH*, p. 50). It would be naïve to suppose that Watson is not fully aware of the comedy in this exchange.

The level of generality which the characters so insistently reach for in their patterns of speech is also present in the author's speech, especially in its imagery, its echoes, its allusions. As already noted in relation to *And the four animals*, the minimalist descriptions rely heavily on imagery associated with the four elements. As noted above in the critical overview and context, this is a pattern which has been fully traced by Margaret Morriss in "The Elements Transcended."[38] In that article, she describes how the novel incorporates earth, air, fire, and water. Morriss also shows symbolic connections with the themes of the novel: "The elements of air and fire are associated with the images of light and glory, and to this extent they are opposed to the fear and darkness related to earth and water" (p. 58). The pattern of "recognition, rejection, and redemption" which Morriss traces in the human characters is also present in elemental nature, so that by the end, "in a microcosm of the regenerative pattern, James moves from dead grass and spraying dust into a meadow of wild hay watered by a hidden spring, upon a stallion that draws life with every breath" (p. 68). Again, the effect is to combine the local with the universal. The fire which destroys Greta is realistic enough, but it is also an elemental fire, a ritualistic, cleansing fire, the "consuming fire" of God, Buddha's "Fire Sermon" out of Eliot's *The Waste Land*. Elemental imagery links the local landscape with every conceivable level of signification.

Literary allusions in *The Double Hook* are a tricky subject. Since Watson has spent a lifetime studying and teaching modernist literature, the temptation is to identify allusions at every turn of phrase. But, as I said before, Watson is more than the sum of her influences. You cannot "explain away" her treatment of the regional novel by reference to Faulkner, any more than you can summarize her theology by invoking Eliot. She is herself, quite rightly, suspicious of critics who dwell on such matters. "I hope you don't think," she said to me once, "that the novel is simply a rewrite of *The Waste Land*." I assured her that I did not; but I couldn't help wondering if it was merely coincidence that both *The Double Hook* and *The Waste Land* use the imagery of drought, that both are in five parts, that in both Part IV is stylistically set apart from the rest, and that in both Part III concludes with purification by fire. "Oh, has it five parts?" she answered mischievously. "I don't remember." And then she went on to tell me that what I should really be paying attention to was Felix's coffee cup. So, consulting these passages, I found Felix sitting "like the round world all centred in on himself" (*DH*, p. 123), celebrating "Time annihilated in the concurrence" (*DH*, p. 33). Not *The Waste Land*, then, but *Four Quartets*: ". . . the still point of the turning world. . . . Where past and future are gathered."[39]

Such references, however, are well in the background of the novel. Religious references, both to the Bible and to the Coyote trickster myths, are much more prominent, and important. The most thorough treatment of the biblical references is to be found in Beverley Mitchell's "Association and Allusion in *The Double Hook*." Going far beyond the direct mentions of Nineveh and Jonah, Mitchell argues that ". . . a close examination of the text of *The Double Hook* will reveal that nearly all the characters have their prototypes in figures from the Old Testament" (p. 66). Only Felix is associated with the New Testament, "as he moves from the comfortable but selfish isolation which he has accepted for himself to an assumption of responsibility for others, realizing the practical application of the liturgy he has never forgotten" (p. 67). For Mitchell, the subtext of biblical reference, both direct quotation and indirect allusion, provides an answer to her opening question. "Why . . . does the reader have the feeling of 'déjà vu' or sense that this story is vaguely familiar?" (p. 63). Again, the local is suffused with the universal, yet the universal is indissolubly realized in the local.

The most contentious point of Mitchell's essay is her treatment of Coyote, whom she identifies with God, or at least with the Old Testament Jehovah. She writes:

Many of [Coyote's] speeches are either explicit or implicit allusions to words spoken by God to the Chosen People. . . . Similarly, the actions of Coyote parallel the actions of God in the Old Testament and can be identified. For the most part, the reactions of the characters in the novel to Coyote are consonant with the reaction of the Chosen People to God, for initially He was feared as the God of vengeance rather than loved as the God of mercy. (p.67)

Mitchell admits that Coyote "has been seen as functioning in Satanic opposition to the Old Testament Jehovah" (p.67), but she chooses to argue against this view, claiming that "just as the God of the Chosen People is revealed fully only in the New Testament as a loving and forgiving Father . . . so, too, Coyote is fully revealed only at the end of the novel . . ." (p.68) in the final words he speaks. It is with some trepidation that I undertake to argue theology with a nun, but I think that Sister Beverley is, like the infant Felix in the lines she cites, on shaky ground here. As I will argue in more detail later, there is nothing in the ending to justify the assertion that Coyote is either loving or forgiving; rather, Coyote is up to his old tricks again, claiming credit to which he has no right. Coyote, "the vainglorious" and "the god-baiter" (*And the four animals*), is as usual fooling himself, and fooling others — including, in this case, the critic. Mitchell is correct to see parallels and allusions between Coyote's speech and Jehovah's, but these parallels do not establish an identification. Rather, they establish the fraudulent nature of Coyote's claim; for Coyote to assume the language of Jehovah is presumptuous parody, seen at its most blasphemous when he welcomes Greta's pitiful suicide with the words of the Song of Solomon, the words traditionally interpreted as the lovemaking of Christ to his church:

And Coyote cried in the hills:
I've taken her where she stood
my left hand is on her head
my right hand embraces her.

(*DH*, p.79)

Coyote is indeed a "God of vengeance"; there is no evidence at all in the text that he is also a "God of mercy."

I prefer to accept the more traditional view put forward by Leslie Monkman in "Coyote as Trickster in *The Double Hook*."[40] Monkman cites, as his main authority, Paul Radin's *The Trickster: A Study in American Indian Mythology*, which traces the appearances of the trickster figure in his various animal incarnations as raven, horse, spider, or coyote. Monkman quotes Radin as saying the trickster "is at one and the same time, creator and destroyer, giver and negator, he who dupes others and who is always duped himself" (p.70). This line is clearly echoed by Watson when she says, through Kip, "that Coyote plotting to catch the glory for himself is fooled and every day fools others" (*DH*, p.55). The trickster, Radin continues, "possesses no values, moral or social, is at the mercy of his passions and appetites, yet through his actions all values come into being" (p.70). Monkman sees this positive aspect of Coyote as emerging indirectly, as if by accident, against his will: "Coyote [is] fooled when suicide, seduction and matricide lead not to despair but to an affirmation of faith and love" (p.72). Coyote's direct influence is more unambiguously negative. He counsels fear, despair, divisiveness, darkness; Monkman speaks of one of his utterances as "a typical benediction on the attractiveness of death" (p.74).

But fear can be faced, and Coyote's illusions destroyed — as Felix remembers, sitting holding his coffee cup, there at the still centre of annihilated time:

> The memory of the time Angel had seen the bear at the fish camp. Seen the bear rising on its haunches. Prostrating itself before the unsacked winds. Rising as if to strike. Bowing to the spirits let out of the sack, Angel thought, by the meddler Coyote. The bear advancing. Mowing. Scraping. Genuflecting. Angel furious with fear beating wildly. Her hunting-knife pounding the old billycan.
>
> He chuckled, remembering the noise and the white face of Angel when he picked up the bear in its devotions. Picked up paper blown off the fish-shack roof. (*DH*, p.33)

Monkman comments on this incident: "The reference here is to Indian myths which relate that the world was originally created as an Eden until Coyote released from a sack the spirits of fatigue, hunger and disease. In spite of her pessimism regarding a benevolent deity or the possibility of communal action and responsibility, Angel will provide the pragmatic element essential to the achievement of those same concepts" (p. 75). The incident is emblematic of the action which must be taken to deal with Coyote. "Fear faced is fear conquered," writes John Grube,[41] and though that is rather an oversimplification, it does indicate the first step. Angel's "pragmatic" action here needs to be complemented by Felix's understanding, and completed by Felix's memory. Her action is in itself meaningless, a reflex of fear; it is Felix who picks up the paper and reveals the bear — and Coyote — for what they are. Felix is often seen as *doing* nothing, but this is, as we shall see, a misconception. Coyote, like the Devil, is a master of lies; the truth is all it takes to make him disappear.

I have summarized some of the major ways in which the local action of the book is generalized: through habits of speech, through literary and religious allusion. It is time now to turn more directly towards that central action, and in order to do so I will refer again to the statement Watson made in 1973:

I'd been away [from Dog Creek] for a long time before I realised that if I had something to say, it was going to be said in these images. And there was something I wanted to say: about how people are driven, how if they have no art, how if they have no tradition, how if they have no ritual, they are driven in one of two ways, either towards violence or towards insensibility — if they have no mediating rituals which manifest themselves in what I suppose we call art forms. And so it was with this that the novel began. ("What I'm Going to Do," p. 183)

To this might be added a casual remark from a private conversation with me, the kind of "casual remark" which is in fact anything but casual: "To be self-centred is an oblivion."

What Watson is describing here is a society fragmented, divided, turned against itself, a society in which each individual is isolated in the oblivion of being self-centred. It is the society adumbrated by the degenerate state of the dogs in *And the four animals*; it is, if you like, Eliot's Waste Land; it is recognizably a twentieth-century society in which religious and social orders have collapsed, and all that is left is this twin drive towards insensibility or violence.

Many of the characters in *The Double Hook* are clearly, at the start of the novel, gripped by a kind of paralysis, a profound surrender of any will towards action, or even understanding. Insensibility has set in: Felix, lost in dreams and misremembered scraps of a ritual that has lost its meaning; Theophil, who has "let fear grow like fur on his eyes" (*DH*, p.52); the Widow Wagner, refusing to admit to herself the obvious fact of her daughter's ninth-month pregnancy; Ara, who can see only death ". . . leaking through from the centre of the earth. Death rising to the knee. Death rising to the loin" (*DH*, p.15). If this last phrase recalls again *The Waste Land* and the Grail legends, then we may find at the centre, not a Fisher King, but a Fisher Queen: the old lady, Mrs. Potter, fishing for spite not food, fishing as a symbol not of redemption but of hostility.

It is in the Potter family that the community's insensibility concentrates into violence. James remembers ". . . the way they'd lived. Suspended in silence" (*DH*, p.37). The few glimpses we are given of the Potter household before the old lady's death are filled with repressed hatred and potential violence:

They'd lived waiting. . . . Moving their lips when they moved them at all as hunters talk smelling the deer. Edged close wiping plates and forks while the old lady sat in her corner. Moved their lips saying: She'll live forever. And when they'd raised their eyes their mother was watching as a deer watches. (*DH*, p.37)

The psychic violence which Mrs. Potter exerts against her own family, and against the whole community, finally erupts into physical violence. James is "driven" into his frantic striking out at all those around him; Greta, more tragically, is driven into striking inwards, at herself. When she has "sat in the old lady's chair" (*DH*, p.37), she finds that nothing has truly changed. In some senses, she has "become" her mother; in other senses, she has only become more fully herself. She attempts to disguise herself in the emblems of growth, wearing a housecoat "All green and gold and purple. . . . Fat clinging clumps of purple flowers. Honey-tongued. Bursting from their green stems. Crowding against green leaves" (*DH*, p.57). But Kip instantly sees through the disguise: "Oh-ho, Kip said. Just the same old Greta. The same old Greta inside some plants and bushes" (*DH*, p.58). The vicious closed system of the Potter household has, it may be presumed, led Greta towards an incestuous love for James; hence her anger and frustration when the death of their mother brings no liberation, but only the prospect of Lenchen. Greta's fury, however, can find no outlet in action. "She wanted to cry abuse through the boards. She wanted to cram the empty space with hate" (*DH*, p.79). But Greta is trapped too deep in the community's paralysis to be capable even of outward-turning violence. She has no course left but to turn all the violence against herself, in a suicide presided over by the spirits of her mother and Coyote.

The only character who initially appears to be free of this insensibility is Kip. Unlike all the other characters named in the opening dramatis personae, Kip is not tied down to one place by the verb "lived." He has no home; he moves freely around; his most characteristic pose is in the saddle of a horse. Kip is a visionary, "reaching to pull down the glory" (*DH*, p.30). He is most often defined in terms of sight: "What in hell are you doing?" Heinrich asks him on his first appearance, and Kip answers, "Looking" (*DH*, p.21). Later he tells Angel, "These eyes seen plenty" (*DH*, p.50). James remembers Kip spying on his assignations with Lenchen: ". . . when he'd looked up he'd seen Kip standing in the pines" (*DH*, p.36). The climax of Kip's sight, and insight, comes in the passage which was, without Watson's agreement,[42] excerpted to stand as an epigraph to the book:

> Kip's mind was on James. . . . He's like his old lady, Kip thought. There's a thing he doesn't know. He doesn't know you can't catch the glory on a hook and hold on to it. That when you fish for the glory you catch the darkness too. That if you hook twice the glory you hook twice the fear. That Coyote plotting to catch the glory for himself is fooled and every day fools others. (*DH*, p.55)

So far so good: Kip's insight here is accurate since James at this stage of the novel has not yet attained the understanding which he will have later on. The idea of the inseparability of glory and darkness, the absolute duality of all experience, is indeed at the centre of the image of the double hook. Kip's mistake, even at this stage, is that he fails to recognize how fully this message applies to himself as well: he is like James in not knowing that his own efforts to reach the glory — standing in his saddle reaching for the thunder, or more mundanely attempting to seduce Lenchen — must also "catch the darkness," and he is like Coyote in not realizing that his own attempts to fool others are only succeeding in fooling himself. Kip's speech here is *not* an authorial statement (this is why Watson objected to its use as such) but the limited statement of a particular character in a fictional situation, governed by a large measure of dramatic irony.

The limitations of Kip's insight become even clearer as the passage continues and shows him paying abject homage to Coyote:

> He doesn't know, Kip thought, how much mischief Coyote can make.
> Coyote reaching out reflected glory. Like a fire to warm. Then shoving the brand between a man's teeth right into his belly's pit. Fear making mischief. Laying traps for men. The dog and his servants plaguing the earth. Fear skulking round. Fear walking round in the living shape of the dead. No stone was big enough, no pile of stones, to weigh down fear. (*DH*, p. 55)

This acceptance of the primacy of fear shows Kip as being truly what Coyote proclaims him to be: "Kip, my servant Kip" (*DH*, p. 29).

So Kip also goes round "making mischief," failing to deliver the message entrusted to him, attempting to reach for the glory himself. His freedom is illusory; if he does not quite share the paralysis and insensibility of the rest of the community, he does share its violence, and he shares it in the most destructive way, as its victim. Later he is able to admit that he brought the violence on himself: "I keep thinking about James, Kip said. I kept at him like a dog till he beat around the way a porcupine beats with his tail" (*DH*, p. 127). The violence is directed against the most vital aspect of Kip's character: his sight. Blinded, he becomes little better than an animal, "Lifting his face windward like an animal.

. . . Finding [his] way by the smell of the water" (*DH*, p. 66). For Kip at the end of the novel there is resignation and acceptance, but no more: he will never again enjoy the freedom, or the illusion of freedom, with which he began.

Insensibility and violence: in the characters we have looked at so far, we see some of the ways in which these ideas are worked out. Together, they form the most sinister of the novel's double hooks, on which the whole community lives suspended, isolated from each other. In the beginning, each of the household groups is alone, set apart in their various houses, united only by their vision of death, by Coyote's illusion of a presence that is really an absence. They are listed, severally, "under Coyote's eye" (*DH*, p. 13). By the end of the book, they will have gathered in one house, Felix's, all except Greta, who is dead, and Theophil, whose insensibility has become terminal. Even the wounded Kip, Coyote's erstwhile "servant," is part of this final unity. The movement of the book is the movement from separate houses to one house; the novel begins with a murder, and closes with a birth.

All the members of the community must participate in this movement, and they do so each in an individual way: William slowly and dully, the Widow Wagner reluctantly, Ara resentfully. But the lead is taken by two characters: James and Felix. Together, they form another of the book's dualities, James representing public physical action, and Felix representing private spiritual meditation. But each of the two also contains elements of the other: the double hook of the two characters is reproduced *within* each of the two characters. James must learn to understand his actions just as Felix must learn to act his understandings.

It is James's violent action of pushing his mother downstairs which initiates the movement of the book. Again, the action is itself a duality: on the one hook, it is the violence stemming from the community's spiritual sterility; on the other hook, it is the first necessary step in the process of the community's regeneration. The old lady dies, the first page tells us, "Pushed by James's will. By James's hand. By James's words" (*DH*, p. 13). The action is, however, an incomplete one for even after her physical death, the old lady continues to appear to the various members of the community, to Greta at the moment of her death, and to James himself. The action of the hand is, for James, easily and quickly completed; but it takes him longer to complete the action of his will and his words.

Thus, James's actions in the first part of the book — the killing of his mother, the blinding of Kip, the assault with the whip on Lenchen and Greta, the escape to the town — are undirected and random. They are the reflex actions of someone still trapped in a world of violence and insensibility, no more meaningful than the words echoed and imitated by Paddy's parrot. So it is no surprise that when he first arrives in town, he still "saw the dark figure of his mother playing her line into the full flood" (*DH*, p. 86).

James goes through the mechanisms of escape, withdrawing his money from the bank, and at the same time, almost consciously, he goes through the mechanisms of avoiding escape, inviting Traff and his friends to steal the money. But it is important to notice that now, for the first time, James's actions follow *after* his thoughts. He knows that he cannot truly escape *before* Lilly and Felicia (whose name is an inverted parody, a mirror image of Felix) actually steal the money. It then becomes his *decision* not to reclaim it, as he easily could have.

The process begins when he feels the temptation to despair, to follow his sister (unwittingly) down the easy path to suicide. "James wanted to go down to the river. To throw himself into its long arms" (*DH*, p. 92). But he still feels, and instinctively rebels against, the identity between this option and his mother's baleful influence: ". . . along the shore like a nightwatch drifted the brown figure he sought to escape" (*DH*, p. 92). It is now that "*for the first time*" (my emphasis) he really tries to understand his own actions, to bring his will and his words into line with the action of his hands. "He asked himself now for the first time what he'd really intended to do when he'd defied his mother at the head of the stairs" (*DH*, p. 92). Coyote is ready with the quick, easy, wrong answer:

> To gather briars and thorns,
> said Coyote.
> To go down into the holes of the rock
> and into the caves of the earth.
> In my fear is peace.
>
> (*DH*, p. 92)

But James now has the strength, and the understanding, to resist
Coyote, to deny the option of suicide, to perceive his mother's
way as life-denying, life-restricting: ". . . his heart cried out
against the thought: This bed is too short for a man to stretch
himself in. The covering's too narrow for a man to wrap himself
in" (DH, pp.92–93). So the next time he stands by the river, the
action is complete: his mother is finally dead; Coyote holds out
no new temptations. "For the first time in his life he felt quite
alone. If his mother was there, he could not feel even a vibration
of her shadow in the darkness" (DH, p.101). Only then does
Lilly arrive to complete in physical action what James already,
profoundly, knows.

So James returns to accept his responsibilities, as Lenchen's
baby's father, and as a member of the reborn community. One
slightly incongruous symbol of his changed attitude is his new
plaid shirt, plaid being a weaving together of various elements
into a unified pattern. The symbol, incidentally, is even more
incongruous in the original edition of The Double Hook, where
one of the most famous misprints in Canadian literature throws a
whole new light on James's character by portraying him wearing
a new plaid skirt (DH, p.124)!

James's return is marked by two decisive comments: first, to
the barn-owner, his acknowledgement of social indebtedness,
"Unless a man defaults, he said, a debt is a sort of bond" (DH,
p.115); and second, his immediate reaction to the sight of the
burned-out house:

> He shut his eyes. In his mind now he could see only the
> seared and smouldering earth, the bare hot cinder of a still
> unpeopled world. He felt as he stood with his eyes closed on
> the destruction of what his heart had wished destroyed that
> by some generous gesture he had been turned once more
> into the first pasture of things.
>
> I will build the new house further down the creek, he
> thought. All on one floor. (DH, p.125)

The imagery is of genesis, a creation myth, the beginning of
things. From a "still unpeopled" volcanic world, James moves to
the Edenic "first pasture," in which everything is, once again,
possible. His own response is, characteristically, one of action:

he will build a new house. Since it will be "further down the
creek," it will be closer to the other houses in the community
(Watson's geography disguises another bad joke: the Potter
house was, of all the houses in the community, the furthest "up
the creek"); and since it will be "all on one floor," it will have
no internal divisions, and no stairs for anyone to be pushed
down.

James's counterpart is Felix, who is first seen in the act of
fishing — not out of spite, like the old lady, but for the natural
and proper reason of providing himself with food. The picture of
him as "Flesh mountainous contemplating. Saint Felix with a
death's head meditating" (DH, p. 18) is simultaneously comic —
since the "death's head" is, not the traditional human skull from
the iconography of hermit saints, but the remains of a fish — and
profoundly serious. In his hesitant, fragmented, and minimal
way, Felix is a saint, the spiritual centre (albeit reluctantly) of the
community's regeneration. The Oxford Dictionary of Saints
informs us that there are no less than sixty-six saints called Felix
listed in the Roman martyrology;[43] I have to confess that my
research here is not exhaustive, but I doubt whether any particular reference is intended!

The symbols of Felix's sainthood are his fiddle and his coffee
cup: the lance and the Grail, as it were, in Watson's domestica-
tion of the legend. The music that Felix plays is practically the
only trace left in the community of what Watson calls those
"mediating rituals which manifest themselves in what I suppose
we call art forms" ("What I'm Going to Do," p. 183). Felix may
not strike the reader as the most vivid representative of the
so-called lively arts, but he's the closest thing they've got. His
music is a link, however tenuous, to the cultural community out
there, in the world beyond even "the town below" (DH, p. 86).
It extends not only in space but also in time: to play music you
have to remember, and Felix is the only member of the community who has any connection with his past. It is he who
remembers the story of Angel and the "bear," and the remembering is just as important as the original happening. And it is
Felix who remembers, or tries to remember, the fragments of the
Roman Catholic mass.

When the coffee cup makes its first appearance, it is immediately associated with the "cup" of Christ's suffering in the

Garden of Gethsemane, and with Felix's failure to accept the Christ-like role:

The cup which Angel had put into his hand, her bitter going, he'd left untouched. Left standing. A something set down. No constraint to make him drink. No struggle against the drinking. No let-it-pass. No it-is-done. (*DH*, p.32)

Avoiding the trials of Gethsemane and of Calvary, Felix believes that he is "Simply redeemed. Claiming before death a share of his inheritance" (*DH*, p.32). This is both true and not true (a double hook): insofar as Felix is still aware of the spiritual dimension, insofar as he can still recall such phrases as "let it pass" and "it is done," he is redeemed; but insofar as he refuses to accept the "cup" of Angel's desertion, insofar as he is unable to translate his slumbering spiritual awareness into action, he is not yet redeemed, and has nothing to claim but death itself.

Holding the cup, he moves into the memory of Angel, and the cup assumes its full symbolic potential:

The remembrance of event and the slash of rain merged. Time annihilated in the concurrence. The present contracted into the sweet hot cup he fondled. Vast fingers circling it. (*DH*, p.33)

If the coffee cup is then the Holy Grail, the incarnation of eternity into the temporal world, then Felix as its guardian is the true Fisher King, counterpointing the false image of Mrs. Potter as Fisher Queen. If one wishes to pursue the analogies further, James could, of course, be seen as the questing knight, but it is Felix himself who has to ask the decisive questions, and who has to meet (as I will shortly show) the traditional number of three challenges.

But, in the meantime, the coffee cup is also, of course, a coffee cup. Late in the book, William and Heinrich, keeping vigil over the ruins of Greta's fire, discuss the coffee cup again. Heinrich begins by stating the conventional view of Felix, that he does nothing; the reader's knowledge of what Felix has by this time done sets Heinrich's comments in an ironic perspective. Heinrich's words also explicitly recall, for the reader, the dimension of the cup as Eliot's "still point of the turning world":

> No one, he said, has asked Felix Prosper. Though what help one could get from Felix I don't know, he said, since Felix sits there like the round world all centred in on himself. (*DH*, p. 123)

William's response, typically, reduces the image from the mystical to the pragmatic. Once he has reduced Felix to the strictly rational level, William is able to dismiss him in a few aphorisms; as always, "William would try to explain, but he couldn't" (*DH*, p. 14):

> He drinks coffee like the rest of us, William said. Though, he said, I'd be hard pressed to know how he comes by the money to pay for it. If you think of it, he said, this case of Felix is a standing lesson for someone to think twice. A man who drinks coffee is dependent on something outside himself. But I myself doubt that he'd be much help to a person in trouble. He has troubles of his own if he cared to pick them up, but he lets them lie on another man's doorstep. He spends all his days lying round like a dog in a strip of sunlight taking warmth where he finds it. (*DH*, p. 123)

Again, the reader's level of awareness tells us that William is wrong: Felix *has* "cared to pick them up," he has accepted the cup of Angel's bitter going; he is *not* like the somnolent dogs of *And the four animals*. Heinrich understands something of this; his view of the world is not as limited as William's is. Heinrich offers some significant modifications to William's rationalist images, but he is still unaware of how fully the truth of what he says does, in fact, already apply to Felix:

> I never heard of a dog brewing himself a pot of coffee, the boy said. The thing about a dog lying in the sunlight is it just lies in the sunlight. Perhaps no living man can do just that. (*DH*, pp. 123–24)

"Perhaps no living man can do just that." "To be self-centred is an oblivion." "A man who drinks coffee is dependent on something outside himself." Felix has to emerge from self into society; he has to act out his understandings as James had to understand his actions. Three times in the course of the book, people come to Felix seeking help, and each time his response becomes fuller, more meaningful.

The first time is when Lenchen takes refuge at his house during the storm. Her presence disturbs him, prompting memories of the "mediating rituals" of civilization. As "His mind sifted ritual phrases. Some half forgotten," he moves from the secular forms of hospitality and common courtesy — "You're welcome. Put your horse in. Pull up" — to the religious forms of worship and congregation — "*Ave Maria. Benedictus fructus ventris. Introibo*" (*DH*, p. 45). These phrases are, of course, highly ironic when applied to the pregnant Lenchen — this scene is one of the most serious in the novel, but it is also its most richly comic — and they lead Felix into a memory as important, if not more so, than his earlier memory of Angel:

Introibo. The beginning. The whole thing to live again. Words said over and over here by the stove. His father knowing them by heart. God's servants. The priest's servants. The cup lifting. The bread breaking. *Domine non sum dignus*. Words coming. The last words. (*DH*, p. 45)

(Felix is, incidentally, the only character in the book with any memory of a father. If there ever was a *Mr.* Potter, not a word is said about him.) Fragmented as it is, this memory does at least constitute the beginning of a spiritual awareness to counter the cosmic nihilism of Coyote. Felix is not yet able, however, to put it into practice very convincingly:

He rolled from his chair. Stood barefoot. His hands raised.
Pax vobiscum, he said.
The girl lifted her head. She licked the saliva from the corner of her mouth.
What the hell, she said. (*DH*, p. 45)

Lenchen's colloquial "hell" responds, theologically, to Felix's hesitant heaven, and the comedy of the scene is enriched by the use of the plural "vobiscum." Felix is repeating words like Paddy's parrot, not knowing their full meaning: "Pax vobiscum" would be addressed by the priest to a whole congregation. The singular form should be "Pax tecum" — except, of course, that Lenchen, being pregnant, is in a sense quite appropriately addressed in the plural!

Words, however, are as far as Felix can go on this first occasion. When he had "Come to the end of his saying. . . . There was nothing else he could do" (*DH*, p. 45). Lenchen goes off into the night, to face James and his whip. The second challenge to Felix comes later, when the blinded Kip seeks his aid, finding him as he sits playing his fiddle and meditating on the cup of time "bound by a glass rim" (*DH*, p. 66). Felix is still unable to give direct aid himself, but neither is he content merely with words. He goes to fetch Angel.

This action, taking up the "cup" of her desertion, is obviously a very difficult one for Felix to take. He has resisted it a long time, even though he has also dreamed about it. "He dreamed that Angel was riding through his gate on a sleek ass. . . . *Dignum et justum est*, he said as he helped Angel down" (*DH*, p. 62). The dream associates the reclaiming of Angel with Felix's vocation as priest: he sees himself as wearing a surplice, even if it is as yet "scratchy" and "straining at his armpits like a garment which had shrunk in a storm" (*DH*, p. 62). The priestly vocation is one which does not yet quite fit him, but he is prepared to try it on. In the same dream, he sees a coyote. Beverley Mitchell, in her attempt to argue that Coyote is in fact Jehovah, points out that "only Felix Prosper finds attractive qualities in the coyote. . . . [He] sees the coyote as another living creature not unlike his hounds and terrier . . ." (p. 68). However, Mitchell does not quote the full passage in which the coyote appears, and thus misses its true meaning. In Felix's dream,

> I mustn't forget, he thought. I mustn't forget.
> He saw a coyote standing near the creek. He wanted to follow it into the hills. He felt its rough smell on his tongue.
> He turned away from the creek and went to the gate.
> (*DH*, p. 62)

Like James, who "wanted to go down to the river" (*DH*, p. 92) when he was tempted to suicide, Felix is here being tempted by the coyote to abandon his mission to bring Angel home. By turning back towards Angel, he is resisting the lure of Coyote, which is also, the passage makes clear, a temptation to *forget*. Memory, as I have already said, is essential to Felix: through his memory, incomplete as it is, he provides the community's only link with the wider culture. Coyote, of course, wants him to forget: Coyote is opposed to tradition, and mediating rituals, and all those aspects of life which stave off insensibility and violence.

It is typical of Felix that he must first *dream* this action before he can perform it. (James does things the other way around.) In the dream, Angel re-enters her home "on a sleek ass," like Christ on Palm Sunday entering Jerusalem; on the double hook of reality, she "did not come riding a sleek ass. She walked beside Prosper on her two feet, her children tagging behind her" (*DH*, p. 80). But she does come; and Felix does go to get her.

The third person who comes is Lenchen again, and this time Felix progresses beyond words, and beyond going to get somebody else to help, to taking direct action himself. Left alone with Lenchen when the time comes for her to give birth, Felix himself delivers the baby — a task which, Angel grudgingly admits, he "didn't do bad for a man" (*DH*, p. 126). That done, he returns to his fishing. But whereas before he fished alone, now he is at the centre of the community; his house has become its focus, the gathering point for all the characters. Whereas before he fished for himself and his dogs, now he fishes for other people. "When a house is full of women and children," he says, "a man has to get something for their mouths" (*DH*, p. 127).

James and Felix, then, come to complement each other. As the development of Felix's character shows, words must be validated by action; but equally, as the development of James's character shows, action must be made meaningful by words. While James and Felix are the dominant characters in this progression, a fuller study of *The Double Hook* would have to give equally detailed attention to the contributions of the minor characters, especially Heinrich and Ara. Heinrich is, as Dawn Rae Downton points out, "the youngest character in the novel," and thus ". . . in his case the process is generation rather than regeneration"

("Messages and Messengers," p. 139). Heinrich is stirred by intimations of the light, the glory, but he doesn't quite know what to
do with them; he is sent by his mother to reclaim Lenchen, but he
never finds her — in his last line of dialogue, two pages from the
end of the novel, he is still asking James, "Tell me . . . what
would a girl do?" (*DH*, p. 126). Downton's claim that "the regeneration of the community is finally accomplished in the figure of
Heinrich, in whom the word and the act, the language and the
morality, have merged" (p. 145) is exaggerated, but the boy is
undoubtedly one of the most interesting of the minor characters.

Another character who demands more attention than accounts
of the novel have hitherto given is Ara.⁴⁴ Ara is usually viewed in
a very negative light, as suggested by the echo of "arid" in her
name. Her childlessness leaves her bitter and self-pitying, but
also keenly aware of the low estimation in which other people
hold her. "Your mother hated me and you pity me," she tells
William. "Where can a women lift herself on two such ropes.
One pulling her down. The other simply holding her suspended"
(*DH*, p. 69). Yet Ara is also a major source of spiritual insight in
the novel, in many ways the complement of Felix. Ara has, as it
were, both the first and the last visionary words in the novel: she
is the first to see the old lady, and to realize her death in the paradoxical terms of the resurgence of life-giving water to the
parched land. "Yet as she watched the old lady, Ara felt death
leaking through from the centre of the earth" (*DH*, p. 15). Her
response to the vision is more immediately practical and directed
towards human communication than is Felix's: "She had to talk
to some living person. She had to tell someone what she felt
about the old lady and the water" (*DH*, p. 27). Ara's vision is
repeated and deepened at the climax of the novel:

> She remembered how she'd thought of water as a death
> which might seep through the dry shell of the world. Now
> her tired eyes saw water issuing from under the burned
> threshold. Welling up and flowing down to fill the dry
> creek. Until dry lips drank. Until the trees stood knee deep
> in water.
> Everything shall live where the river comes, she said out
> loud. And she saw a great multitude of fish, each fish
> springing arched through the slanting light. (*DH*, p. 108)

Again Ara's vision is followed by practical concerns, the urge towards community, as she goes to help the Widow Wagner: "I might as well be what use I can" (*DH*, p. 109). Finally, it is also Ara who has the last word in the novel, the last paradoxical vision of Coyote—which brings us to consider the ambiguities of the novel's resolution.

All this talk of "regeneration," of which I have done my share, perhaps implies that the final situation in the novel is more definite than in fact it is. The movement in the book — from the death at the beginning to the birth at the end, from the characters scattered in isolation to the characters gathered together around the baby Felix — is indeed the major thematic movement which *The Double Hook* presents. But, as always, there is a double hook.

Thus, the achievement of a sense of community has come at a quite drastic cost: one murder, one suicide, one blinding. Nor is it complete: Theophil remains isolated, obstinately *out*side the community. The last page of the novel is full of uncertainty: as Lenchen sees James (literally? or in her mind's eye?) "lifting the baby in his two hands," Ara suddenly feels excluded. "The girl wasn't speaking to her any longer . . ." (*DH*, p. 128). Ara perhaps is bitterly reminded of her own childlessness, her own aridity. In a novel about the growth of human community, the last line to mention any of the characters by name is "Ara didn't want to look at James" (*DH*, p. 128).

Instead, she turns away, and hears again the voice of Coyote, undaunted, unperturbed by the setback he has suffered, making his same old confident, confidence trickster claims:

I have set his feet on soft ground;
I have set his feet on the sloping shoulders
of the world.

(*DH*, p. 128)

It is indeed ironic that it is Ara who has this vision, Ara who has seen as clearly as anyone the regenerative vision, but who has also been described herself as "made to beat her hands against rock faces and to set her foot on sliding shale" (*DH*, p. 75). Mitchell describes these lines as "Messianic prophecy" (p. 66), but they are so only in the sense of blasphemous parody with which Coyote always appropriates divine diction. How Coyote can take any credit for Felix's birth is not clear, nor are *"soft* ground" and *"sloping* shoulders" the most stable of foundations for the infant Felix's feet. Coyote's claim is as usual a lie, but he does make it, and he does have the last word. Coyote is never completely defeated; fear and division, insensibility and violence, exist still for every generation. They are the issues which will confront the infant Felix in his turn, as he sets out on his life's path into the world of the double hook, duality and duplicity, under Coyote's eye.

NOTES

[1] Hugh Kenner, *The Invisible Poet: T. S. Eliot* (New York: Citadel, 1964).

[2] "Sheila Watson: A Biography," in *Figures in a Ground: Canadian Essays on Modern Literature Collected in Honor of Sheila Watson*, ed. Diane Bessai and David Jackel (Saskatoon: Western Producer Prairie Books, 1978), pp. 1–3. The essay is unsigned. All further references to this work appear in the text.

[3] Sheila Watson, "What I'm Going to Do," *Open Letter*, 3rd ser., No. 1 (Winter 1974–75) [*Sheila Watson: A Collection*], pp. 182–83. All further references to this work appear in the text.

[4] Diane Bessai, "Wilfred Watson." I am grateful to Professor Bessai for providing me with a copy of this as yet unpublished manuscript.

[5] Henry Kreisel, "Sheila Watson in Edmonton," in Bessai and Jackel, eds., *Figures in a Ground*, p. 4.

[6] *Dubbelkroken*, trans. Artur Lundkvist (Stockholm: Tidens Verlag, 1963); and *Sous l'oeil de coyote*, trans. Arlette Francière (Montréal: La Presse, 1976).

[7] Kreisel, p. 4.

[8] These names are as they appear on the masthead of the first issue: *White Pelican*, 1, No. 1 (Winter 1971).

[9] *Sheila Watson: A Collection* [*Open Letter*, 3rd ser., No. 1 (Winter 1974–75)].

[10] "Sugar Heart" and "Be Fruitful and Multiply," in *Stories from Québec*, ed. Philip Stratford (Toronto: Van Nostrand Reinhold, 1974), pp. 11–19.

[11] Sheila Watson, *And the four animals*, MS Editions [First Draft May

1980] (Toronto: Coach House, 1980). All further references to this work appear in the text.

[12] *Four Stories* (Toronto: Coach House, 1979), p. 48. All further references to this work (*FS*) appear in the text.

[13] Sheila Watson, "About Pelicans," *White Pelican*, 1, No. 1 (Winter 1971), 3–4.

[14] "A Note from the Publisher," in *The Double Hook* (Toronto: McClelland and Stewart, 1959), [p. 5]. All further references to this work (*DH*) appear in the text.

[15] *Creative Writing in Canada*, rev. ed. (Toronto: Ryerson, 1961), p. 267.

[16] Hugh McPherson, "Fiction 1940–1960," in *Literary History of Canada: Canadian Literature in English*, 2nd ed., gen. ed. and introd. Carl F. Klinck (Toronto: Univ. of Toronto Press, 1976), II, 225.

[17] *Our Nature — Our Voices: A Guidebook to English-Canadian Literature*, Volume 1 (Toronto: New, 1972), p. 150.

[18] Jan Marta, "Poetic Structures in the Prose Fiction of Sheila Watson," *Essays on Canadian Writing*, No. 17 (Spring 1980), pp. 46–47.

[19] Douglas Barbour, "Editors and Typesetters," *Open Letter*, 3rd ser., No. 1 (Winter 1974–75) [*Sheila Watson: A Collection*], p. 184.

[20] John Grube, Introd., *The Double Hook*, New Canadian Library, No. 54 (Toronto: McClelland and Stewart, 1966), pp. 5–14.

[21] Margaret Morriss, "The Elements Transcended," *Canadian Literature*, No. 42 (Autumn 1969), p. 57. All further references to this work appear in the text.

[22] Leslie Monkman, "Coyote as Trickster in *The Double Hook*," *Canadian Literature*, No. 52 (Spring 1972), pp. 70–71. All further references to this work appear in the text.

[23] Beverley Mitchell, S.A.A., "Association and Allusion in *The Double Hook*," *Journal of Canadian Fiction*, 2, No. 1 (Winter 1973), 63–69. All further references to this work appear in the text.

[24] Nancy J. Corbett, "Closed Circle," *Canadian Literature*, No. 61 (Summer 1974), pp. 46–53.

[25] Barbara Godard, " 'Between One Cliché and Another': Language in *The Double Hook*," *Studies in Canadian Literature*, 3 (Summer 1978), 149. All further references to this work appear in the text.

[26] Dawn Rae Downton, "Messages and Messengers in *The Double Hook*," *Studies in Canadian Literature*, 4 (Summer 1979), 137–46. All further references to this work appear in the text.

[27]Joyce Wayne, "The Atwood Generation: Notes on Surfacing from the Underground," *Quill & Quire*, Feb. 1981, pp. 4–8.

[28]See above, note 9.

[29]See above, note 23.

[30]See above, note 21.

[31]I heard MacLennan tell this story in a lecture, years ago. I may not have recalled the wording exactly.

[32]The translations are from the Jerusalem Bible (1966).

[33]Martin Kiddle, *The Revelation of St. John* (New York: Harper and Row, 1940), pp. 90–91.

[34]The Jerusalem Bible, commentary on iv.6.

[35]G. B. Caird, *A Commentary on the Revelation of St. John the Divine* (London: Adam and Charles Black, 1966), p. 64.

[36]Richmond Lattimore, trans., *The Revelation of John* (New York: Harcourt, Brace & World, 1962).

[37]See above, note 23.

[38]See above, note 21.

[39]T. S. Eliot, "Burnt Norton," Pt. II, in *Collected Poems 1909–1962* (London: Faber and Faber, 1963), p. 191.

[40]See above, note 22.

[41]Grube, p. 10.

[42]See Barbour, "Editors and Typesetters," p. 184.

[43]David Hugh Farmer, *The Oxford Dictionary of Saints* (Oxford: Clarendon, 1978), p. 148.

[44]For the view of Ara's character sketched here, I am much indebted to the work of Maureen Scobie.

SELECTED BIBLIOGRAPHY

Primary Sources

Watson, Sheila. *The Double Hook*. Toronto: McClelland and Stewart, 1959.

——. "About Pelicans." *White Pelican*, 1, No. 1 (Winter 1971), 2–4.

——, trans. "Sugar Heart" and "Be Fruitful and Multiply." By Madeleine Ferron. In *Stories from Québec*. Ed. Philip Stratford. Toronto: Van Nostrand Reinhold, 1974, pp. 11–19.

——. *Sheila Watson: A Collection* [*Open Letter*, 3rd ser., No. 1 (Winter 1974–75)].

——. *Four Stories*. Toronto: Coach House, 1979.

——. *And the four animals*. MS Editions [First Draft May 1980]. Toronto: Coach House, 1980.

Secondary Sources

Barbour, Douglas. "Editors and Typesetters." *Open Letter*, 3rd ser., No. 1 (Winter 1974–75) [*Sheila Watson: A Collection*], p. 184.

Bowering, Angela. "Figures Cut in Sacred Ground: *Illuminati* in *The Double Hook*." *Line*, 2 (Fall 1983), 43–60.

Bowering, George. "Sheila Watson, Trickster." In *The Mask in Place: Essays on Fiction in North America*. Winnipeg: Turnstone, 1982, pp. 97–112.

Corbett, Nancy J. "Closed Circle." *Canadian Literature*, No. 61 (Summer 1974), pp. 46–53.

Downton, Dawn Rae. "Messages and Messengers in *The Double Hook*." *Studies in Canadian Literature*, 4 (Summer 1979), 137–46.

Godard, Barbara. "'Between One Cliché and Another': Language in *The Double Hook*." *Studies in Canadian Literature*, 3 (Summer 1978), 149–65.

Grube, John, introd. *The Double Hook*. New Canadian Library, No. 54. Toronto: McClelland and Stewart, 1966, pp. 5–14.

Kreisel, Henry. "Sheila Watson in Edmonton." In *Figures in a Ground: Canadian Essays on Modern Literature Collected in Honor of Sheila*

Watson. Ed. Diane Bessai and David Jackel. Saskatoon: Western Producer Prairie Books, 1978, pp. 4–6.

Marta, Jan. "Poetic Structures in the Prose Fiction of Sheila Watson." *Essays on Canadian Writing*, No. 17 (Spring 1980), pp. 44–56.

McPherson, Hugh. "Fiction 1940–1960." In *Literary History of Canada: Canadian Literature in English*. 2nd ed. Gen. ed. and introd. Carl F. Klinck. Toronto: Univ. of Toronto Press, 1976. II, 205–33.

Mitchell, Beverley, S.A.A. "Association and Allusion in *The Double Hook*." *Journal of Canadian Fiction*, 2, No. 1 (Winter 1973), 63–69.

Monkman, Leslie. "Coyote as Trickster in *The Double Hook*." *Canadian Literature*, No. 52 (Spring 1972), pp. 70–76.

Morriss, Margaret. "The Elements Transcended." *Canadian Literature*, No. 42 (Autumn 1969), pp. 56–71.

Neuman, Shirley. "Sheila Watson." In *Profiles in Canadian Literature*. Ed. Jeffrey M. Heath. Vol. IV. Toronto: Dundurn, 1982, 45–52.

Pacey, Desmond. *Creative Writing in Canada*. Rev. ed. Toronto: Ryerson, 1961.

"Sheila Watson: A Biography." In *Figures in a Ground: Canadian Essays on Modern Literature Collected in Honor of Sheila Watson*. Ed. Diane Bessai and David Jackel. Saskatoon: Western Producer Prairie Books, 1978, pp. 1–3.

Thomas, Clara. "Sheila Watson." In *Our Nature — Our Voices: A Guidebook to English-Canadian Literature, Volume I*. Toronto: New, 1972, pp. 150–51.